D1037978

PHILLIES ESSENTIAL

Everything You Need to Know to Be a Real Fan!

Rich Westcott

Library of Congress Cataloging-in-Publication Data

Westcott, Rich.
Phillies essential : everything you need to know to be a real fan / Rich Westcott.
p. cm.
ISBN-13: 978-1-57243-819-4 (hard cover)
ISBN-10: 1-57243-819-3 (hard cover)
1. Philadelphia Phillies (Baseball team)—History. 2. Philadelphia Phillies (Baseball team)—Miscellanea. I. Title.

GV875.P45B56 2006
796.357'640974811—dc22

2005034164

This book is available in quantity at special discounts for your group or organization. For further information, contact:

Triumph Books
542 South Dearborn Street
Suite 750
Chicago, Illinois 60605
(312) 939-3330
Fax (312) 663-3557

Printed in U.S.A.
ISBN-13: 978-1-57243-819-4
ISBN-10: 1-57243-819-3
Design by Patricia Frey
Editorial production by Prologue Publishing Services, Oak Park, Illinois
All photos courtesy of AP/Wide World Photos except where otherwise indicated.

To Margot and Nicole.
Two new members of the family.
May your lives be filled with glory.

Introduction

The great Phillies pitcher Robin Roberts spent nearly 14 years in Philadelphia, where he was one of the most popular players ever to pull on a uniform. Such admiration was, of course, entirely understandable. Few players ever graced a Philadelphia baseball diamond with the success that Roberts—on his way to the Hall of Fame—did. Nor did anyone carry himself with any more class or dignity. Those are reasons enough to put a Philadelphia player in the good graces of the local fans. But with Roberts, the admiration was a two-way street.

"I loved playing in Philly," he said. "I have nothing but positive feelings. The first time that I walked out of the clubhouse onto the field at Shibe Park [later called Connie Mack Stadium], I thought it was the most beautiful sight I'd ever seen. Talk about your field of dreams. The Phillies gave me the opportunity to pitch, and playing in Philadelphia has always meant something very special to me."

When it comes to sports, Philadelphia is indeed a special place. Tough, yes. But in a city that worships the good players and teams and spits out the bad ones, Philadelphia has always put its favorites on a high pedestal.

In recent decades that pedestal has become cluttered with delegates from a variety of sports, not the least of which are football, basketball, and ice hockey. Professional teams and dozens of colleges pack the area. Some colleges began playing football in the 1870s and basketball in the 1890s, and the city's Big Five has for 50 years been one of the preeminent roundball alliances in the country. Professional football, basketball, and ice hockey teams first appeared in the city in the 1920s.

The city that's been around since the late 1600s and is often referred to as "the Cradle of Liberty" had horse racing in the mid-1700s. By then, rowing was also a major sport in the area. Boxing was popular as far back as the 1850s, tennis took hold in the city in the 1880s, and golf began to become fashionable in the 1890s. There was even professional auto racing on city streets for a few years in the early 1900s. Since then, other sports have gained in popularity while countless major events on a national level in all the sports have been common occurrences in the area.

No sport, however, has been more dominant in Philadelphia and held center stage for a longer period than baseball. When it comes to sports, baseball is really the king of the local kingdom.

It should be. It's had an uninterrupted run in the city since the 1830s, when club teams began to sprout. The first recorded game in Philadelphia took place in 1860 when a team called Equity beat the Pennsylvanians in anything but a tight pitchers' duel, 65–52.

In 1865 Al Reach—later to become the first owner of the Phillies—became baseball's first professional player. He played for a team called the Athletics, which in 1871 became the champion of the first professional baseball league, the National Association.

It was in that league in 1875 that an Athletics pitcher named Joe Borden hurled the first no-hitter in pro ball. One year later, the first National League game ever played took place in Philadelphia with Borden—now pitching for the Boston Red Caps—beating yet another team called the Athletics, 6–5.

A third team called the Athletics joined the newly formed American Association in 1882 and won the league title the following year. That year, the Phillies came into existence as a new entry in the National League. In 1890 there were three major league teams playing in Philadelphia—the Phillies, the Athletics, and the Quakers of the short-lived Players, or Brotherhood, League. All played home games within a few city blocks of each other.

When the American League began in 1901, still another Athletics team was one of the charter members. That club remained in the city through 1954, along the way winning nine pennants and five World Series. The Athletics, whose presence guaranteed that there would always be a big league game going on in Philadelphia, was the dominant team in the city until the Phillies won the National League pennant in 1950.

Further solidifying Philadelphia's position as a baseball leader was the presence of Negro League teams. African American club teams played in the city going back to the 1860s. Then, beginning in 1902, professional teams known as the Philadelphia Giants, the Hilldale Daisies, and the Philadelphia Stars performed at different times in the city. The Stars' demise in 1952 ended what had been a glorious half century of black baseball in Philadelphia.

All of which brings us back to the Phillies, a team that entering the 2006 season has been around for 123 years. It has been 123 years of peaks and valleys, with, unfortunately, the valleys outnumbering the peaks by a considerable amount.

Those valleys have often created heaping sums of discontent among the—you'll pardon the expression—City of Brotherly Love's rabid sports fans, who, while being among the most knowledgeable in the country, have over the years elevated the crude noise of booing to a level unheard in any other city.

Naturally, the fans have had their favorite targets. Del Ennis was one. So was Dick Allen. Early in his career, Mike Schmidt felt boos ringing in his ears. And of late, David Bell has borne the brunt of the more vocal fans.

You could build a pretty good case that none of these fine players deserved such rude treatment. On the other hand, legions of others were certainly worthy recipients. Without them, the Phillies wouldn't have enjoyed such an ignominious record of having lost 100 or more games 13 different times—including five in a row—and finishing in last place 31 times.

To be sure, though, Phillies fans have had ample opportunity to cheer and to be supportive of a team that has had some truly exciting moments and players. Who can forget the 1980 World Series and the parade that followed the next day when an estimated 2 million fans gathered to watch the Phillies roll down Broad Street? Or who cannot notice that the club has drawn more than 2 million in seasonal attendance 16 times since 1976, including twice above 3 million?

During that 16-year period, the Phillies won six division titles, three of their five National League pennants, and their only World Series. And they featured some of the best players in Phillies history, including

Schmidt, the best all-around third baseman baseball ever had, and Steve Carlton, one of just 22 of baseball's 300-game winners.

In the best of times, playing for the Phillies and in the sport-rich city of Philadelphia can be an exhilarating experience. "It is very exciting playing here," said current star Bobby Abreu. "What makes it so good is the organization, the stadium, the city itself, the good weather, the fans. When you're working hard and playing well, the fans appreciate it. It's just a nice place to play, and I'm thankful that the Phillies gave me the opportunity to prove that I could play in the big leagues."

The Phillies moved into Citizens Bank Park in 2004. The new park is the fifth ballpark the Phillies have called home in their 123-year history.

The bottom line is that the team that once featured Grover Cleveland Alexander and Chuck Klein and Richie Ashburn is a franchise that, in spite of the losing seasons, has had a fascinating and sometimes glorious history. Only two other teams—those currently known as the Cincinnati Reds and Chicago Cubs—have been around longer than the Phillies, and in that time no team in the city of Philadelphia has been more interesting or more colorful.

From Recreation Park to Citizens Bank Park, from Ed Delahanty to Bobby Abreu, from Al Reach to David Montgomery, from last-place finishes to pennants, the Phillies have, for the most part, offered the best game in town.

This, then, is their story. It is a story about a team, some of its players, and the special events that have made it a significant part of baseball's and the city's history.

It's 1883, and the Phillies Have Arrived

Although he was born in London, England, the son of a cricket player, Al Reach was an American success story. He was a left-handed second baseman who became not only the top player of his era but also baseball's first professional player. Eventually, he also became a millionaire sporting goods manufacturer and the Phillies' first owner.

Born in 1840, Reach came the following year to the United States with his parents. He grew up in Brooklyn, a poor kid who sold newspapers to help his parents make ends meet. Later, he worked 12 hours a day at an iron foundry.

Reach stood just 5'6". But he was attracted to baseball and eventually became good enough to play for the Brooklyn Eckfords, one of early baseball's most prominent teams. By the time he had reached his midtwenties, Reach was regarded as the best player in the game. In fact, he was so good that, in 1865, a team called the Philadelphia Athletics—no relation to the future American League team of the same name—offered him $1,000 for the season. The left-handed second sacker took the deal and thus became the first player to be paid to play baseball.

Al was worth the money. He was usually good for three or four hits per game. And as the key drawing card, he helped the Athletics attract huge crowds to their games, including one totaling 20,000. So great was that crowd that spectators were forced to climb trees, perch on roofs, or clamor to the tops of buggies to watch the action.

In 1871 Reach, hitting what was later calculated to be .353, led the Athletics to the championship in the maiden season of the first professional league, the National Association. He then played four more years before retiring after the 1875 season to devote full time to his growing business empire.

DID YOU KNOW . . . That the newly formed American League's first five batting champions were all former members of the Phillies? They were Nap Lajoie (1901, 1903, and 1904), Ed Delahanty (1902), and Elmer Flick (1905).

Reach was no dummy. While making a name for himself on the field, he invested his money wisely, first opening a sporting goods store in center city Philadelphia, then launching a business that manufactured sporting goods with Ben Shibe, a maker of whips, as his partner.

The A. J. Reach Company, as it was named, became enormously successful. Although it made a variety of sports equipment, its main product was baseballs. Shibe devised a cork-center ball that was mass-produced and eventually became the official ball of the American League. (The official ball of the National League was made by A. G. Spalding and Bros., a company that merged with Reach in 1892. Ironically, despite their different names, the balls were made in the same plant in Philadelphia.)

In 1882 an old friend of Reach's paid him a visit. Col. A. G. Mills, an early baseball player himself who had become a prominent New York attorney, was also the president of the National League, formed in 1876. At the time, the league had teams in places such as Troy, New York, and Worcester, Massachusetts. Mills knew that having teams in such cities was a bad proposition. "We've got to get New York and Philadelphia in the league," he said. "They have tremendous futures, and someday their populations will be in the millions."

Soon afterward, both the Troy and Worcester teams were disbanded, and a new team emerged in New York (where it was later named the Giants). Then Mills approached Reach, wondering if he'd be interested in running a team in Philadelphia. "If you can get the backing and build a ballpark, I'll put a team in Philadelphia," Mills told Reach.

Consider it done, or words to that effect, said Reach. Enlisting as his partner Col. John Rogers, a lawyer and member of the governor of Pennsylvania's staff, Reach quickly jumped into action.

He bought a run-down old ballpark that had been around since at least 1860 and had been used as an encampment by Union soldiers during the Civil War. At one time serving as a site for a horse market, Recreation Park was situated on a city block that, because of its odd shape, gave the field a set of unfathomable dimensions. It was 300 feet down the left-field line and 331 to dead center. The field then swerved to a distance of 369 feet in right center before slicing back to 247 feet down the right-field line.

Once refurbished, the park had a seating capacity of 6,500. There were no dugouts. Players sat on benches in front of the stands. Nor were there any locker rooms. The uniformed personnel dressed in their rooms at nearby hotels, riding in horse-drawn buggies to the ballpark. Reach hung large red signs around the ballpark forbidding transgressions such as gambling, pick-pocketing, profanity, and insults to players, umpires, and other patrons.

Reach decided to call the team the Phillies. Now for the next problem: who will be the manager? Al made his choice. The first Phillies skipper would be Bob Ferguson, a former player and teammate of Reach's in Brooklyn and a National League manager during the previous seven seasons.

Ferguson had the unusual nickname of "Death to Flying Things." It was never really determined how he got that name. One theory was that as a player he caught everything hit his way. That was probably not the case inasmuch as Ferguson made more than 600 errors during 14 years as a player. A more plausible explanation was that Ferguson had the uncanny knack of being able to kill all bugs that got near him.

By far, Reach's most difficult task was to assemble a team. Because other league teams had quickly signed players from the failed Worcester club, no players came with the franchise. Reach had to start from scratch. "That is not a problem," he told anybody who would listen.

How wrong Reach was. Al scoured the hinterlands. Minor leaguers, has-beens, and local sandlot players got looks. So did nearly anybody else who owned a pair of spikes and knew how to pull on a pair of knickers.

One of Reach's big catches was a kid named Sid Farrar who was found working in a Massachusetts box-making factory. According to reports of the day, Reach offered Farrar $1,000. The then-23-year-old first baseman with no professional experience took the offer. The factory owner promised to hold Farrar's job open for one year in case he struck out in baseball.

Farrar didn't strike out. He played eight years in the big leagues. He did, however, have the unusual distinction of batting ninth in the club's lineup.

TRIVIA

Who was the first Phillies player ever to win a home-run title?

Answers to the trivia questions are on page 190.

Sid's chief claim to fame came not from what he did on the field, but from what he did off it. He sired a daughter named Geraldine who, for the first three decades of the 20th century, was the premier opera singer in America. Described as a "dark beauty" with "electrifying stage presence," she had legions of adoring fans while performing in all of the top operas of the day. When Sid, who became a bank president, died in 1935, his obituary contained more information about Geraldine than it did about him.

Unlike today, when teams travel to affluent resort areas for spring training, the Phillies spent their first spring training at good old Recreation Park. Then, on May 1, 1883, the Phillies made their National League debut, facing the powerful Providence Grays and Charles "Old Hoss" Radbourn at Recreation Park. Although they had a 3–0 lead after seven innings, the Phillies lost 4–3 as the Grays rallied with four runs in the eighth. It was the start of a *loooong* season.

After the Phillies lost 13 of their first 17 games, Reach relieved Ferguson of his duties, replacing him with center fielder Bill "Blondie" Purcell. Ferguson continued for the rest of the season as the club's second baseman, where he made 88 errors.

Under Purcell, the Phillies lost one game to Boston, 29–4. In the highest-scoring shutout in major league history, the team was ravaged by Providence, 28–0. And in yet another mismatch, the Phillies committed 27 errors (although walks, wild pitches, and passed balls counted in those days as errors) in one game.

By the end of the season, the Phillies had won 17 games. They lost 81. With a winning percentage of .173, the team finished in eighth place, 46 games out of first.

Nobody had a more disastrous season than John Coleman. The Phillies' starting pitcher in 65 of their 98 games, he was on the losing end 48 times (with 12 wins). Coleman completed 59 games while hurling 538 innings and allowing 544 runs and 772 hits. The losses, runs, and hits are all-time major league records that will never be erased.

The Phillies tried eight other pitchers during the season. One of them, Art Hagen, posted a 1–14 record. Only one player—catcher Emil

By the NUMBERS

37—The number of Hall of Famers who spent at least parts of their careers with the Phillies. Those members are the following:

Year Inducted	Player	Position with Phillies	Years with Phillies
1937	Nap Lajoie	1B, 2B	1896–1900
1938	Grover Cleveland Alexander	P	1911–1917, 1930
1945	Dan Brouthers	1B	1896
1945	Ed Delahanty	LF, 1B, 2B	1888–1889, 1891–1901
1945	Hugh Duffy	LF, Manager	1904–1906
1945	Hugh Jennings	SS, 1B	1901–1902
1946	Johnny Evers	2B	1917
1946	Tom McCarthy	OF	1886–1887
1948	Herb Pennock	GM	1943–1948
1949	Kid Nichols	P	1905–1906
1951	Jimmie Foxx	1B, P	1945
1953	Chief Bender	P	1916–1917
1953	Harry Wright	Manager	1884–1893
1961	Billy Hamilton	CF	1890–1895
1963	Elmer Flick	RF	1898–1901
1963	Eppa Rixey	P	1912–1917, 1919–1920
1964	Tim Keefe	P	1891–1893
1966	Casey Stengel	RF	1920–1921
1967	Lloyd Waner	CF	1942
1970	Earle Combs	Coach	1954
1971	Dave Bancroft	SS	1915–1920
1974	Sam Thompson	RF	1889–1898
1975	Bucky Harris	Manager	1943
1976	Roger Connor	1B	1892

(continued on next page)

Year Inducted	Player	Position with Phillies	Years with Phillies
1976	Bob Lemon	Coach	1961
1976	Robin Roberts	P	1948–1961
1979	Hack Wilson	RF	1934
1980	Chuck Klein	RF	1928–1933, 1936–1939, 1940–1944
1990	Joe Morgan	2B	1983
1991	Ferguson Jenkins	P	1965–1966
1994	Steve Carlton	P	1972–1986
1995	Richie Ashburn	CF	1948–1959
1995	Mike Schmidt	3B	1972–1989
1996	Jim Bunning	P	1964–1967, 1970–1971
2000	Sparky Anderson	2B	1959
2000	Tony Perez	1B	1983
2005	Ryne Sandberg	2B	1981

In addition, the following members of the local media have also been honored by the Hall of Fame:

Ford C. Frick Award—By Saam (1990) and Harry Kalas (2002)

J. G. Taylor Spink Award—Allen Lewis (1981), Ray Kelly (1988), and Bus Saidt (1992)

Gross—hit above .300 (he hit .307). The season was a disaster at virtually every turn, and many observers of the carnage expected the team would not return for a second season. In fact, quite a few urged Reach to throw in the sponge.

Reach, however, was undaunted. "We spent a year finding ourselves," he said. "Of course, it was expensive. We made mistakes, but we learned from our experiences. Philadelphia has the population and interest to support this club. And someday, the Philadelphia National League club will be famous. More famous than the Athletics."

To help facilitate such matters, Reach made what would turn out to be the best move of his ownership by luring Harry Wright away from the

Providence club. Already a manager of considerable renown, Wright—also a native of England and a former cricket player—was the skipper of baseball's first all-professional team, the 1869 Cincinnati Red Stockings. He then enjoyed highly successful runs as manager of the Boston Red Caps and Providence, en route to a career that would lead him to the Hall of Fame.

Immediately, Harry began to straighten out the sorry state of affairs at Recreation Park. His main focus was, of course, the roster, which he overhauled from top to bottom. Included in the new group was pitcher Charlie Ferguson, who would win 21 games in 1884 and 99 over a four-year period. Ferguson, who also pitched the Phillies' first no-hitter, died tragically of typhoid fever in 1888 at the age of 25.

Under Wright, the Phillies moved up to sixth place in 1884, then finished third, fourth, and second over the next three years. "I'll tell you one thing, Al," Wright told Reach. "It's only a matter of time before I can give you a championship. I make that promise."

As it turned out, it was an idle promise. Wright never gave the Phillies a championship. Neither did the next eight full-time managers...or even Reach, one of three would-be pilots who, in 1890, stepped briefly into the skipper's seat to fill in for Wright after he experienced a temporary case of blindness.

Wright retired after the 1893 season. In 1901, as their sporting goods company flourished, Shibe—with Reach's blessing—became the majority owner of a new Philadelphia Athletics team in the newly formed American League. The teams would go on to wage a bitter fight for players and fans.

Reach and Rogers—who by then had become the more conspicuous member of the owners tandem but no longer on friendly terms with Reach—sold the team in 1903 for the grand sum of $170,000.

The Oldest Nickname in Professional Sports

When Al Reach gave his new Philadelphia team its nickname in 1883, there's no way he could have imagined how long that name would survive.

Reach picked the team's name for geographical reasons. "Let's call the team the Phillies," he decided. "That way, people will know it's from Philadelphia." Good call, Al. The name has connected the team with the city for more than 123 years since Reach made that fortuitous decision. What's more, no other team in all of sports has ever been called Phillies.

Of even more significance, Phillies is the oldest, uninterrupted, one-city nickname in professional sports. Two teams—the National League's Chicago and Cincinnati clubs—have been around longer than the Phillies. But neither has used the same nickname throughout its existence.

That's not to say that the Phillies' nickname streak has never been threatened. At least three times over the years, attempts were made to change the name. Obviously, all of them failed.

The first attempt came in 1909 and was the misguided recommendation of team president Horace Fogel. A former sportswriter who went straight, Fogel had put together a group and, using money mostly from the Taft family in Cincinnati, had purchased the team for a reported $350,000.

After his installation as team president, Fogel quickly swung into action. He fired the manager and made trades. Somehow it dawned on him that the team name should be changed to Live Wires. The name, Fogel proposed, would be an apt description of what he hoped would be the spirited play of the newly energized team.

Nice try, Horace. Fans and Fogel's pals in the media totally ignored the name. Phillies it was, and Phillies it would stay. And Live Wires quietly slipped out the side door, never to be heard from again. (Three years later, Fogel also slipped out the side door after he was banned for life from organized baseball for making disparaging comments about the National League.)

TRIVIA

Which last name is the most common in Phillies history?

Answers to the trivia questions are on page 190.

The name Phillies went unchallenged until 1942, when Hans Lobert was appointed manager. A former Phillies third baseman and an interim manager in 1938, Lobert was taking over a team that had just finished in eighth place four times in a row. The club had lost more than 100 games in each of those seasons.

There was, concluded Hans, a desperate need to change the image of the team. After all, how could a team win any respect if it carried the same name as all those losers? "Let's call this team the Phils," Lobert told club officials, who agreed that was not such a bad idea.

An attempt was made to change the name. Even the wording on the uniforms was switched from Phillies to Phils. But the name was never officially changed. And, although it has remained since then as a backup nickname for the club, it, too, drifted away after the '42 team lost 109 games and finished in last place, 62½ games out of first place, resulting in a quick end to Lobert's tenure with the Phillies.

Soon, though, the name Phillies met more opposition. This, it turned out, was the most serious threat to the old nickname that was ever mounted.

After William Cox, in 1943, had become the second Phillies president to have been banned from baseball forever (for betting on Phillies games), Bob Carpenter took over as the team's president. Despite their seventh-place finish that year, the team was still hanging out with the dregs of the National League.

As he tried to upgrade the club in every way possible, Carpenter decided it was time for a name change. "We need a new name," he said. "It's time to get rid of the old one."

TOP TEN

Highest Career Batting Averages with the Phillies

	Name	Average
1.	Billy Hamilton	.361
2.	Ed Delahanty	.348
3.	Nap Lajoie	.345
4.	Elmer Flick	.338
5.	Sam Thompson	.334
6.	Chuck Klein	.326
7.	Spud Davis	.321
8.	Fred Leach	.312
9.	Richie Ashburn	.311
10.	John Kruk	.309

As a believer in a democratic system, Carpenter rejected the idea of providing the name himself. No, indeed, this time the fans would make the decision. The 28-year-old Carpenter held a contest. When the votes were finally tabulated, some 5,064 ballots had been cast. And the winner was...Blue Jays!

The team moved quickly to make the change before the 1944 season began. The team logo was changed. The words *Blue Jays* were printed on the caps. Even the stationery was changed to reflect the new name.

For the most part, though, no one really seemed to care. With one exception—the student body at Johns Hopkins University in Baltimore. Teams at Hopkins had been called Blue Jays for 68 years. Nobody as downtrodden as the Phillies was going to use that name, the students protested.

The students passed a resolution. Carpenter's use of the name Blue Jays "is a reprehensible act which brings disgrace and dishonor to the good name of Johns Hopkins University," the resolution said in part. It added that calling the Phillies the Blue Jays is an insult to the good name of the blue jay itself.

The protest notwithstanding, the team never officially adopted the name. Nor did it file for a name change. For several years, though, Blue

Jays stayed as a kind of unofficial secondary name. But by 1949 it had run its course and disappeared from the scene.

The name remained out of sight until a new American League team was formed in Toronto, the city where the Phillies ran a farm club from 1948 through 1950.

Since the Blue Jays caper, no attempts have been made to dump the name Phillies. And although the club has been called the Whiz Kids, the Wheeze Kids, and various other names, the one that Al Reach gave it continues to stand on its own.

Often Last, but Seldom Dull

Despite their frequent visits to the dungeons of the National League standings, the Phillies have never really been what you'd call boring. Dreary at times, yes. Exciting once in a while, certainly. But this is a franchise that could always be described as often last, but seldom dull.

How else could you explain the presence of a guy like Jack Clements, a left-handed catcher who played in 14 seasons with the Phillies in the late 1800s? Or a player like Sherry Magee, who once knocked out an umpire, then became one himself a couple of years later? Or a third baseman like Joe Mulvey, who made 135 errors over two seasons?

The esteemed first baseman John Kruk, who claimed to chew as many as 20 sticks of gum during a game, was once berated by a woman as he sat in a restaurant eating a big dinner, partaking of a few drinks, and smoking cigarettes. No professional athlete should be doing those kinds of things, the lady scolded. "I ain't no athlete, lady," Kruk responded. "I'm a ballplayer."

The Phillies had a reserve second baseman named Dave Johnson who hit two pinch-hit grand-slam homers during the 1978 season. Johnson, a solid player before he came to the Phils and a capable manager afterward, claimed to be an avid reader—he even read *War and Peace*, he said. Teammates thought they'd give him a test. "Who wrote that book?" someone asked. "Why, it was Leo Toystore," Johnson said confidently.

After joining the Phillies in the mid-1960s, noted comic Bob Uecker once said that he got drunk and was picked up and fined by Philadelphia police. "Five hundred dollars for being drunk," he explained, "and $100 for being with the Phillies." Uecker also claimed that Phillies fans would

IF ONLY . . . The Phillies had signed Philadelphia-area natives, such as Mike Piazza or Reggie Jackson or Mickey Vernon or Roy Campanella or Eddie Stanky or Jimmy Dykes or Ray Narleski or Jamie Moyer. It's a safe bet that if any of these guys had played with the Phillies, in certain years the team would've been better than it was.

boo kids who came up empty-handed in an Easter egg hunt and would target unwed mothers on Mother's Day. "I've even seen people standing on street corners booing each other," he said.

Billy Sunday once played in the outfield for the Phillies. Shortly afterward, he retired from the game and launched a career that would make him a world-famous evangelist. Another Phillies outfielder was Earle "Greasy" Neale. Later, he became the head coach of the Philadelphia Eagles, leading the team to its first two NFL championships.

A former Phillies pitcher named Pete Sivess was one of the original members of the CIA and a key player in that organization for 25 years. Stan Baumgartner pitched for the pennant-winning Phillies in 1915, then covered the team for many years for the *Philadelphia Inquirer,* often wearing a Phillies cap in the press box.

First baseman Dick Stuart was widely noted as a fielder of disastrous proportions who earned the nicknames "Stonehands" and "Dr. Strangeglove." Once, he sidled over to the mound to have a word with Jim Bunning, who had just thrown a couple of pickoff attempts. "Don't throw it so hard," he pleaded.

When asked what he and fellow reliever Tug McGraw talked about in the bullpen, Al Holland replied, "Neither of us has an elevator that goes to the top floor, so most of the time we talk from the waist down." When talking about a Phillies victory, infielder Solly Hemus explained it by saying, "Even monkeys fall out of trees once in a while."

After getting the hit that set a new National League record, Pete Rose got a congratulatory call from President Ronald Reagan. "Pete, this is President Reagan," said the voice on the other end of the phone. "Hey, how ya doin'?" Rose responded. And when outfielder Ethan Allen, one of the few major leaguers with a master's degree, was asked for his thoughts on the fine art of hitting, he said, "I always felt that when you were hitting, you could hit anybody. When you weren't hitting, you couldn't hit your Aunt Katie."

Likeable outfielder Jeff Stone had a special way with words. Once, while traveling on the team bus to Wrigley Field, Stone spotted Lake Michigan. "Is that the Atlantic or Pacific Ocean?" he inquired. After a season playing winter ball in Venezuela, Stone decided not to bring his new television set home with him. Why? "They only talk Spanish on it," he said. Offered a shrimp cocktail once, Stone declined. "No thanks," he said. "I don't drink."

What team besides the Phillies could possibly have colorful nicknames such as Tight Pants, Shucks, Weeping Willie, Earache, Handle Hit, Dirty Jack, Possum, Candy, Bareback, What's the Use?, Losing Pitcher, Fidgety Phil, Horse Face, Boom Boom, or Wagon Tongue? Or Putt-Putt, Nibbler, Pretzels, Cactus, Buckshot, Squirrel, Cupid, Runt, Wild Thing, Gnat, Dude, Crash, Head, or Sarge?

Or what team had a player (Hans Lobert) race a horse around the bases, only to lose by a nose after stumbling while coming around

TOP TEN

Best Phillies Teams in the 20th Century (by Percentage)

	Year	Record	Percentage
1.	1976	101–61	.623*t*
	1977	101–61	.623*t*
3.	1993	97–65	.599
4.	1916	91–62–1	.595
5.	1901	83–57	.593
6.	1915	90–62–1	.592
7.	1950	91–63–3	.591
8.	1913	88–63–8	.583
9.	1917	87–65–2	.572
10.	1964	92–70	.568

Note: Ties not included in percentage calculations.

DID YOU KNOW . . . That like a number of other cities, Philadelphia once had two major league teams? The Athletics joined the newly formed American League in 1901 and, after winning nine pennants and five World Series, moved to Kansas City after the 1954 season (they later became the Oakland A's). Although they were once the city's most popular team, the Athletics dropped well behind after the Phillies won the pennant in 1950. From then on, it was a Phillies town.

second base? Or a left-handed shortstop such as Bill Hulen? Or a Dan Casey, a pitcher who until his dying day steadfastly maintained that he was the subject of Ernest Thayer's famous poem *Casey at the Bat*?

The Phillies once had an executive who bent his elbow with a fair degree of regularity. He was said to hold the team record for "doubles." And his favorite players, it was claimed, were Jack Daniels and Jim Beam.

Phillies managers were often highly quotable. "I don't want to go off on a transom," suggested Frank Lucchesi. "Nobody's going to make a scrapgoat out of me," informed Lucchesi when he was fired. Skipper Nick Leyva described outfielder Lenny Dykstra as being "like a mosquito when you're outdoors. You're always waiting for it to bite." While piloting the Phillies, Larry Bowa was asked about a statement pitcher Mike Timlin had made, in which he said the players weren't having any fun. "If you want to have fun," Bowa fumed, "join a last-place team."

When probed about his team having a problem with morale, Danny Ozark advised the press that "on this team, morality is not a factor." Ozark once said outfielder Mike Anderson's "limitations were limitless." Another time, he claimed, after the Phillies had been swept in a series, that the team's performance "was beyond my apprehension." "I've got a great repertoire with my players," he said another time.

General manager Paul Owens once got a ride back from the airport, and along the way he asked the driver to turn the car radio "up a few disciples." When asked about the comment later, Owens said, "Oh, I was just kidding. I knew it wasn't disciples. I knew the word was decimals."

Late in the 1964 season, the Phillies obtained first baseman Vic Power in a trade with the Los Angeles Angels for pitcher Marcelino Lopez and a player to be named later. At the end of the season, Power

John Kruk's colorful career epitomized the notion that the Phillies—whether they were winning or losing baseball games—have rarely lacked personality.
Photo courtesy of MLB Photos via Getty Images.

became one of the few players ever traded for himself when he was returned to L.A. as the player to be named later.

When the Phillies made a trade that sent Von Hayes to the Angels, Dykstra was asked for his reaction to the deal. "Good trade, good trade," he declared. "Who'd we get?"

Pitcher Curt Simmons once said that trying to sneak a fastball past Hank Aaron "is like trying to sneak the sunrise past a rooster." And Robin Roberts, whose one flaw as a pitcher was serving up an untidy number of home runs, revealed that, "In the long history of organized baseball, I stand unparalleled for putting Christianity into practice."

In 1921, in an away tilt with the Pittsburgh Pirates, the Phillies were part of the first game ever broadcast. The Phillies played in the major league's first night game in 1935 in Cincinnati. A former Phillies player (Eddie Grant) was the first major leaguer killed in World War I. Phillies pitcher Hugh Mulcahy was the first big leaguer drafted into World War II. Team president Gerry Nugent's wife, Mae, became, in 1932, the first woman executive in baseball. And in 1946 the Phillies hired Edith Houghton as baseball's first female scout.

Ralph Kiner once told his listeners that two-thirds of the world was covered by water, and one-third was covered by Phillies center fielder Garry Maddox.

When reading a list of Phillies who hit inside-the-park home runs, a writer wondered if anything unusual had happened to aid slow-footed Bob Boone's trip around the bases. "Yes, there was," answered the club's public relations director Larry Shenk. "Three outfielders died."

Thinking he would enjoy having multiple choices, a teammate took ice cream lover Jackie Brandt to one of those stores that features a gazillion flavors. Instead of some exotic choice, Brandt ordered a vanilla cone. Outfielder Jimmy Wasdell once decked a teammate because he wouldn't stop singing on the team bus. Reliever Larry Andersen kept a collection of wigs that he sometimes wore onto the field before a game.

When they brought him to the big club in 1945, infielder Putsy Caballero was just 16 years old. Flint Rhem, a pitcher in the 1920s, once tried to avoid a starting assignment with the claim that he'd been kidnapped, when in reality he was on a three-day binge. And a Phillies scout rejected the chance to sign Honus Wagner, saying, "He's too clumsy to play in the National League."

By the NUMBERS

51—The number of minutes it took for the Phillies and the New York Giants to complete a nine-inning game on the last day of the season in 1919. The shortest game on record, it was won by the Giants, 6–1, before an announced crowd of 20,000 at the Polo Grounds. There were 18 hits in the game.

Five Phillies played professional basketball, either in the Basketball Association of America or the NBA. They were Frankie Baumholtz, Howie Shultz, Dick Groat, Gene Conley, and Ron Reed. NBA great Neil Johnston and All-American Johnny O'Brien also spent time in the Phillies' system. And Bob Finley and Chuck Essegian both played football in Rose Bowls, while Alvin Dark was an All-American gridder.

Unfortunately, the Phillies had the habit of often signing the wrong brother. They nabbed Ken Brett instead of George, Mike Maddux rather than Greg, Vince DiMaggio in place of Joe or Dom, and Jeremy Giambi but not Jason. Mark Leiter was a Phillie instead of Al, Rick Surhoff got the call in place of B.J., Frank Torre suited up for the Phils rather than Joe, Emil Meusel played in place of Bob, and Harry Coveleski was a Phil, but Stan wasn't.

Of, course, there were some good moves. The Phillies' regular lineup included Dick Allen as opposed to either Ron or Hank. It had Ed Delahanty instead of any of his four brothers. And Granny Hamner ranked well ahead of Garvin.

This was proof that all was not always lost in Philliesland. Much of the time, though, the franchise was anything but ordinary.

The Hall of Fame Outfield

The Phillies once fielded an outfield in which all three players made the Hall of Fame. One year, all three hit above .400.

For five seasons, from 1891 through 1895, Ed Delahanty patrolled left field for the Phils, Billy Hamilton tracked down balls in center, and Sam Thompson was stationed in right. Most experts agree that it was the greatest outfield ever assembled.

During a period when the underachieving Phillies were stuck mostly in fourth place, the terrific trio gave disappointed Phillies fans a reason to come to the ballpark. "The pride and delight of the Philadelphia crowds was the crack outfield," sportswriter Fred Lieb wrote.

Delahanty was the most prominent member of the group. Owner of the fourth-highest career batting average (.346) in major league history, he won two batting championships and hit over .300 in 11 of his 13 full big league seasons. He was the second big league player ever to hit four home runs in a single game, and in another game, he lashed six hits in six trips to the plate. Today, Delahanty still ranks among the leaders in most of the Phillies all-time career offensive statistics.

Delahanty's four-home-run game in 1896 was so impressive that even opposing pitcher Adonis Terry of the Chicago Colts joined the crowd at home plate to shake the slugger's hand after his fourth blast. Nor did Ed's achievement go unrecognized by the Phillies. The club gave him four boxes of chewing gum—one for each homer.

He was easily the most interesting character, too. One of five brothers to make the big leagues—although Big Ed was far and away the best of the group—he was a restless sort. He broke in as a second baseman, spent most of his time in the outfield, but also liked to take a turn playing first base.

"It's fun to be right in the middle of the game," he said. "In the outfield, you have to wait too long for a fly ball, and when you get a bad pitcher in there, you run until your tongue hangs out."

Once, Delahanty ignored manager Harry Wright's signal to bunt and swung away, hitting a home run. Wright fined him for not paying attention to the sign.

Twice during his career, Delahanty jumped leagues, once in 1890 to join the short-lived Players League and again in 1902 when lured away to the one-year-old American League. Delahanty, who liked to hang out in center city Philadelphia with his friends, met an early demise in 1903, one year after winning a batting title with the Washington Senators. After being thrown off a train because of rowdy behavior, he plunged from a bridge into the Niagara River, eventually washing over Niagara Falls. It has never been clearly established whether Delahanty, by then a heavy gambler and drinker, fell, jumped, or was pushed to his death.

Delahanty's outfield mates were less celebrated, but were nonetheless players of considerable note. Hamilton, nicknamed Sliding Billy, was a 12-time .300 hitter who hit .344 during his career and won two batting titles. While leading the league in stolen bases five times, he swiped more than 100 sacks in three different seasons and ranks in third place on baseball's all-time stolen base list. In 1894 he set a still-standing all-time record with 192 runs scored. In six seasons with the Phils, he never scored less than 110 runs.

Thompson, a career .331 hitter with two home-run crowns and one batting title to his credit, was the first National League player to hit 20 home runs in one season, to get 200 hits in a single year, and to record 300 total bases in one campaign. He hit over .300 seven times while slamming the most home runs (127) of any 19th-century player.

It was in 1894, though, that the future Hall of Famers (Delahanty elected in 1945, Hamilton in 1961, and Thompson in 1974) made their most indelible mark in baseball. That was the year all three hit over .400.

By the NUMBERS

7—The number of bases Billy Hamilton stole in one game in 1894. The thefts rank as a club record and tie the major league mark.

Ed Delahanty is probably the greatest Phillie not named Mike Schmidt. He was unquestionably one of the two or three best players of the pre-1900 era and posted a career batting average of .346, fourth highest all-time. He was one of five brothers who played major league baseball. Photo courtesy of National Baseball Hall of Fame Library, Cooperstown, New York.

In a never-to-be-repeated performance, Delahanty and Thompson each hit .407, while Hamilton posted a .404 mark. And to add to this incredible achievement, reserve outfielder Tuck Turner batted .416 in 339 trips to the plate.

During the season, Hamilton had a 27-game hitting streak, stole seven bases in one game, and set a major league record that still stands with 192 runs scored. Thompson (141) and Delahanty (131) ranked second and third in the league in RBIs.

Amazingly, there was no batting championship in Philadelphia that year. Boston's Hugh Duffy won top honors with a .440 mark. The Phillies captured the next four spots in the league.

Despite a team batting average of .349—the highest in major league history—the Phillies finished in fourth place, 18 games behind the first-place Baltimore Orioles.

More than one-half century later, the Phillies came close to fielding another Hall of Fame outfield. Its members would have come from the quartet of Richie Ashburn, Hank Aaron, Al Kaline, and Carl Yastrzemski.

How, you say? In the 1950s, Ashburn, of course, was already with the team, a homegrown product who had come up through the club's farm system. And the Phillies could have signed each of the others.

The Phils gave Aaron a tryout, then said, "Don't call us, we'll call you." They never did. Kaline impressed the Phillies brass in a tryout, but the club was also interested in a young pitcher. When it came down to who would get the $100,000 bonus that the team was offering, the pitcher, Tom Qualters, was chosen over Kaline. Qualters never won a game for the Phillies. Finally, after trying out with the club, Yastrzemski was offered a $90,000 bonus to sign. His father asked the Phils to throw in another $10,000 to make it an even $100,000, but the request was denied, and Yaz, like Aaron and Kaline, became a marvelous player elsewhere.

Some years later, the record book would show that if the Phillies had signed this threesome, they might have had an outfield to rival the legendary group of the 1890s.

TOP TEN

Phillies Career Leaders in Assists by an Outfielder

	Name	Assists
1.	Ed Delahanty	221
2.	Sam Thompson	202
3.	John Titus	181
4.	Cy Williams	173
5.	Roy Thomas	172
6.	Chuck Klein	170
7.	Gavvy Cravath	168
8.	Richie Ashburn	154*t*
	Jim Fogarty	154*t*
10.	Johnny Callison	153

Home, Not-So-Sweet Home

Of all the ballparks that the Phillies called home, none was more unusual or the site of more bizarre incidents than the one in which the team played the longest. For most of its life, the park was called Baker Bowl. Eventually, the name became synonymous with the worst in Phillies baseball.

The Phillies played at Baker Bowl for 51½ years. When it was opened in 1887, it was considered the finest stadium in the nation, a magnificent showplace that people came from far and wide to see and that was the envy of cities throughout the country. When the Phillies moved out in 1938, it was the laughingstock of baseball, the oldest park in the game and a run-down, obsolete relic that was derisively called names such as "the toilet bowl," "bandbox," and "cigar bowl."

Baker Bowl was one of five ballparks that have serviced the Phillies during their 123-year existence. Recreation Park (1883–1887) was the first. After Baker Bowl came Shibe Park, later to be renamed Connie Mack Stadium (1938–1970). That was followed by Veterans Stadium (1971–2003), and finally Citizens Bank Park.

Of the five, Baker Bowl was certainly the most unique, the most interesting, and the one with the craziest history. And to think, it cost just $101,000 to build.

Perhaps foretelling the future, the ballpark was built on a dump at Broad Street and Lehigh Avenue. It took 120,000 wagon-loads of dirt to fill the dump and the creek bed that ran through the lot. Originally, the park held 12,500 before the seating capacity was later raised to 18,800.

The park was first called Philadelphia Base Ball Park or Huntington Street Grounds (a side street where the main gate was located). In 1913, after William Baker had bought the team, he named the park after himself.

While it stood, Baker Bowl was the site of one World Series, in 1915. The second game of that Series against the Boston Red Sox was attended by President Woodrow Wilson, making him the first United States chief executive to watch a World Series game. President Wilson, accompanied by his future wife, Edith Galt, bought his own ticket and program.

Undoubtedly, Baker Bowl was the place that gave birth to Philadelphia's legendary boo birds. Along with showing their discontent vocally, fans of this era also demonstrated their displeasure by throwing seat cushions onto the field.

Once, a heckler dressed in farmer's clothing sat in the stands during batting practice, unmercifully riding the Phillies. "I can do as good as you can, you bums," he shouted. "You can't hit, you can't do nothin'." When challenged to back up his words, the farmer came down on the field, walked up to home plate, borrowed a bat, and proceeded to hit balls all over the lot. Then he disappeared, never to be seen again. Fans wondered what had happened to the hard-hitting farmer. Little did they realize that the "farmer" was noted prankster and Phillies right fielder Casey Stengel.

Through much of its life, Baker Bowl was the home of some awful teams. Fans responded accordingly. Often, there were no more than 1,000 to 1,500 at a game. And the team would draw between 200,000 and 300,000 for the season, sometimes even less.

"Sometimes," said pitcher Bucky Walters, "there were so few fans in the park that you'd say, 'Where is everybody? They must all be down at the shore.'"

In the 1930s, when the team was drawing its smallest crowds, many of the paying customers were local gamblers. To keep things interesting, they'd bet on virtually everything. "Ten cents it's a strike," somebody would yell. The takers would raise their hands.

Over the years, the most distinguishing feature of the ballpark was its right-field wall. Made of metal with a stone base, it ran from foul territory in right field to straightaway center. Originally, the wall was 40 feet high (later, Baker added a screen to bring the height to 60 feet). Through most of its life, the wall stood either 280 or 272 feet from home plate.

That, of course, meant that pop flies often went for home runs and screaming line drives often wound up being singles or doubles. "You had to pitch altogether differently than you would at any other field," said

DID YOU KNOW . . . That the Phillies won their first game of the 20th century, 19–17, in 10 innings over the Boston Braves? With each team using only two pitchers, the Braves slammed 25 hits while the visiting Phillies collected 19. The Phils lost the first game of the 21st century, falling to the Arizona Diamondbacks and Randy Johnson, 6–4, in Phoenix.

pitcher Claude Passeau. "It was never any fun. Even the right-handers would square off against you and hit to right."

The wall was so close that famed sportswriter Red Smith, who covered the Phillies in the 1930s, once wrote, "It might be exaggerating to say that the outfield wall casts a shadow across the infield. But if the right fielder had eaten onions for lunch, the second baseman knew it."

The right fielder played so close to the infield that Chuck Klein had 44 assists one year. And, of course, scores of games typically were high. The Phils won a game 28–0. They lost by scores of 28–6 and 20–16. In one 20–14 victory over the St. Louis Cardinals, there were 10 home runs in the game. One year, there wasn't a shutout thrown all season. The average score of games that year was 8–7, with the Phillies on the losing end.

Opposing pitchers disliked the wall as much as the home crew did. Dazzy Vance of the Brooklyn Dodgers refused to pitch at Baker Bowl when his club played there. In a classic understatement, he said it "hurt my record." Manager Wilbert Robinson usually granted the pitcher's wishes.

"The game was never over at Baker Bowl," Walters said. "Somebody was always likely to poke one over that short right-field fence. It was a hitter's paradise, and the hitters always fattened up their averages at Baker Bowl."

Cheap home runs were so frequent that the Phillies had a standing policy. If you were driving on Broad Street (which the wall paralleled) and a home run crashed into your windshield, you could come around to the main entrance and get reimbursed for the breakage.

The wall was also noted for the signs that hung on it. One sign in the 1915 era advertised a fly-catching product using the Phillies' center fielder in the copy. "Dode Paskert caught 309 flies last season," the sign said. "Our fly-catcher caught 1,237,345."

The most famous sign displayed a huge ad for Lifebuoy soap. It ran top to bottom on the wall and across a long section of the outfield. The sign read, "The Phillies Use Lifebuoy." At one point, some wag painted underneath: "And they still stink."

In sharp contrast, the left-field wall for most of the time was 341 feet down the line. With the power alleys veering off even farther, home runs to left were not an ordinary feat. In fact, only four balls during the entire life of the ballpark were ever hit out of the stadium in left.

Baker Bowl was also noted for its strange clubhouse arrangement. The locker rooms were in center field, making the ballpark one of only three big league parks ever to use that location. The Phillies clubhouse, eventually located on the second level, contained a swimming pool. Players would dive in to cool off after a game. Once, Hugh Jennings, a coach at the time, dove in only to find there was no water in the pool. Fortunately for him, his injuries were minimal.

There was always plenty of action outside the stadium. With no parking lots available and space at a premium, those who drove to a game turned over their cars to members of a neighborhood group called the Unholy Seven. In what was an early version of a valet service, they would drive the cars away to spots located many blocks from the ballpark.

A special character on the outside was a guy called Ball Hawk George. He made his living chasing down balls hit over the roof and onto the street. After retrieving them, Ball Hawk would return them to the Phillies, earning as much as 75¢ for a clean ball. Often, George had to

ALL-STADIUM TEAM

Baker Bowl

Position	Player
Left Field	Ed Delahanty
Center Field	Billy Hamilton
Right Field	Chuck Klein
First Base	Fred Luderus
Second Base	Nap Lajoie
Shortstop	Dick Bartell
Third Base	Pinky Whitney
Catcher	Jimmie Wilson
Right-handed Pitcher	Grover C. Alexander
Left-handed Pitcher	Eppa Rixey

By the NUMBERS

$1.65—The cost of a box seat at Baker Bowl in the 1930s. Grandstand seats were priced at $1.10, and bleacher seats set a customer back 50¢.

fight off neighborhood kids to grab the balls, pushing and elbowing them out of the way to get there first.

Baker Bowl was the site of several major catastrophes. A fire in 1894 required much of the ballpark to be replaced. The rebuilt park was the first to use mostly steel and brick and to feature a cantilever pavilion, a radical new architectural technique. These features again made the park a showplace and gave it notoriety as the most modern in baseball.

In 1903 a group of young girls was teasing several inebriated men outside the park. When one of the drunks lurched after one of the girls, he fell on top of her. Cries of "help" and "murder" arose from the girls, causing curious fans inside the park to race to a 100-foot-long wooden deck that hung 30 feet above the street. As more fans crowded onto the deck, it began to give away. Under all the weight, it crashed to the street. Twelve fans were killed, and 232 were injured.

The ballpark was the site of many other memorable moments. Babe Ruth played his last major league game there. The Phillies won their first and only World Series game in their first 97 years at Baker Bowl. Phillies pitcher Joe Oeschger hurled all 20 innings in a 9–9 tie with the Brooklyn Dodgers there. Sherry Magee slugged an umpire during a mêlée that occurred just four years before the Phillies outfielder became an umpire himself. Grover Cleveland Alexander, the winner in the World Series win, won a game there that was his 33rd victory, his 16th shutout, and his 38th complete game of the year. And Gavvy Cravath, Cy Williams, and Klein won home-run crowns there.

By the 1920s, Baker Bowl had become a neglected antique that was falling apart at the seams. While calling it a "cobwebby House of Horrors," future Pulitzer Prize–winner Red Smith wrote that the old ballpark "bore a striking resemblance to a rundown men's room."

The Phillies left the park in the middle of the 1938 season, moving seven blocks down the street to Shibe Park. Baker Bowl, which was also the first home of the Philadelphia Eagles, was used for various activities thereafter, before its ultimate demise in 1950.

A Pennant Finally Arrives

The Phillies' first pennant in 1915 offered a strong argument for the merits of disrupting the status quo. It was a classic case of out with the old, in with the new.

The club made some key alterations to its roster. It hired a new manager. Changes were made in the way the players conducted themselves both on and off the field. The team even came up with a new location for spring training.

No change was more important than the one in which Pat Moran replaced Charlie "Red" Dooin as manager. Dooin had been the team's pilot since 1910, but despite the appearance of being a pennant-contender after a second-place finish in 1913, the Phillies had placed a disappointing sixth in 1914. Owner William Baker had seen enough of his former star catcher.

"I don't blame Charlie for everything that happened last year," Baker said. "But he lost control of the team, and I think a change is advisable and necessary. Fortunately, we didn't have to go far in looking for a successor."

Moran was already on the team. A former backup catcher who had been with the club since 1910, he was a Phillies coach. Because he preferred beverages with a kick, Pat was nicknamed Whiskey Face.

"I've watched Pat, and I like the way he goes about his work," said Baker. "He knows a lot of baseball, and I think he'll make us a fine manager."

Moran did indeed know baseball. According to Fred Lieb, a noted sportswriter of the day, Pat "was wise, sagacious with just enough of the Irish psychic in him to give him good hunches and enable him to look through people. No phony ever got anywhere with Moran."

The Phillies also made other off-season changes. Although the club had to give up star left fielder Sherry Magee and third baseman Hans Lobert, among others, it made trades that brought them left fielder George "Possum" Whitted, third baseman Milt Stock, second baseman Bert Niehoff, and pitcher Al Demaree. They also bought minor-league shortstop Dave Bancroft.

This group gave the Phillies an entirely new mix, even in terms of the players' backgrounds. For instance, Demaree, an off-season cartoonist, was a native of Scotland. Pitcher Erskine Mayer was one of the era's rare Jewish players, and hurler Ben Tincup was a Cherokee Indian. Pitchers Eppa Rixey (Virginia), Stan Baumgartner (Chicago), and Joe Oeschger (St. Mary's of California) were all college graduates, with the latter possessing a master's degree from Stanford.

The team had three future Hall of Famers—Grover Cleveland Alexander, Bancroft, and Rixey. Much later, Stock would be the third-base coach of the Brooklyn Dodgers and the man who made the ill-advised decision to send Cal Abrams home in the final game of the 1950 season. And right fielder Gavvy Cravath would go on to win six home-run titles en route to becoming baseball's top home-run swatter until Babe Ruth appeared.

Since 1910 the Phillies had held spring training at a different location each year. In 1915 the team switched its spring headquarters to St. Petersburg, Florida, where it played in a little old park well removed from downtown, called Coffee Pot Park. The park, located on a bayou and surrounded by orange groves, held just 500 fans. In the locker room, there was only one shower.

Immediately, Moran set up some new rules. Players would walk the two miles from their hotel to the ballpark and back. Oeschger and Baumgartner tried to ride bicycles, but Moran soon caught them and made them walk an extra mile each day.

By the NUMBERS

21—The number of innings John "Mule" Watson pitched in a 2–1 loss to the Chicago Cubs in a game in 1918. While setting a Phillies record, Watson allowed 19 hits (18 singles). After allowing one run in the first inning, he pitched 19 scoreless innings.

The Phillies' one and only pennant over a 68-year period was in 1915. Rookie shortstop Dave Bancroft, a future Hall of Famer, was a big reason Philadelphia took the pennant that year. Bancroft was in the top 10 in five offensive categories, including home runs, runs, and walks. He is generally regarded as the best shortstop of the 1910s and 1920s.

TRIVIA

Who holds the Phillies career record for hitting the most inside-the-park home runs?

Answers to the trivia questions are on page 190.

Practice consisted of morning and afternoon sessions, with the hotel delivering lunch that often featured horrible tasting fish with the heads still intact. Players often dumped the fish and picked oranges for their lunch. Once in a while, roast beef was served, but that was wholly unappetizing, too, as Alexander ably demonstrated when he removed a piece from his sandwich and nailed it to the soul of his shoe.

Calling it "inside play," Moran drilled his team in the fundamentals of the game. Among a variety of pioneering techniques, he became one of the first managers to give his pitchers and catchers combination signs. He also had his players endlessly practicing cutoffs, breaking up double plays, throwing to second and third on bunts, and working on plays in different situations. The pitchers were drilled on pickoffs, covering first base, and backing up other bases, and they were taught to keep records on opposing hitters.

During a game, everybody on the bench had a specific job, whether it was trying to steal the other team's signs, noting the traits of the opposing pitcher, or observing the habits of the enemy hitters. Once, when Rixey spent too much time fooling around on the bench instead of watching the rival pitcher, Moran strolled over and rapped a fungo bat across his toes.

Although the team was heavily stocked with fun-lovers, team discipline was extremely important to Moran. That was evident when Rixey, Tincup, Oeschger, and Baumgartner rented a boat one night and got stuck on a sandbar in Tampa Bay. They didn't return to the hotel until 8:00 AM, at which time a furious Moran fined the quartet.

Nevertheless, the team did have fun. Players sometimes stuck dead birds in catcher Bill Killefer's mitt. Center fielder Dode Paskert often spit tobacco juice into an electric fan. And once some unknown prankster dropped a bag of water out of a hotel window onto Rixey's head.

All the while, Moran, who had banned big-money craps and poker games from the clubhouse, kept repeating the same message. "This is not a sixth-place team," he said over and over. He would then add, "This is your bread and butter as well as mine."

DID YOU KNOW . . . That the Phillies have had more no-hitters pitched against them than any team in baseball? Starting with Noodles Hahn's whitewash in 1900, there have been 17 no-hitters of nine innings or more fired at the Phils. The last one was tossed by Bob Forsch in 1978.

Sometimes players failed to heed their leader's admonitions. Such was the case when infielder Beals Becker twice tried to steal third base with a Phillies player already there. Or when Alexander tried to swipe third with the bases loaded. Or when Cravath, in a fit of anger that contradicted the manager's keep-calm philosophy, fired a bat through a clubhouse window.

When the season began, the Phillies got off to a fast start, winning 11 of their first 14 games, then moving in and out of first place until permanently taking over the top spot on July 13. A little more than two months later, the Phillies coasted to the first pennant in their 33 years, finishing seven games ahead of former Phils manager George Stallings' defending world champion Boston Braves.

Alexander won the clincher with a 5–0 victory while hurling his fourth one-hitter of the season. It had been an awesome season for the ace right-hander. He led the league in wins (31), complete games (36), innings pitched (376), strikeouts (241), shutouts (12), and ERA (1.22).

Mayer won 21, Demaree 14, and Rixey 11. Cravath's 24 home runs set an all-time record that would not be broken until Ruth belted 29 in 1919. First baseman and captain Fred Luderus led the team with a .315 batting average.

The Phillies' opponent in the World Series was the Boston Red Sox, a team loaded with stars, not the least of whom was a young pitcher named Babe Ruth, an 18-game winner making his first postseason appearance. The first two games were staged at Baker Bowl. Alexander beat the Red Sox, 3–1, in the opener, but the Phillies would not win another Series game until 1980.

With Alexander subsequently ineffective because of a sore arm, the Phillies lost the next four games, all by one run, and three in a row by 2–1 scores. The third and fourth games were played at Braves Field—the Series was moved there because the park held more people than the Red Sox's Fenway Park.

Back at Baker Bowl for the fifth game, the Phils lost, 5–4, on Harry Hooper's second home run of the game. Like the first one, it bounced into the temporary stands (for a ground-rule homer) that Baker had installed across center field to increase the number of ticket sales.

Tough as it might have been to take, the Phillies, who earned losers' shares of $2,520.17 apiece, were hardly crestfallen after the final game. Beer kegs were rolled into the clubhouse, and the players drank themselves silly. One after another passed out as the party stretched far into the night.

Killefer won top party-boy honors, passing out and getting carried to the nearby station, where he was packed onto a train that would carry him home to Michigan. Reindeer Bill, as he was called, didn't awake until the train was traversing the famous horseshoe curve in Altoona.

16 Shutouts in One Season

One of the best players ever to throw a little round sphere at a man holding a wooden stick was a guy with the epic name of Grover Cleveland Alexander. He was a Nebraska farm boy, one of 13 children, and he could throw a baseball so well that some of his records will never be broken.

He was named after a sitting president, and, in his own way, Alexander was certainly presidential, too, reigning over a population of hitters who had no chance of initiating a recall.

Alexander's place in baseball history was assured in 1938 when he was among the members of the second group elected to the Hall of Fame, just the fourth pitcher—behind Cy Young, Walter Johnson, and Christy Mathewson—to enter the baseball shrine. Only Young and Johnson won more games than Alex, who tied with Mathewson in career victories with 373. Alexander lost 208 while finishing his career with a sparkling 2.56 ERA.

The best part of Alexander's career came while hurling with the Phillies in the pitchers' nightmare called Baker Bowl. Old Pete, as he came to be known, won 190 games for the Phils, including 30 or more in three straight seasons and 22 or more three other times. Only Steve Carlton and Robin Roberts won more games in Phillies uniforms.

In each of his seven seasons with the Phillies, Alex never failed to work in at least 300 innings—his high being 388⅔ in 1916—and he led the National League in innings pitched six times, and in wins, complete games, shutouts, and strikeouts each five times.

A sidearmer who occasionally went overhand, Alex had masterful control, which he developed as a youth, bringing dinner home for his family by throwing rocks at rabbits. During his entire 20-year career, when he was a nine-time 20-game winner, he walked only 951 in 5,190 innings.

TOP TEN

Most Strikeouts in One Season by a Phillies Pitcher

	Name	Year	Strikeouts
1.	Curt Schilling	1997	319
2.	Steve Carlton	1972	310
3.	Curt Schilling	1998	300
4.	Steve Carlton	1980	286*t*
	Steve Carlton	1982	286*t*
6.	Steve Carlton	1983	275
7.	Jim Bunning	1965	268
8.	Jim Bunning	1967	253
9.	Jim Bunning	1966	252
10.	Grover C. Alexander	1915	241

"He could throw through the eye of a needle," former Chicago Cubs second baseman Sparky Adams once said. "He wasn't too fast, but he could throw wherever he wanted, hitting the same spot every time. I wish I had six Alexanders on my team."

Alexander threw a fastball; a curve, which although it broke just a few inches, was fast and virtually unhittable; a sinker; and a screwball. His motion was effortless. "When he pitched, it looked like he was throwing batting practice," said former Boston Braves pitcher Tim McNamara.

Unquestionably, the preeminent feat in Alexander's career came in 1916 when he tossed 16 shutouts en route to a 33-win season. No pitcher has ever come close to duplicating that feat; none ever will.

"It was," said baseball writer and historian Allen Lewis, "probably the greatest accomplishment in one season of any pitcher in the modern era."

During the season, Alexander blanked the Cincinnati Reds five times, the Braves three times, and the St. Louis Cardinals, Brooklyn Dodgers, and Pittsburgh Pirates each twice.

He ended the record with a 2–0 victory over Boston in a game in which he threw 17 ground-outs.

Late in the season, he beat the Reds in the first game of a doubleheader. "I'll have to ask you to pitch the second game, too," advised

Grover Cleveland Alexander was a 30-game winner three times and a 20-game winner three additional times for the Phillies in the 1910s. In all, he won 190 games for the Phillies in seven seasons before being traded to the Cubs in 1917. In 1915 and 1916 he led the National League in wins, ERA, and strikeouts, despite pitching in the hitter-friendly Baker Bowl and battling ongoing problems with epilepsy and alcoholism.

DID YOU KNOW . . .

That the Phillies played in the first games at Ebbets Field in Brooklyn in 1913, at the Houston Astrodome in 1965, at Montreal's Olympic Stadium in 1977, and at Enron Field (now Minute Maid Park) in Houston in 2000? They also played in the last games at New York's Polo Grounds in 1963 and Cincinnati's Riverfront Stadium in 2002. The Phils participated in the first baseball game broadcast on radio in 1921 in Pittsburgh and in the first major league night game in 1935 in Cincinnati.

manager Pat Moran. "But we've only got a little more than an hour to catch the train. Get it over fast." The game took 58 minutes to play, with Alex firing a shutout.

Alexander finished the 1916 campaign with a league-leading 1.55 ERA, firing 38 complete games in 45 starts. He led the league in seven different categories. He was also credited, years later, with recording three saves.

Alexander's magnificent feat was, of course, one of many remarkable achievements during his career. As a rookie in 1911, he threw four straight shutouts on the way to winning 28 games. When the Phillies captured their first pennant in 1915, Old Pete not only won 31 games, but hurled four one-hitters. The Cardinals' Art Butler hit a pop fly single with two outs in the ninth in one of those games. Another came with a week to go in the season and gave the Phillies a pennant-clinching 5–0 win over Boston. Nine days later, Alex beat the Red Sox, 3–1, to give the Phillies their only victory in a World Series game in 97 years.

When he came to the Phillies, Alexander was one of the club's biggest bargains. And his signing was somewhat accidental. Patsy O'Rourke was randomly scouting the New York League for the Phillies and stopped at Syracuse to watch a game. "See anything up there that caught your eye?" asked team president Horace Fogel. "You bet," said O'Rourke. "A fine pitcher. One of the greatest pitching prospects I've ever looked at."

"If you're talking about Chambers, save your breath," Fogel said, referring to George Chambers, who would post a 25–6 record that season at Scranton. "We've already got him."

"Chambers is good," replied Patsy, "but the fellow I'm talking about is even better." Fogel was unimpressed, but O'Rourke persisted. "All I can say is that you better grab this Alexander before someone else does."

Finally relenting, Fogel purchased Alexander's contract from Syracuse. He paid $750.

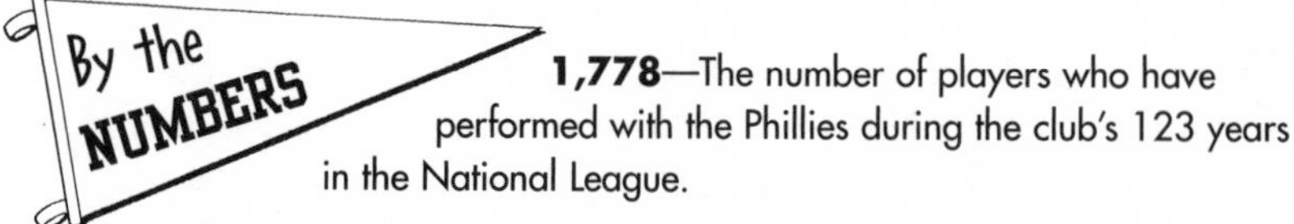

1,778—The number of players who have performed with the Phillies during the club's 123 years in the National League.

In the twilight of his career, Alex gained fame as the pitcher who shuffled in from the bullpen to strike out the New York Yankees' Tony Lazzeri with the bases loaded in the seventh game of the 1926 World Series.

Over the years, Alex was accused of being hungover from a drinking binge the previous night and had to be awakened from a deep slumber in the Cards' bullpen before entering the game. Old Pete always denied the claim.

"I don't want to spoil anybody's story," he said. "But I was cold sober the night before, although there were plenty of other nights before and since when I wasn't. I wasn't any more drunk than the fellows who wrote that story."

In 1930, by then suffering from a serious drinking problem and bouts with epilepsy, which he had battled for many years, the 43-year-old Alexander returned briefly to the Phillies before drawing his release after pitching in nine games.

In the ensuing years, Alex pitched for the House of David and various other independent teams. Eventually, with his fondness for strong liquid refreshments taking a powerful hold on his activities, he wandered from town to town, holding a variety of unattractive jobs.

At one point, several years after his induction into the Hall of Fame, Alexander was discovered working as a shill at a flea circus near Times Square in New York City. A disbelieving writer asked the once-great pitcher how he could work in such dismal surroundings.

"It's better living off the fleas than having them live off you," Alexander explained.

Two years after he died in 1950, Alex's life was portrayed in a movie, *The Winning Team,* with Ronald Reagan playing the part of the Hall of Fame hurler. How fitting that a future president would play the namesake of a former one.

Managers of All Stripes

No one could ever accuse the Phillies of lacking managers with unusual and often colorful ways. Indeed, many of them were more colorful than they were successful.

A few of them were brilliant strategists. Others were downright mediocre. And some of them had the brains of an ant.

Phillies managers (not counting interims) held the job for an average of 2.4 years. Only 12 of them lasted four years or more. Thirty-eight of them came to the Phils with no prior managing experience, and 36 of them never managed in the big leagues again. Forty played in the big leagues, 19 of whom spent time with the Phillies. Just 10 full-time skippers had winning records.

Among those who managed the Phillies were the man called "the Father of Baseball," an alleged bigamist, a former medical school student, a dentist, three future umpires, a former Phillies ticket-taker, a vaudeville singer, a former college professor, the son of a former Phillies player, the owner of baseball's highest single-season batting average, three Hall of Famers, and two All-Star shortstops.

Phillies managers had nicknames such as Whiskey Face, Wild Bill, Cactus, Stuffy, Blondie, Stud, Chief, Doc, Pope, Tito, and, of course, the inimitable Death to Flying Things.

A Phillies owner (Al Reach) once piloted the club for 11 games. That year, because manager Harry Wright had a spell of blindness, the Phillies had four managers, including a rookie player (Bob Allen) who led the club for 35 games.

Four men managed the Phillies twice. Four were native Philadelphians. And all five who piloted All-Star teams won.

Among the men who led the Phillies, here are some of the least ordinary:

Harry Wright (1884–1893) was called the Father of Baseball, in part because he managed the first all-pro team, the Cincinnati Redlegs in 1869. He also created flannel uniforms, colored stockings, and knickered pants. "What I had in mind," he said, "was fewer clothes. You couldn't play ball with inches of flannel flapping around your ankles." (Tell that to today's players.) Wright set the club on the right course after he took over in the Phils' second year. He had seven winning seasons.

Arthur Irvin (1894–1895) was another unusual skipper. He had the highest winning percentage (.575) of any Phils manager who led the team for two years or more. He was also an alleged bigamist. Irvin, a former star shortstop who was one of the first players to wear a fielder's glove, was believed to have jumped to his death in the Atlantic Ocean while riding a ship between his families in Boston and New York.

George Stallings (1897–1898) was a former medical school student, the son of a Confederate general, and a gentleman off the field but an abusive tyrant on it. Players hated him. Their dissent reached a point in 1898 when they threatened to go on strike if Stallings wasn't removed. He was. Stallings, however, went on to manage, among others, the "Miracle Braves," upset winners in the 1914 World Series.

Billy Shettsline (1898–1902) rose from Phillies ticket-taker to manager and eventually to team president. Not a bad manager who had just one losing season out of five, the vastly overweight Shettsline, who was anything but agile, was once so happy over his team's victory that on the way home, according to one report, "he fell out of the carriage and got a mud bath."

DID YOU KNOW . . . That three of the Phillies' full-time managers were born in Philadelphia? They were Billy Shettsline (1898–1902), Jimmie Wilson (1934–1938), and Lee Elia (1987–1988). Two others, Hans Lobert (1938 and 1942) and Dallas Green (1979–1981), came from nearby Delaware. Part-timer Jack Clements (1890) was also born in Philadelphia.

Eddie Sawyer (right), here with Dick Sisler, managed the Phillies to their first pennant in 35 years when he guided the 1950 Whiz Kids into the World Series against the Yankees. Sisler hit the home run that got them there.

Charlie Dooin (1910–1914), an excellent catcher for the Phillies, had better luck as a singer than he did as a manager. Although expected to drive the team to its first pennant, he never did. Dooin, whose Irish tenor voice could often be heard in the clubhouse and during the off-season on vaudeville, wound up back in show business, where he performed for many years after leaving the Phillies.

Pat Moran (1915–1918) was not only a former Phillies backup catcher who led the club to its first pennant in 1915, but he also instilled the kinds of fundamentals often overlooked in his day. Whiskey Face caught batting practice and from that position got his pitchers to think about what they were doing. He also banned gambling from the clubhouse. Moran was the manager of the Cincinnati Reds, winners in the 1919 World Series over the infamous Chicago Black Sox.

Burt Shotton (1928–1933) was in his first big league managerial job when he became the only Phillies pilot to lead his team to a winning season (1932) over a 32-year period. Once, mindful that some players were sneaking out of the hotel via a fire escape to go dancing after hours, Shotton painted the railing green. Those who showed up for breakfast the next day with green hands were promptly chastised. Shotton later managed the Brooklyn Dodgers when Jackie Robinson broke in and was the pilot of that team when it lost to the Phillies in 1950 on the last day of the season.

James "Doc" Prothro (1939–1941) may have been one of the worst managers in Phillies history, although his teams were always far short on talent. They lost more than 100 games in each of his three seasons, including a club record 111 in 1941. A practicing dentist during the off-season, Prothro's chief claim to fame was that he sired a son, Tommy, who was a prominent football coach in the college and pro ranks.

Bucky Harris (1943) had one of the shortest tenures of any Phillies manager, but was one of the best the team ever had. Trouble was, the owner, William Cox, didn't like the way Bucky managed. When Cox fired Harris in late July of his first season, the future Hall of Famer mentioned to the press how Cox bet on Phillies games. The remark led to an investigation that resulted in Cox getting thrown out of baseball for life.

TRIVIA

Which Phillies managers won All-Star Games?

Answers to the trivia questions are on page 190.

TOP TEN

Winningest Phillies Managers

	Name	Years	Wins
1.	Gene Mauch	1960–1968	646
2.	Harry Wright	1884–1893	636
3.	Danny Ozark	1973–1979	594
4.	Jim Fregosi	1991–1996	431
5.	Red Dooin	1910–1914	392
6.	Eddie Sawyer	1948–1952, 1958–1960	390
7.	Burt Shotton	1928–1933	370
8.	Billy Shettsline	1898–1902	367
9.	Larry Bowa	2001–2004	337
10.	Pat Moran	1915–1918	323

Eddie Sawyer (1948–1952, 1958–1960) ranks as one of the Phillies' finest skippers. The former college professor led the Whiz Kids to the National League pennant in 1950. "I tried to treat my players like I wanted to be treated when I was a player," said the former New York Yankees farmhand. Despite his rating, Sawyer had only two winning seasons with the Phils, and his fatherly presence turned against him. He quit the team after one game in his second term in 1960.

Mayo Smith (1955–1958) was so unknown when he was hired that a chorus of "Mayo who?" sounded when he was introduced at his initial press conference. One newspaper even called him "Ed Mayo Smith" in a headline. Smith was hired to try to get the Phillies back to respectability after they plummeted following the 1950 season, but he could never quite do it. Instead, he went on to greener pastures, leading the Detroit Tigers to the World Championship in 1968.

Danny Ozark (1973–1979) was the guy who said after a particular losing streak that "even Napoleon had his Watergate." Despite his frequent verbal blunders, Ozark was generally an easygoing soul who should—but often doesn't—get credit for guiding the Phillies to three straight division titles. Ozark, a former Los Angeles Dodgers coach, is more often remembered as the manager who failed to substitute Jerry Martin for Greg Luzinski in the 1977 League Championship Series.

Dallas Green (1979–1981) will forever be known as the manager who drove the Phillies to their only World Championship. Said to be as "subtle as a crowbar," Green whipped and hollered the Phils to the title, but he was also highly complimentary when a player did something good. His screaming fit late in the 1980 season helped to turn a sagging club around. The outspoken Green, a one-time Phillies farm-system director, went on to the unlikely status of managing both the New York Yankees and Mets.

Jim Fregosi (1991–1996) led the Phillies to their fifth and last pennant in 1993. A "player's manager" who left his underlings alone to play their own game, the former All-Star shortstop could be curt and aloof at times and jovial at others. But he knew the game, and he was respected for that. Fregosi also managed the California Angels, Chicago White Sox, and Toronto Blue Jays.

Larry Bowa (2001–2004) was a fiery, intense skipper whose aggressiveness sometimes got in the way of his managing. That alienated many of his players. Bowa, another former All-Star shortstop, posted 86–70 records in two of his four years as manager. None, however, was quite good enough to get the Phillies into the playoffs, a place so many expected them to be. Bowa, who often criticized his players publicly, was fired after four stormy seasons.

Among other Phillies managers worth noting, there were **Jimmie Wilson** (1934–1938), a hometown former Phils catcher who couldn't win, in part because his good players always got traded; **Steve O'Neill** (1952–1954), a World Series winner in 1945 with the Tigers, but over the hill when he became, at the age of 60, the Phils' oldest manager; **Frank Lucchesi** (1970–1972), an enormously popular but largely unsuccessful pilot who called himself "Skipper" and used phrases such as "you can't serve water with a pitchfork"; and **Terry Francona** (1997–2000), whose dad, Tito, also played for the Phillies, was one of the nicest guys you'll ever meet. He went from taking the heat in Philadelphia for the team's lack of success to being manager of the World Champion Boston Red Sox in 2004.

Bleak Years and Cheap Times

Nearly every team in sports has at one point suffered through an unbearable losing period. The Phillies are no exception. The only trouble with their losing period is it lasted for 32 years.

During that time, a sixth-place finish by the Phillies was considered a remarkable achievement. Even a seventh-place spot in the standings wasn't considered too bad. Neither happened very often, though. Between 1917, when they finished second, and 1949, when they placed third, the Phillies wound up in the National League basement no less than 16 times. They finished seventh eight times.

Only once during that incredibly long period were the Phils able to sneak out of the second division. That was in 1932 when they made an amazing jump all the way up to fourth place with shortstop Dick Bartell and right fielder Chuck Klein, starters the following year in the first All-Star Game, leading the way. The Phils even had a winning record (78–76) that year.

The rest of the time the Phillies were the unchallenged flops of the league. Along with their misery on the field, they played in a ballpark that had become the worst in the major leagues. And during those bleak years, they played under 16 managers, only five of whom lasted more than two seasons.

"Sometimes I'd go home at night after playing hard all day," said Bartell. "We'd lost 10–4 or something like that, and I'd be bleeding. I'd say to myself, 'I'm just not going to do this anymore.' But I'd be back the next day, and we'd do the same thing all over again. It was really depressing."

At times, it could also get really bizarre. For instance, in the early 1920s the Phillies took an 11-game losing streak into a series with the Brooklyn Dodgers at Ebbets Field. But sometime between their previous

TOP TEN

Worst Phillies Seasons of All Time (by Percentage)

	Year	Record	Percentage
1.	1883	17–81–1	.173
2.	1942	42–109	.278
3.	1941	43–111–1	.279
4.	1928	43–109	.283
5.	1939	45–106–1	.298
6.	1945	46–108	.299
7.	1938	45–105–1	.300
8.	1961	47–107–1	.305
9.	1923	50–104–1	.325
10.	1940	50–103	.327

Note: Ties not included in percentage calculations.

game and their arrival in Brooklyn, the player's trunks had gotten lost. The Phils had to use the Dodgers' equipment and wear their away uniforms. Thusly disguised, the team went out and won the first game of the series. After the trunks showed up the next day, the club regained its losing habits and dropped the next 12 games in a row.

In 1930 the club had a team batting average of .315—the third highest in major league history—but over the entire season the Phils were outscored by an average of 8–6. They finished in dead last, 40 games out of first place. That year, the club's woeful pitching staff had an ERA of 6.71.

Although losing 100 or more games during the long years of ineptitude was fairly common—the team hit the century mark in losses six times between 1921 and 1936—the darkest days of the era occurred from 1938 to 1942. The Phillies not only finished in last place in each of those five seasons, but also lost more than 100 games each year. The low point came in 1941 when the Phils dropped 111 decisions while winning just 43 games. The following year, the team was 42–109.

"Win a few games in a row, and it might be cause for a congressional investigation," said second baseman Danny Murtaugh.

Despite their sorry times, the Phillies did have a few bright spots. Just a few, though. Gavvy Cravath won six home-run titles. Cy Williams won three. Klein won a Triple Crown and three other home-run crowns.

Lefty O'Doul won a batting title with a .398 average while setting a league record (since tied) for most hits (254) in a season. Fred Leach hit above .300 four straight years. And Danny Litwhiler became the first outfielder ever to play 150 or more games and field a perfect 1.000 for the season.

On the other side of the diamond, the Phillies seldom had a pitcher win more than 15 games in a season. In fact, between 1918 and 1945, no one on the staff won in double figures five different seasons. Hal Kelleher allowed 12 runs in one inning. Bill Kerksieck gave up four home runs in one inning. And Hugh Mulcahy lost 76 games in four years, once dropping 22 and another time 20. Is it any wonder his nickname was "Losing Pitcher"?

Before a game in 1930, team captain Fresco Thompson filled out the lineup card and delivered it to plate umpire Bill Klem. In the pitcher's spot, Thompson, who escaped his miserable surroundings to become a vice president with the Dodgers, wrote, "Willoughby and others."

Most of the Phillies' problems stemmed from a case of extreme poverty. Under owners William Baker and then Gerry Nugent, neither of them wealthy, the team was always just one step away from bankruptcy.

Crowds at Baker Bowl, the Phillies' home park, seldom reached 300,000 for the year. Five times, the team even drew well under 200,000. Most of the time, a single game would draw between 1,500 and 2,000.

To the detriment of the Phillies, their lack of fans in Philadelphia was also enhanced by the presence of the American League's Athletics. In the two-team city, the A's were not only the dominant, but easily the much more popular club, and they remained that way until the Phillies won the National League pennant in 1950.

Under such circumstances, Phillies management often had to take extreme steps just to stay alive. One of its regular devices was to sell or trade its best players. Ones such as Klein, Bartell, Bucky Walters, Claude Passeau, and Dolph Camilli were shipped off with the club always getting in return a few lesser players and a sizeable chunk of cash. Usually, the money would be the only way the Phils could stay afloat all season.

43—The number of doubleheaders the Phillies played in 1943. It's a major league record never to be broken.

In one of the strangest yet shrewdest set of deals, the Phillies in 1933 swapped Klein to the Chicago Cubs for players and $65,000 cash, then two and one-half years later, they got the future Hall of Famer back along with $50,000.

In one of their more unfathomable moves, the Phillies sold Johnny Moore to the Los Angeles Angels of the Pacific Coast League after the slugging outfielder had just hit over .300 in four straight years. It turned

The 1920s Phillies didn't win many games, but they could hit. Outfielder Lefty O'Doul led the National League in hitting in 1929, when he batted .398 for the Phillies.

IF ONLY . . . In the 1930s the Phillies hadn't dealt away most of their top players, including Lefty O'Doul, Dick Bartell, Pinky Whitney, Chuck Klein, Bucky Walters, Johnny Moore, Dolph Camilli, and Claude Passeau. The decade wouldn't have been nearly as bleak on the field, but off the field the team probably would've faced bankruptcy because of the salaries it would've had to pay those stars.

out that the L.A. club was the highest bidder. "Several other major league clubs were interested in me," Moore recalled, "but L.A. offered more money."

The Phillies sold the office furniture one year to pay for spring training. And on road trips, they would use the cheapest form of transportation and stay in the most inexpensive hotels.

Kirby Higbe, a Phillies pitcher in 1939 and 1940, claimed that the hotel rooms were so small "that you had to go out in the hall to change your mind. You could dust off the mirror in the bathroom with your eyelashes," he added.

The Phillies scrimped in many other ways, too, including in matters at Baker Bowl. Players, for instance, hung their clothes in the locker room on nails. "Some years, we'd even get a new nail," said pitcher Passeau.

Added pitcher Pete Sivess, "After a game, you had to stand in line to take a shower. There were only four showerheads."

A classic case of Phillies frugality happened in the early 1920s. With no money available to pay extra workers to help maintain the playing field, head groundskeeper Sam Payne was forced to take a radical step. He hired three sheep—two ewes and a ram—to help keep the grass trimmed. The sheep lived under the stands in left field.

At the time, one of the Phillies executives was an exceptionally portly gentleman named Billy Shettsline. A former manager and later club president, Shettsline was still employed by the club when the sheep were on the job. One day, Shettsline was walking across the outfield when the ram decided to charge. Running as fast as he could with the wooly critter in hot pursuit, Shettsline finally made it to safety.

The next day, however, the three sheep were handed their unconditional releases. And so went another bizarre incident in what was the Phillies' bleakest, and certainly its strangest, era.

Home Runs Are Not Welcome

Chuck Klein may be the only batter in baseball history who played for a team on which the owner tried to reduce his own slugger's home-run production.

That seriously contradicts the homer-happy mentality of today, not to mention that of many teams in Klein's era, too. But then, there have been few owners as cheap—or as unorthodox—as the Phillies' William Baker.

Baker owned the Phillies from 1913 to 1930. Rarely was he ever inclined to spend more money than the absolute minimum, a practice that was reflected in the sorry teams that took the field most of the time during his reign.

One of many who suffered from this practice was Klein, a slugger of considerable talent and one of the best batsmen the Phillies ever had. Klein became a member of the Hall of Fame in 1980, carrying a .320 lifetime batting average with 300 home runs into the baseball shrine.

A sturdy farm boy from Indiana who built his muscular frame by tossing around metal ingots weighing several hundred pounds in a steel mill, Klein came to the Phillies in 1928. He had been tearing apart the Midwestern-based Class B Central League while playing with the Ft. Wayne Chiefs when a scout decided that the former high school basketball star would look mighty good in a Phillies uniform. Somehow, he persuaded Baker to spend $5,000 to buy the kid's contract.

A few days later, Klein showed up in the Phillies' clubhouse carrying a battered suitcase in each hand. "I'm Klein," he announced. "They call me Chuck Klein."

As usual, the Phillies were buried deep in the National League standings, heading for their seventh last-place finish in the last 10 years. So new manager Burt Shotton was anxious to see if the kid was for real. "All right, Klein," he said. "Get in uniform. They tell me you can hit. Goodness knows, we need hitters. In fact, we need everything."

In his first at-bat in the big leagues, Klein popped out as a pinch-hitter. The next day, he smacked a home run and double, and the Phillies had themselves a keeper.

Nobody ever hit better in his first five years in the majors than Klein. During that stretch, he averaged 36 home runs, 224 hits, 139 RBIs, and 132 runs a season with a batting average of .359 and a slugging percentage of .639. He won four home-run titles, a batting crown, and led the league in runs three times and in RBIs twice.

"Lefties, righties, it didn't matter who was pitching," said teammate and shortstop Dick Bartell. "He hit them all."

In 1930 Klein hit .386 but didn't even win the batting title. He finished third as Bill Terry led the league with a .401 mark. That year, Chuck also collected 250 hits, 40 homers, 59 doubles, 170 RBIs, and 158 runs in what was, at least statistically, his finest season.

Although he was an extraordinary hitter—he still holds or is tied for NL marks for a left-handed batter for total bases (445), extra-base hits (107), runs (158), RBIs (170), and most games with one or more hits in a season (135)—it was as a home-run hitter that Klein attracted the most attention. He lofted balls over the right-field wall at Baker Bowl with monotonous regularity.

The fact that the right-field wall stood just 280 feet from home plate had a lot to do with the pull-hitting Klein's home-run totals. Sometimes, the so-called experts shrilly belittled his accomplishments. One of them was the miserly Baker.

Babe Ruth had hit 60 home runs in 1927, and Baker was well aware of the salary the New York Yankees slugger commanded after that record. Hence, as Klein was heading for the league lead in home runs in his first full season in 1929, Baker decided to try to curtail his right

By the NUMBERS

8—The number of times Phillies players have hit for the cycle. The special swatters are Lave Cross (1894), Sam Thompson (1894), Cy Williams (1927), Chuck Klein (1931 and 1933), Johnny Callison (1963), Gregg Jefferies (1995), and David Bell (2004).

fielder's long-distance clouting. If Klein moved up to Ruth's class as a home-run basher, Baker rationalized, his salary demands would become excessive. And if that happened, everybody else on the team would want higher pay, too.

Baker Bowl's tin right-field wall was 40 feet high. To that, the owner added another 20 feet of screen. When asked why he did that, Baker was ready with an alibi. "Home runs have become too cheap at the Philadelphia ballpark," he alleged.

The ploy worked. Instead of hitting an expected 50 homers, Klein had to settle for 43. That was a new Phillies record. But it was not enough

Outfielder Chuck Klein, exploiting the short dimensions of Baker Bowl, hit 191 home runs for the Phillies over a six-year period, starting in 1928, and won the Triple Crown in 1933. Traded to the Cubs after the 1933 season, his offensive numbers declined significantly, leading many at the time to wonder if Klein wasn't simply a creation of Baker Bowl. Photo courtesy of National Baseball Hall of Fame Library, Cooperstown, New York.

DID YOU KNOW . . . That seven Phillies outfielders have fielded a perfect 1.000 during an entire season? In 1942 Danny Litwhiler became the first major league outfielder to play a full season without making an error. He was followed by Tony Gonzalez (1962), Don Demeter (1963), Johnny Callison (1968), Milt Thompson (1994), Jim Eisenreich (1995), and Doug Glanville (2002).

to get Klein the substantial pay raise he richly deserved. And it was surely the only time an owner ever attempted such an absurd tactic as restricting his own player's home-run output.

Although Klein hit no more than 40 home runs in any future season, his big bat continued to flourish. He belted more than 200 hits and drove in more than 100 runs five years in a row. He hit for the cycle twice.

"Klein was one of the greatest players of his day," said Ralph Bernstein, retired Pennsylvania sports editor for the Associated Press.

In 1930 Klein had one of baseball's most unusual hitting streaks. He hit in 26 straight games, then was stopped, hit in another five in a row, was stopped, then had a 13-game streak, was stopped, and finally hit in another 26 consecutive games. During the surge, Klein had hit in 70 of 73 games.

In 1931 *The Sporting News* named Klein the National League's Most Valuable Player.

The following year, both *TSN* and the Baseball Writers' Association of America chose Klein as the loop's MVP. In 1933, while hitting .368 with 28 home runs and 120 RBIs, Klein won the Triple Crown. In one of the rarest of rarities, Jimmie Foxx (.356-48-163) of the Athletics won the Triple Crown in the American League that year, making Philadelphia the only city ever to have Triple Crown winners from each league in the same season.

Klein had his finest day at the plate in 1936 when he became the first National Leaguer in the 20th century to smack four home runs in one game in a 9–6 Phillies' victory over the Pittsburgh Pirates on a rainy day at Forbes Field. Klein's leadoff homer in the top of the tenth provided the Phillies with the winning run in a game in which the slugger drove in six runs and barely missed a fifth homer with a long foul fly that was caught against the wall in the second inning.

TRIVIA

The Phillies played in the first legal Sunday game in Philadelphia. When and where did that happen?

Answers to the trivia questions are on page 190.

The next morning, the *Philadelphia Inquirer* provided an unusual description of the fourth home run. "Score tied, tenth inning. Klein the first hitter, [Bill] Swift, the Pirates' third pitcher, on the mound. The storm, which had been brewing most of the afternoon, broke suddenly. Rain began to fall as Chuck came up. He took one look—Swift wound up—over came the pitch, and bang went the first ball, even farther than any of the other three."

The home run made Klein the second of three Phillies (the others were Ed Delahanty and Mike Schmidt) to hit four home runs in one game.

Klein, who was no slouch in the field—he holds the National League record for most assists (44) in one season—has one other mark of distinction. He was a member of the Phillies three different times.

The Phillies traded him to the Chicago Cubs after the 1933 season. Klein returned to the Phils in a trade in 1936. Released by the Phils during the 1939 season, Chuck joined the Pirates but was released at the end of the campaign. He then returned to the Phillies in 1940 and stayed with the club as a player/coach through 1944.

Team Presidents Were a Varied Group

The year that Bob Carpenter became president of the Phillies he took over a forlorn franchise that was trapped in a three-decade funk. It was late in 1943, World War II was raging, and the Phillies were as feeble as any major league baseball team could possibly be.

The team had achieved just one winning season since 1917. Its roster was made up mostly of youngsters, old men, and cripples. It had no money, no general manager, no farm system, and no direction.

Less than one year earlier, the team had been a ward of the National League, its ownership dissolved and its operations handled by league perfunctories. The following season, the team's new owner—lumber dealer William Cox—was banned from organized baseball for life for betting on his own team.

Carpenter's timing may not have been impeccable, but his heart—and, more importantly, his bank account—were in the right place. Ultimately, he would yank the Phillies from the pits of disaster, and in so doing, he would elevate the team into the elite circle of National League franchises.

When he took over after his ultra-wealthy father, Robert R. M. Carpenter Sr., had purchased the team for $400,000, the junior Carpenter was just 28 years old, the youngest team president in major league history. "It [the Phillies] was probably the worst major league club I've ever seen, including the old St. Louis Browns," he told Skip Clayton. "We had 25 second-division players and one minor leaguer named Turkey Tyson. It was a terrible team."

One of the first orders of business for Carpenter, whose father—married to one of the du Ponts and a high-ranking executive in the family company—had run a farm team in Wilmington, Delaware, for his good friend Connie Mack, was to hire former pitcher and Boston Red Sox farm director Herb Pennock as the club's first full-time general manager. The two then dove into their first task, that of putting together a farm system.

In 1943 the Phillies had only one full-time scout and a working agreement with just one team. Carpenter, who put Pennock in charge while he left to serve in the army, quickly authorized the formation of a farm system, which by 1946 included nine teams. The club also built a sizeable scouting staff, which in 1946 included Edith Houghton, baseball's first woman scout.

Before long the Phillies had ceased to be the perennial doormats of the league. By the late 1940s, the Phils had affiliations with 15 farm teams, and the system was producing outstanding young players. In 1950 all the hard work paid off when the Phillies—by then known as the Whiz Kids—won the National League pennant.

Following the 1954 season, the Phillies' chief competition in town since 1901—the American League's Philadelphia Athletics—moved to Kansas City. Although the Phillies never captured another pennant under Carpenter, they at least had the full attention of the city's baseball fans.

In Carpenter's 29 years as president, the Phillies finished at or over .500 12 times. They achieved nine first-division finishes, yet placed last six times and seventh three. They also never made much money, even though Carpenter did once offer the St. Louis Cardinals $500,000 for Stan Musial.

"If anybody goes into this business for money," said Carpenter, who never collected a salary, "he should have his head examined."

Carpenter gave out tons of money in bonuses to untested youngsters, many of whom never earned a penny in the big leagues. He also had a penchant for signing big, strong-armed pitchers. Sometimes—as in cases such as Robin Roberts, Curt Simmons, Jack Sanford, Jack Meyer, Dick Farrell, Don Cardwell, Art Mahaffey, Ray Culp, Chris Short, and Rick Wise—they worked out splendidly. Other times, they didn't.

If Carpenter had one serious fault, it was his reluctance to sign black players, a shortcoming that for years prevented the Phillies from ranking among the league's top teams. The Phillies were the last NL team to integrate, failing to take that step until a full 10 years after Jackie Robinson had made his big league debut.

TRIVIA

Who played the most games at Veterans Stadium?

Answers to the trivia questions are on page 190.

TOP TEN

Phillies' Highest Season Home Attendance

	Attendance	Year
1.	3,250,092	2004
2.	3,137,674	1993
3.	2,775,011	1979
4.	2,700,070	1977
5.	2,665,304	2005
6.	2,651,650	1980
7.	2,583,389	1978
8.	2,480,150	1976
9.	2,376,394	1982
10.	2,290,971	1994

"I'm not opposed to Negro players," Carpenter said. "But I'm not going to hire a player of any color or nationality just to have him on the team."

Nevertheless, Carpenter, a major figure behind the construction of Veterans Stadium, is in many respects the most celebrated of Phillies owners. At least among those prior to his tenure, such a designation is unchallenged with the exception of the club's first president, Al Reach.

Between the two, the Phillies were run by men such as Billy Shettsline, who rose from ticket-taker to manager to team president; Horace Fogel, a former sportswriter who ultimately was barred from baseball for, among other things, claiming that the 1912 pennant race was fixed and that umpires favored certain teams; William Baker, a former New York City police commissioner and notorious tightwad; Gerry Nugent, a former shoe salesman and then a front-office assistant who obtained majority control of the team after Baker died and left stock to Nugent's wife and son; and assorted others whose names ring no bells in the annals of Phillies history.

Two others who came close to being in charge would surely have altered the team's history had they taken over. One was Ty Cobb. The other was Bill Veeck.

Cobb was slated to become manager and co-owner of the Phils following the end of his playing career in 1928 with the Athletics. Hoping to

By the NUMBERS **36**—Hard to believe, Harry, but this is how many hits the Phillies lashed in a 29–4 victory over the Louisville Colonels in a game in 1894. Sam Thompson led the way with six, while Billy Hamilton, Joe Sullivan, and Mike Grady each had five. The total is an all-time major league record.

return to baseball, he and Philadelphia real estate tycoon Reynold H. Greenburg had seemingly worked out a deal with Baker to buy the club for $900,000. Cobb spent several weeks in town preparing for his new assignment. While he did, the Phillies went on a road trip, won eight games, and soared from eighth place to sixth. Buoyed by the team's sudden success, Baker decided it was worth more than the agreed-upon figure and upped the price $100,000. Furious, Cobb packed his bags and left town, ending any chance of his running the team.

Veeck, whose father was president of the Chicago Cubs, was the top bidder for the Phillies in 1942 when the club was being swallowed by debt. According to his autobiography, *Veeck as in Wreck*, written many years later, the would-be owner planned to stock the team with stars from the Negro League, including Josh Gibson, Judy Johnson, Roy Campanella, Satchel Paige, and various others. Although some researchers doubt that such a plan ever existed, Veeck claimed that he revealed his idea to commissioner Kenesaw Mountain Landis, who had toiled vigorously for many years to keep blacks out of the big leagues. When Landis heard the plan, he persuaded Nugent to sell the team to the league for $500,000. Then, with the help of National League president Ford Frick, a group led by Cox was awarded the franchise. Before the end of 1943, Cox was banished for life from baseball. And what could have been a profound change in the game was thwarted.

After Carpenter bought the Phillies late that year, the team belonged to the family until 1981. Bob retired in 1972 and was succeeded by his 32-year-old son, Ruly. The young Carpenter, a former Yale football player and baseball captain, had been employed in the team's front office for 10 years, working much of that time in the minor league department with farm director Paul Owens.

He knew the team intimately. And under his guidance, the Phillies put together their greatest era. While developing top players in their farm system and making trades for others, the team won four division titles, one pennant, and one World Series.

Ruly played a major role in the success of the team. But in 1981—the year of a prolonged baseball strike—he made the stunning announcement that he was tired of all the contract squabbles, labor negotiations, and philosophical differences with other owners and was selling the team.

"Rather than continue to beat our heads against the wall, we have decided to sell," he said.

A group headed by vice president Bill Giles stood ready. They bought the team for $30 million. With Giles serving as president, the Phillies won two more pennants with a collection of players acquired mostly from other teams.

Both before and during his presidency, Giles was widely acclaimed as a promotional genius. He created the Phillie Phanatic, stationed attractive ballgirls on the foul lines, and devised numerous other ways to entertain fans, especially with pregame extravaganzas, not the least of which were two legendary walks across the top of Veterans Stadium by high-wire artist Karl Wallenda. The 900-foot-long, 150-foot-high excursion was as exciting as it was terrifying to viewers, many of whom couldn't bear to watch all of the astounding feat.

After he stepped down in 1997, Giles made one other lasting contribution to Phillies baseball. He was the driving force behind the planning and building of Citizens Bank Park.

Giles' successor, Phils vice president David Montgomery, oversaw the move into the club's new home in 2004. In its first season there, the team drew a record 3,250,092 fans.

Under Montgomery, the Phillies boldly entered the big-contract market, bringing in top players such as Jim Thome, David Bell, and Billy Wagner. As that happened, the Phillies also regained a place as one of the top franchises in the league.

Why'd You Do It, Baby?

Eddie Waitkus never had a chance to dodge the bullet. It was fired at close range in a Chicago hotel room from a .22 rifle by a crazed woman who had a secret crush on the Phillies' first baseman.

The bullet pierced Waitkus' chest, passed through a lung, and lodged in a muscle near his spine. As it did, it touched off one of the strangest and most heavily publicized off-the-field events baseball has ever seen.

Over the years, the Phillies have had their share of off-hours tragedies. Ace pitcher Charlie Ferguson died of typhoid fever in 1888 after winning 99 games in the previous four years. Pitcher Dutch Ulrich died of pneumonia in 1929, catcher Walter "Peck" Lerian was hit and killed by a pickup truck in the same year, pitcher Hal Carlson succumbed to a case of severe indigestion in 1930, and second baseman Mickey Finn died of complications after undergoing surgery for an ulcer in 1933.

The wound to Waitkus was not fatal. But it shocked anyone who was paying attention to the sport on that frightful night of June 14, 1949.

Waitkus, in his fourth big league season, had just come to the Phillies in an off-season trade in December 1948 with the Chicago Cubs. He was the first baseman the club sorely needed. A marvelous fielder and a dependable hitter, the man who spoke five different languages was a major part of the Phils' plan to climb the National League ladder after years and years of ineptitude.

The Phillies were finally respectable again as they traveled to Chicago to meet the Cubs. The team stayed at the fancy Edgewater Beach Hotel just off Lake Michigan. Following an afternoon game at

Wrigley Field, the players scattered for dinner. Then, as Waitkus returned to the hotel just before midnight, his roommate, Russ Meyer, handed him a note. It was from a woman who claimed to be from Eddie's hometown of Cambridge, Massachusetts.

The groupies who lust for athletes and entertainers, Baseball Annies as they are called, have never been shy about following baseball players. But this woman seemed different. Her note made a meeting with Waitkus appear to be urgent.

"Mr. Waitkus," it said, "it is extremely important that I see you as soon as possible. We're not acquainted, but I have something of importance to speak to you about. I think it would be to your advantage to let me explain it to you. As I'm leaving the hotel the day after tomorrow, I'd appreciate it greatly if you could see me as soon as possible. My name is Ruth Anne Burns, and I'm in room 1297A. I realize this is a little out of the ordinary, but as I said, it's rather important. Please come soon. I won't take up much of your time."

A 29-year-old bachelor, Waitkus was curious. He called the woman's room. "What's this all about?" he asked. The woman said she could wait and see him the next day. But when Waitkus told her he couldn't come then, the pair decided to meet immediately.

Still thinking the woman was somebody from his hometown, Waitkus went to the room. When he knocked on the door, the woman invited him in. She said she had a surprise for him as he crossed the room and sat down in a chair.

Did she ever. As Waitkus waited for an explanation, the woman went to a closet and yanked out the rifle that she had bought at a pawn shop for $21. She shot him in the chest.

"I thought it was a joke," he said later. "I was laughing when she shot me. I didn't believe what was happening."

DID YOU KNOW . . . That Lee Meadows, who pitched for the Phillies from 1919 to 1923, is credited with being the first major leaguer to wear eyeglasses while playing? Perhaps that is why they called him "Specs."

By the NUMBERS

9—The number of batting titles that have been won by players wearing the Phillies uniform. The big belters are Billy Hamilton (1891 and 1893), Ed Delahanty (1899), Sherry Magee (1910), Lefty O'Doul (1929), Chuck Klein (1933), Harry Walker (1947), and Richie Ashburn (1955 and 1958).

The woman then called the front desk and told the clerk she had just shot somebody. Waitkus was rushed to a nearby hospital in critical condition.

As newspapers throughout the country carried the story on their front pages, police learned the next day that the woman was really a crazed 19-year-old stenographer from Chicago. Her real name was Ruth Anne Steinhagen. She was obsessed with Waitkus, kept pictures of him in her bedroom, sat in the stands at Wrigley Field and watched his every move when he played with the Cubs, and often followed him.

"Why'd you do it, baby?" Waitkus asked when police brought the woman to the hospital for him to identify. "I'm not sure," she replied. Then, admitting she always wanted to be in the limelight, Steinhagen stated that if she couldn't have Waitkus, nobody could.

"I liked Eddie because he was clean cut, and I liked the way he played baseball," she added. "And I was in love with him. I planned this very carefully and knew what the consequences would be. I really intended to commit suicide, but Eddie was moaning on the floor, and I couldn't find another bullet. Now, for my sake, I hope he recovers. But if he can't play baseball, I hope he dies."

Although the shot nearly ended his life, Waitkus held on. He had five operations, and his weight had dropped from 180 to 145 pounds by the time he was honored in September with a special night at Shibe Park. After Phillies president Bob Carpenter paid for a winter of rehabilitation in Florida with the team's trainer Frank Wiechec, Waitkus made his comeback the following year. He batted .284 while playing in 154 games and helping the Phillies win a pennant.

Meanwhile, Steinhagen was committed to a mental hospital, spending several years there before returning to Chicago, where she lived the life of a recluse.

Waitkus was traded by the Phillies to the Baltimore Orioles in 1954, returned briefly to the club in 1955, then retired after that season with a .285 career batting average. After his death in 1972, an autopsy revealed that he had died of lung cancer, probably a result of that shot fired many years earlier.

One final note: *The Natural,* a novel written in 1952 by Bernard Malamud and many years later turned into a movie starring Robert Redford, was patterned after the tragedy that befell Eddie Waitkus that fateful night in Chicago.

Whiz Kids Take the Prize

Of all the Phillies teams that have paraded across the baseball universe, none was more popular than the 1950 club known as the Whiz Kids. Even today, the team is fondly remembered as the one that, after years of futility, finally put Philadelphia baseball back on the map.

Dubbed the Whiz Kids by sportswriter Harry Grayson because of the presence of so many young players on the club—the average age was 26—the team was largely the product of a Phillies farm system that had been virtually nonexistent until Bob Carpenter assumed the presidency of the team in late 1943. Carpenter's heavy expenditures in building a farm system that was now producing a bevy of good players gave the team a homegrown flavor that captured the hearts and fancy of not only the fans but also the local press.

Before the start of the 1950 season, the Phillies were not really considered contenders. After all, the club hadn't won a pennant since 1915. So why should this season be any different? Most experts picked the Fightin' Phils, as they were also known, to finish fourth.

The logic was reasonable. Until they finished third in 1949, the Phils had placed in the first division just once since 1917. This was a franchise that had an excessively long history of being in shambles. Moreover, at least on paper, there were a number of strong teams in the league, not the least of which were the Brooklyn Dodgers, New York Giants, and Boston Braves. Each had jumped to the forefront by signing African American players, a step the Phillies would fail to take until 1956 and which hurt the franchise for the next decade.

Until 1950, the Phillies weren't even Philadelphia's favorite team. That distinction belonged to the American League's Athletics, whose

Consistently among the league leaders in home runs, Del Ennis, here in 1957, was a key bat in the middle of the Whiz Kids lineup. He is second on the Phillies all-time home-run list.

nine pennants and five World Championships had made them enormously more popular than the forlorn Phillies.

But that all changed in 1950. With an exciting, young Phillies team and Athletics teams that for the most part had been awful since the mid-1930s, the Phils became Philadelphia's favorite team. And the A's were banished to obscurity, a fate that eventually resulted in their leaving town after the 1954 season.

The Whiz Kids roster was certainly appealing. It featured youngsters such as future Hall of Famers Robin Roberts and Richie Ashburn, Del Ennis, Granny Hamner, Willie Jones, and Curt Simmons. The team was not, however, without its share of veterans, including Andy Seminick, Eddie Waitkus, Dick Sisler, Jim Konstanty, Russ Meyer, and Ken Heintzelman. All got along. There were no special factions on the club.

"We all had so much in common," said shortstop Hamner, the team's fiery young captain. "And we all showed up at the park to win. I think that made us closer. There is nothing a player appreciates more than a guy trying his best. We all did that."

Added right fielder Ennis, "It was like a family. We pulled for each other, and when we won games, it was not an individual effort. We went out together at night. Sometimes we'd be sitting around talking baseball, and [Eddie] Sawyer would come by and buy us a beer. We had 25 guys on that club, and every one stuck up for one another. It was wonderful to play with a bunch of guys like that."

Sawyer was an integral part of the formula. A Phi Beta Kappa at Ithaca College, he had played in the minors but never reached the big leagues. He was a college professor during the off-season and a likeable, fatherly type during the season.

"I think Sawyer was the greatest major league manager I ever saw as far as keeping a club together and getting them to pull together," said Hamner. "He was a great motivator and knew how to get everything out of each guy."

Sawyer was equally effusive. "We had our battles with other teams, but none with each other," he said. "The players started out young and developed friendships, and they played most of their careers together. The older players who came along later just fit in. Everybody got along."

Like any team, of course, the Phillies had players with unusual backgrounds. First baseman Waitkus had been shot the year before by a crazed admirer and was trying to make a comeback. Ennis was a native Philadelphian who had been awarded the National League's Rookie of the Year in 1946 by *The Sporting News* and would win the RBI title in 1950, but was often loudly booed by the local fans who were always especially demanding of hometown players. And promising second baseman Mike Goliat, a clutch performer during the season, was in his first full year in the big leagues, but would be gone from the Phillies the following year and out of the majors for good early in 1952.

TRIVIA

Who is the youngest player ever to appear in a game with the Phillies?

Answers to the trivia questions are on page 190.

The roster was filled with colorful characters. One was Konstanty, whose stellar performance (16 wins, 22 saves) would, at the end of the year, make him the first relief pitcher ever to win the Most Valuable Player award. The 33-year-old hurler, who had always been a starter before joining the Phillies in 1948, summoned an undertaker friend from upstate New York whenever he experienced a problem with his deliveries. The undertaker, a man with no baseball experience whatsoever, would rush to Philadelphia, pull on his catcher's mitt, catch some pitches, and diagnose the trouble.

Meyer, called the Mad Monk, was another original thinker. Once, the veteran pitcher needed 10 stitches in his nose after a girl with whom he was breaking up bit him there. Another time, he punched a photographer who had just taken his picture. Meyer's most notorious act occurred a few years later when he heaved a rosin bag in the air as he was being lifted from a game. The bag dropped directly onto Meyer's head, leaving a white cloud around his cap.

Jones was another character. Called Puddin' Head, the third baseman was a country boy from South Carolina who always seemed to have aching feet. He also liked to drink beverages stronger than milkshakes. Once, he arrived at the ballpark feeling a bit peeked. But after a nap, a rubdown, and a cold shower, he went out and got five hits in nine trips to the plate, including a triple and two doubles, during a steamy afternoon doubleheader. Jones was also the guy who once told a writer that he wanted his pregnant wife to come home right away from a trip to Canada. Why? Because if the baby was born in Canada, said Willie, "he won't be able to grow up to be president of the United States."

By the NUMBERS

5—In 1949 the Phillies hit five home runs in one inning, a club record. In a 12–3 victory over the Cincinnati Reds and former teammate Ken Raffensberger, Andy Seminick blasted two homers, while Willie Jones, Schoolboy Rowe, and Del Ennis each socked one in the eighth inning at Shibe Park.

One time, Hamner was followed by a detective as he drove home. When he reached his house, Hamner went inside, grabbed a gun, and snuck around the side and up to the flatfoot's car. "What are you doing?" he demanded to know while pointing the gun at the man's head. It turned out Carpenter had hired the PI to follow Jones, but since Willie and Granny Hamner had the same model Cadillac, he had followed the wrong car. Shortly afterward, the wayward detective was fired.

There was seldom a dull moment with the Whiz Kids. "We grew up together, and we always had fun," said Roberts.

There were times, though, when it wasn't so much fun during the season. At one point, pitcher Bubba Church took a smash to the face off a wicked line drive by slugger Ted Kluszewski and had to be carried off the field. Pitcher Bob Miller missed some action when he slipped and injured his back at a train station in Boston. Simmons, enjoying his best season to date, was pulled into the National Guard and missed most of the final month of the season. And Seminick played the final weeks of the season with a badly damaged ankle on which he could barely walk, much less catch.

Nevertheless, the Phillies bounced back and forth between first and third during the early months, then took over first place to stay with a doubleheader victory on July 25 over the Chicago Cubs. With 20 wins in 28 games, the Whiz Kids' lead reached six and one-half games by the end of August.

On September 3 an estimated crowd of 30,000 greeted the Phillies at Philadelphia Airport when they returned from a road trip in which they won 11 of 14 games. "We still have 27 games left," admonished Sawyer. "We haven't won the pennant yet."

How right he was. The Phillies' lead began to slip. But with 11 games left in the season, the lead jumped back up to seven and one-half games with the help of a dramatic 8–7, 19-inning victory over the Cincinnati Reds in the second game of a doubleheader at Shibe Park. Incredibly, Konstanty pitched 10 innings in relief.

After the Phillies had swept that doubleheader, however, the lead tumbled again, and finally, with two games left in the season, it was down to two games.

In the final game of the season, with their lead down to one game, the Phillies beat the Dodgers, 4–1, in 10 innings with Ashburn's heroic throw to the plate to squelch the winning run, Sisler's three-run homer, and Roberts' courageous complete-game pitching performance leading the pennant-clinching victory.

The World Series was almost like an afterthought. The Phillies were swept in four games by the New York Yankees, losing three games by one run. Because the pitching staff was exhausted, Konstanty got an unexpected start in the opener and pitched brilliantly before losing, 1–0. Roberts lost the second game, 2–1, on Joe DiMaggio's tenth-inning home run. The Phillies continued to get standout pitching, this time by Heintzelman, but little hitting as reliever Meyer lost the third game, 3–2. Then a 5–2 loss ended the Series in Game 4.

Contrary to the expectations of most observers that the Phillies would be a major contender throughout the decade, the Whiz Kids' courtship with glory was over. The Phils were rarely a serious contender, never finishing higher than a third-place tie in 1953 and ending the decade with two last-place finishes.

ALL-STADIUM TEAM

Shibe Park/Connie Mack Stadium

Position	Player
Left Field	Del Ennis
Center Field	Richie Ashburn
Right Field	Johnny Callison
First Base	Dick Allen
Second Base	Tony Taylor
Shortstop	Granny Hamner
Third Base	Willie Jones
Catcher	Andy Seminick
Right-handed Pitcher	Robin Roberts
Left-handed Pitcher	Chris Short
Relief Pitcher	Jim Konstanty

The Throw That Saved a Pennant

During a playing career that included 12 years with the Phillies, Richie Ashburn was an outstanding leadoff hitter, base stealer, and collector of fly balls that were hit beyond the reach of normal center fielders.

Ashburn won two National League batting titles and led the league in hits three times. He was usually among the league leaders in stolen bases, winning one title in that department. And he topped the circuit in walks four times.

In the field, Ashburn holds the major league record for most years (four) with 500 or more putouts. He is tied for the ML mark for most years (nine) with 400 or more putouts. And he led the National League in chances eight times and in putouts nine times.

All of these are achievements that earned Ashburn a place in the Hall of Fame in 1995. But despite his glowing records with the bat and glove, it was a throw by Ashburn that provided his single most memorable moment in baseball. Ironically, throwing was by far the weakest part of Richie's game.

The throw came on October 1, 1950, in the last game of the season. The first-place Phillies were playing the second-place Brooklyn Dodgers at Ebbets Field. Having surrendered a seven-and-one-half-game lead with 11 games left in the season (does this have any resemblance to 1964?), the Whiz Kids, as they were called, clung to a one-game lead. A loss would drop the Phils into a tie for first place, necessitating a best-of-three playoff for the pennant. The exhausted and badly slumping Phillies, who had held first place since July, wanted no part of a playoff.

And so, as they entered the season finale, the Phillies were in a must-win position. It was a tense situation, to say the least, and it got even more tense as the game progressed.

By the NUMBERS

$4,081.23—The losers' share each Phillies player got from the World Series in 1950. Today, this sum would be roughly the amount the lowliest sub makes for one regular-season game.

As the bottom of the ninth inning began, with Robin Roberts and Don Newcombe still on the mound for their respective teams, the score was tied, 1–1. Cal Abrams led off for the Dodgers with a walk, then went to second on a single by Pee Wee Reese. Duke Snider followed with a line shot to center.

Although he would normally have been playing deeper, Ashburn was stationed in shallow center. He snared the drive on one hop. Milt Stock, the third baseman on the Phillies' last pennant-winner in 1915, was coaching third for the Dodgers. With none out, he injudiciously waved Abrams home.

"I was thinking one thing with the winning run on second," Ashburn told Skip Clayton some years later. "I knew Snider wouldn't bunt, so I shortened up a step or two. The ball came right to me. The Dodgers used bad judgment sending Abrams home. I was never known to have a strong arm, but I had an accurate one. I got rid of the ball quickly."

Ashburn made a perfect throw to catcher Stan Lopata. Abrams, ironically a native Philadelphian, was out by 15 feet as Lopata moved up the line to nail him. The throw cut down what would have been the winning run. And when Roberts retired Carl Furillo and Gil Hodges—after intentionally walking Jackie Robinson—the game moved into extra innings. In the tenth, Dick Sisler's three-run homer gave the Phillies a 4–1 victory and the pennant.

It was a victory, though, that wouldn't have happened without what has been unanimously regarded as the greatest single throw in Phillies history.

Ashburn, of course, had other noteworthy feats while wearing a Phillies uniform. He was Rookie of the Year in 1948, when he finished second in the batting race to Stan Musial with a .333 average. He hit .300 or more eight times as a Phillie. He laced more than 200 hits in a season three times, reaching a high of 221 in 1951. Ashburn had a career batting average of .308 with 2,574 hits. He hit just 22 home runs with the Phils; seven of them were inside-the-parkers.

"Every at-bat was life or death to him," said Maje McDonnell, a Phillies coach when Ashburn played. "He didn't give in to anyone. And what a competitor he was. I don't remember a game when he didn't compete 100 percent. He just bore down every day."

The Nebraska native was also durable. In 12 years with the Phillies, he played in 97 percent of the team's games. He holds the club record for most consecutive games, a streak that ended at 730 when he collided with left fielder Del Ennis while chasing a fly ball in a preseason game in 1955 in Wilmington.

There was nothing more sacred to Ashburn than his bats. Once, many years after his playing days had ended and he was serving as a Phillies broadcaster, Richie and colleague Harry Kalas were discussing bats on the air. "How important is your game bat?" Kalas asked Ashburn.

"When I was on a hot streak, I didn't trust anybody with my bat," Ashburn responded. "I didn't leave it around the clubhouse or the dugout. I always took it with me. If I was on the road, I'd often take it back to the hotel. I'd even take it to bed with me."

Kalas expressed surprise at the last statement. "Actually," Ashburn replied, "I've gone to bed with a lot of old bats."

Ashburn was especially adept at using his bat to foul off pitches. Once, he fouled off 14 in a row. Another time, he drilled a ball into the stands, hitting a fan named Alice Roth directly in the nose. Mrs. Roth's husband, Earl, was, at the time, the sports editor of the *Philadelphia Evening Bulletin*. As medics carried the injured woman out of the stands on a stretcher, Ashburn hit another foul ball into the stands. This one struck the very same woman.

The speedy Ashburn had a sprint race one time against Roger Bannister, not long after the British runner had broken the four-minute mile. Richie beat him.

When Ted Williams first saw Ashburn play, he marveled at how fast the rookie ran. "He runs like he has twin motors in his pants," said the great slugger of the Boston Red Sox. "He goes putt-putt, putt-putt, putt-putt." From that day on, Ashburn's nickname was "Putt-Putt."

TRIVIA

Who was the Phillies' first winner of a Gold Glove?

Answers to the trivia questions are on page 190.

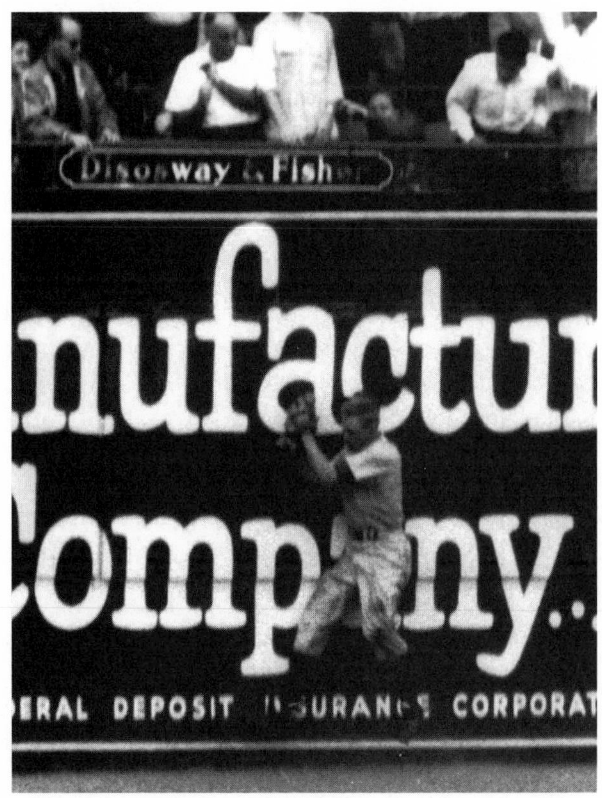

Outfielder Richie Ashburn, here making a leaping grab of a fly ball at Ebbets Field in 1953, was the penultimate leadoff hitter, leading the league in hitting twice and walks four times. A five-time All-Star, he spent 12 years with the Phillies before ending his career with the infamous 1962 Mets.

Had it not been for a few strange twists, Ashburn might never have become either a center fielder or a Phillie.

Ashburn was originally a catcher. In high school in 1943, in Nebraska, he attended a tryout camp conducted by the St. Louis Cardinals. Then the following year, at the age of 17, he was signed by the Cleveland Indians. But baseball commissioner Kenesaw Mountain Landis nullified the deal because Ashburn was underage. One year later, the Chicago Cubs signed the youngster, but again the agreement was voided, this time because of what was said to be an irregularity in the contract.

Soon afterward, with Ashburn having enrolled as a journalism student in a junior college, he was signed by the Phillies. In 1945 he reported to the club's farm team at Utica, where future Phillies pilot Eddie Sawyer was the manager. Sawyer took one look at Ashburn flying down the base path and made an immediate decision. Ashburn was not going to be a catcher, not with that blinding speed. Henceforth, Richie was an outfielder.

Three years later, having become an accomplished fly-chaser, Ashburn arrived in Philadelphia as the Phillies' regular center fielder. In spring training, he had beaten out defending National League batting champ Harry Walker for the job, due in part because of the latter's extended holdout. By the time Walker reported to camp, it was too late to catch up to the fast-rising star.

Ashburn's parents came to Philadelphia, too. Then and for several years thereafter, they rented a house for the summer. Not only did Ashburn stay there each year, but so did several of his young teammates who were also far from home.

That group helped to form the backbone of the team later known as the Whiz Kids. It was a team for which Ashburn's legendary throw saved a pennant.

DID YOU KNOW . . .

That in 1947 the Phillies were so anxious to sign Curt Simmons that owner Bob Carpenter sent the team to the young pitcher's hometown near Allentown to play a game against Curt and a local team? Simmons struck out 11 Phillies in a game that ended in a 4–4 tie. Soon afterward, the Phils gave him a $65,000 bonus to sign with them.

The Home Run That Won a Pennant

Of the thousands and thousands of home runs hit during the life of major league baseball, the one hit by Dick Sisler in 1950 ranks as one of the most memorable.

It may stand just a notch below the legendary homers smote by Bill Mazeroski, Bobby Thomson, Hank Aaron, and a few others. But it's right up there near the top. And without a doubt, it's the most memorable, most dramatic, most significant home run anybody ever hit for the Phillies.

The blow came on October 1, the last day of the 1950 season. It gave the Phillies their first National League pennant in 35 years, and only the second flag during the club's first 68 years.

The Phillies, affectionately called the Whiz Kids that year, were locked in a do-or-die struggle with the Brooklyn Dodgers as the pennant race drew to a close. What at the end of August had been a six-and-one-half-game lead for the Phillies, had disintegrated into a mere two-game pad with just two games—both against the Dodgers at Ebbets Field—left in the season.

After the Phils lost the first game, their lead was down to one game. A loss in the final game would throw the race into a tie, forcing a best-of-three playoff. For the fading and depleted Phillies and their decimated pitching staff, a playoff spelled almost certain defeat.

Thus, in a must-win situation on a sunny, fall afternoon in Brooklyn, manager Eddie Sawyer sent his ace, Robin Roberts, to the mound against the Dodgers' star moundsman, Don Newcombe. Both pitchers were seeking their 20th wins of the season. For Roberts, it was his third start in the last six days and his sixth attempt to win 20.

Sisler was in left field, batting third in the lineup on a team in which he was not viewed as one of the main cogs. That distinction belonged to

TRIVIA

Who has the most walk-off home runs of any Phillies player?

Answers to the trivia questions are on page 190.

future Hall of Famers Roberts and Richie Ashburn, as well as right fielder Del Ennis, shortstop Granny Hamner, and relief pitcher Jim Konstanty.

"If I hadn't hit that home run," Sisler said many years later, "I don't think people would have remembered me. I was just another ballplayer, maybe a little bit better than average."

Sisler certainly had good genes. His father was Hall of Fame first baseman George Sisler, one of the greatest hitters of all time. In fact, George, who had another son, Dave, who would become a big league pitcher, was in the stands on that final day of the season. George was a scout with the Dodgers.

The comparisons between Dick and his father were inevitable. "It was tough being the son of George Sisler," Dick said. "When I was a kid, I got a lot of this, 'Aww, your dad wouldn't have struck out' or 'Your dad wouldn't have popped up.' It got to me then. But later I had a talk with my dad. He said, 'Dick, you're always going to have that on you, so you might as well get used to it.' I finally did. I just figured, I can't change my dad, so I kind of put the whole thing out of my head. I knew I had to make good on my own."

Dick, a rookie in 1946 with the World Champion St. Louis Cardinals, had come to the Phillies in 1948 in a trade that sent undistinguished infielder Ralph LaPointe and $20,000 to the city on the Mississippi River. Ultimately, the trade was regarded as one of the best the Phillies ever made.

Sisler played first base in 1948 but moved to left when the Phils acquired Eddie Waitkus in a trade with the Chicago Cubs. After Waitkus was shot in 1949, Sisler moved back to first, but he returned to left in 1950 when Waitkus resumed his starting role.

A sturdy left-handed batter, Sisler hit .274 in 1948 and .289 the following year. He had his best year in the majors in 1950, finishing with a .296 batting average.

At one point during the season, Sisler lashed eight straight hits, going five for five in one game with a homer and five RBIs. By the time the last game of the season appeared, though, nothing that Dick had done during the season mattered. It was really now or never for him and his teammates.

A crowd of 35,073—many of them Phillies fans who had traveled from Philadelphia—jammed into tiny Ebbets Field. It was estimated that another 30,000 were turned away at the gates.

Both Roberts and Newcombe pitched brilliantly. Sisler singled and came around to score on singles by Ennis and Willie Jones to give the Phils a 1–0 lead in the sixth. A controversial, ground-rule home run by Pee Wee Reese that lodged at the base of a wire screen in right-center field tied the score in the bottom of the sixth.

Outside of Philadelphia, the Whiz Kids may have been forgotten if not for Dick Sisler, the Phillies left fielder who hit a dramatic tenth-inning, game-winning home run at Ebbets Field on the final day of the 1950 season to give the Phillies the pennant. Dick was the son of Hall of Famer George Sisler.

TOP TEN

Phillies Batters with Most Hits in One Season

	Name	Year	Hits
1.	Lefty O'Doul	1929	254
2.	Chuck Klein	1930	250
3.	Ed Delahanty	1899	238
4.	Chuck Klein	1932	226
5.	Chuck Klein	1933	223
6.	Sam Thompson	1893	222
7.	Richie Ashburn	1951	221
8.	Billy Hamilton	1894	220
9.	Ed Delahanty	1893	219*t*
	Chuck Klein	1929	219*t*

The score was still 1–1 when Cal Abrams walked and then, trying to score from second, was thrown out at the plate by a wide margin by Ashburn. The throw saved the day—and the pennant—for the Phillies. After Roberts escaped the inning with no damage, the game moved into extra innings.

Roberts led off the tenth with a single. He went to second on a hit by Waitkus but was thrown out at third on an attempted sacrifice by Ashburn. That brought up Sisler.

Dick already had touched Newcombe for three singles. "I always had pretty good luck against Newcombe," recalled Sisler, who was playing with a badly sprained wrist that had sidelined him three weeks earlier and that he had aggravated sliding into second in the fourth inning. "He was a fastball pitcher, and I was a fastball hitter."

Newcombe got two quick strikes, then threw a ball. His next pitch was a fastball high and away. Sisler swung. "I just wanted to make contact," he said. "But the ball sailed out to left field. I didn't think it would go out, so I just kept running."

As he rounded first base, Sisler watched the ball sail into the bleachers over the head of Abrams, the Brooklyn left fielder. It was a three-run homer, and it gave the Phillies a 4–1 lead.

"As I circled the bases, I thought that would be enough for Roberts because he was tough that day," remembered Sisler. "You talk about competitors. He was dead tired, but he was able to dig down and come up with a little extra in that last inning. He just reached back and fired with everything he had."

Sisler's crystal ball couldn't have been more accurate. Roberts retired the Dodgers in order in the bottom of the tenth. The Phillies had the pennant. And pandemonium erupted in the stands and back in Philadelphia in what was the biggest celebration the city had ever seen. Horns honked, sirens screamed, tugboats in the Delaware River tooted, and ecstatic fans spilled out into the streets for a party that would reach far into the late hours of the night. Sisler's dramatic home run had given the Phillies and their fans the most memorable moment in the team's history up to that point.

Back in the stands, Dick's dad George had watched the home run with mixed emotions. "I don't know exactly how I felt," he said later. "Here I am working for one ballclub, and my son wins the pennant for the other one. I felt awful and terrific at the same time."

In the deliriously jubilant Phillies locker room, Sisler was the center of attention. "I've hit some better, but none ever meant so much," he said. "It's the biggest hit I ever got. It's a dream. It's a dream. Oh, how I love this park."

And, oh, how Phillies fans loved Dick. They flocked to his home the next morning, lining the street in front of his house. When he appeared on his front porch to wave, he noticed that someone had hung a sign on the house. It said, "We love that man."

Rightfully so. In the annals of Phillies home runs, he had just hit the biggest one of them all.

DID YOU KNOW . . . That all three Phillies coaches in 1950—Benny Bengough, Dusty Cooke, and Cy Perkins—played at one time or another for the New York Yankees, the team the Whiz Kids met in the World Series? Manager Eddie Sawyer played in the Yankees' farm system.

28 Complete Games in a Row

When Robin Roberts was an eighth grader in Springfield, Illinois, his school had a special guest speaker at its sports banquet. The kids were told that the visitor was a famous former big league pitcher. The man was staying at a hotel in town.

Roberts didn't know much about the guy. But he did know his name was Grover Cleveland Alexander.

Alexander, by then nearly a decade removed from the big leagues, stood in front of the class and told his listeners about the game he had played so well. As his talk neared the end, the Hall of Fame hurler gave the class some words of encouragement. "You don't know," he said, "maybe some of you youngsters will be pitching in a World Series in a few years."

Roberts and Alexander never met again. But the old pitcher proved to be an excellent prophet. Some time later, one of the students did pitch in a World Series. And it was for the same team with which Alexander made his first Series appearance.

Like the speaker, Roberts also went on to gain a place in the Hall of Fame after fashioning a career that made him the top pitcher in Phillies history.

Roberts' numbers with the Phillies were remarkable. Although he pitched much of the time on mediocre teams, he won 20 or more games six years in a row. He led the National League in wins four times, in complete games and innings pitched five times apiece, in strikeouts twice, and in shutouts once. Rare was the year when Robbie didn't complete at least 30 games and pitch in more than 300 innings.

The strong-armed right-hander was chosen for seven All-Star teams and started an unprecedented five of them. Twice he was named National

DID YOU KNOW . . . That the cost to build Baker Bowl in 1887 was $101,000? It cost $315,000 to put up Shibe Park in 1909. By 1971 the price tag for Veterans Stadium had risen to $52 million. Far exceeding all of them was the $345 million needed to erect Citizens Bank Park in 2004.

League Pitcher of the Year—a forerunner of the Cy Young Award—and once he was selected Major League Player of the Year.

Most importantly, Roberts was the winning pitcher on the day the Phillies clinched the 1950 NL pennant, halting the Brooklyn Dodgers with 10 gritty innings of work. Overall, Roberts posted a career record of 286–245 in 19 big league seasons, including a 234–199 mark in 14 years with the Phillies. He completed 305 of the 609 games he started.

Of all his glittering statistics, none was more impressive than his run of 28 consecutive complete games.

We live today in a time when a pitcher is celebrated for lasting six innings. If he exceeds 100 pitches, the modern mound gurus make it seem like his arm will fall off. As for complete games, whole pitching staffs don't complete half as many games during an entire season as Roberts did during his streak.

The complete game is no longer a badge of honor. Rather, it is something to be avoided. Even if a hurler has a three-hit shutout after eight innings, he most likely will be replaced in the ninth by the ubiquitous refugee of the bullpen known as a closer.

Roberts, though, came from a different era. It was an era when durability counted for something. And no one was more durable than the big hurler with the pinpoint control.

"He wanted to pitch every day," Phillies manager Eddie Sawyer once said.

Roberts' streak began on August 28, 1952, when he beat the St. Louis Cardinals, 10–6. Two starts later, in perhaps the most astonishing game of his career, Roberts pitched all 17 innings of a 7–6 win over the Boston Braves. Robbie allowed 18 hits.

The Phillies' ace ended the season with his eighth straight complete game, beating the New York Giants, 7–4, for his 28th win of the season. It was the most wins in one season for a Phillies pitcher since Alexander

TOP TEN

Phillies' All-Time Leaders in Games Won

	Name	Wins
1.	Steve Carlton	241
2.	Robin Roberts	234
3.	Grover C. Alexander	190
4.	Chris Short	132
5.	Curt Simmons	115
6.	Curt Schilling	101
7.	Charlie Ferguson	99
8.	Al Orth	98
9.	Kid Carsey	95*t*
	Tully Sparks	95*t*
	Jack Taylor	95*t*

copped 30 in 1917. Since 1952 only Steve Carlton, with 27 wins in 1972, has come close to Roberts' total.

Roberts lost the 1953 opener to the Giants, 4–1, but his streak was still intact. It continued until July 9, when Roberts was pulled in the eighth inning with the Phillies trailing the Dodgers, 5–4. (The Phils rallied to win, 6–5.)

During the streak, Roberts pitched 264 innings without being relieved. He won 21 of the games. Three were shutouts. Twice he pitched with just two days' rest. And three times in the midst of the streak he made relief appearances.

Although the streak fell short of the major league record of 39 set by Jack Taylor in 1904, it was, by modern standards, a truly amazing feat. But then, amazing feats were a staple of Roberts' career.

Robbie never threw a no-hitter, but he hurled three one-hitters. In one, he gave up a leadoff home run to the Cincinnati Reds' Bobby Adams, then retired 27 batters in a row. In another, the only hit was a bouncer by the Giants' Felipe Alou that third baseman Joe Morgan (not the Hall of Famer) backed up to field, gloved the ball, then tripped and fell on his back. The third one-hitter resulted from a third-inning double by Del Crandall of the Milwaukee Braves.

Robin Roberts won 20 games six straight years and was the anchor of the Whiz Kids' pitching staff. His 20 wins in 1950 represented the most wins by a Phillies pitcher since 1917.

Roberts also lost no-hitters in the eighth inning against the Chicago Cubs and in the ninth against the Giants.

Ironically, Roberts was originally more noted as a basketball player. He attended Michigan State University on a basketball scholarship, but also played baseball in college and during the summer, where he was spotted by big league scouts. The Phillies eventually signed him, shelling out a $25,000 bonus.

Roberts pitched just one-half of a season in the minors at Wilmington, Delaware, before getting summoned to the big club. The pitcher, who had won his first professional game 19–1 with 17 strikeouts, was with the Blue Rocks in Hagerstown Maryland, when he was awakened by a caller telling him he was going up.

"I had to go back to Wilmington to get my clothes, then the next day, I got a train to Philadelphia," Roberts said. "I arrived in town at 4:30, checked into the hotel, and by the time I got to the ballpark it was 6:00. The manager, Ben Chapman, came up to me in the clubhouse and said, 'Can you pitch tonight?' I said I could. So by 8:00 I was on the mound."

In his first big league game, Roberts lost to the Pirates, 2–0. "I have never been so nervous," the pitcher recalled. In his next start, Roberts won his first game with a 3–2 decision over the Reds.

Roberts went from there to post wins in double figures in 12 straight seasons. His 28–7 record in 1952 gave him second place in the MVP voting. Then, starting with the following season, he won 23 each in three straight years.

If there was one chink in Robbie's armor, it was his propensity for serving gopher balls. He refused to deliver brushback pitches. As a result, hitters dug in at the plate, and before it was broken, Roberts held the major league record for giving up 46 home runs in one season. He still

By the NUMBERS

6—Proving that the starting lineup played virtually all the time, six players had at least 500 at-bats during the 1950 season. Eddie Waitkus led with 641, followed by Granny Hamner (637), Willie Jones (610), Del Ennis (595), Richie Ashburn (594), and Dick Sisler (523).

owns the major league mark of having yielded the most homers (505) in a career.

No game in Roberts' long career is more memorable than his victory over the Dodgers in the last game of the 1950 season. Roberts scattered five hits—three by Pee Wee Reese—as the Phillies won, 4–1, on Dick Sisler's tenth-inning home run.

Not only did Roberts pitch one of his familiar complete games, he escaped a jam in the ninth with the aid of Richie Ashburn's spectacular throw to the plate that nailed Cal Abrams. And, while lost in the glitter of the Phils' victory, it was Roberts who began the tenth inning with a single. After Eddie Waitkus singled, Ashburn bunted. Racing to third, Roberts was thrown out sliding headfirst into the bag and came up with an eyeful of lime. Despite a considerable amount of pain, he stayed in the game and retired the Dodgers in order in the bottom of the tenth.

"I just kept bearing down," he said. "After all the pressure, I was kind of relaxed. After going through what we went through, with a three-run lead, three outs didn't seem that tough."

Exhausted after carrying much of the Phillies' pitching load through the final weeks of the season, Roberts sat out the first game of the World Series against the New York Yankees. He got the call in the second game and worked nine nearly spotless innings before losing, 2–1, on a game-winning home run by Joe DiMaggio in the tenth inning.

It turned out to be the only World Series start in Roberts' career. Despite the loss, though, Mr. Alexander would've been proud of him.

Disaster in the '60s: A Decade to Forget

Eddie Sawyer was the manager in 1950 when the Phillies won the National League pennant for the first time in 35 years. The Whiz Kids were an immensely popular team, and the scholarly Sawyer was greatly admired as the man who piloted the club out of the dregs of the league.

When the performance of the Phillies began to unravel in 1952, Sawyer was relieved of his duties. But the club rehired him in 1958 with the hope that his special touch would restore the club to respectability.

It didn't. That year and the next, the Phillies finished dead last, each year fielding pitiful teams that were about as competitive as a three-legged racehorse.

After the Phillies lost the opening game of the 1960 season, Sawyer took a long look down the road. It wasn't a very pleasant sight. Not wanting to be part of the landscape, Sawyer abruptly quit.

"I'm 49, and I want to live to be 50," he explained.

Sawyer proved to be an expert prophet. The 1960 Phillies, as well as the '61 team, finished last. And although the team would improve greatly over the next few years, the decade of the 1960s was the most painful one that the team ever experienced.

Disaster struck quickly. In 1961, under Gene Mauch, who had replaced Sawyer, the Phillies set an all-time record for futility when they unceremoniously lost 23 games in a row.

"You couldn't imagine anything worse," said pitcher Art Mahaffey. "It was just awful."

Dubbed the "Team from Hell," the Phillies lost to good teams. They lost to other bad teams. Mahaffey was the only pitcher to win in double figures (11)—but he lost 19—and Tony Gonzalez had the team's highest batting average at .277.

The team finished in last place in the National League in batting, home runs, and slugging percentage. Its pitching staff had the highest ERA and the fewest complete games. Larry Merchant, writing in the *Philadelphia Daily News,* called the team the "Manayunk Mugwumps."

It was said that first baseman Pancho Herrera led the league in dinners. Left fielder Tony Curry led the league in missed fly balls. And pitcher Chris Short led the league in bad clothes.

During the season, Mauch released Hall of Fame–bound pitcher Robin Roberts, owner at the time of a 1–10 record. "He throws like Dolly Madison," Mauch said.

The first loss of the 23-game streak came against the San Francisco Giants after Mauch ordered pitcher Don Ferrarese to walk Willie Mays in the first inning. That loaded the bases, and, of course, the next batter, Orlando Cepeda, hit a grand slam. The Giants won, 4–3.

In the second game, Mauch didn't have Jim Owens walk Mays intentionally. So Willie smashed a home run that led the Giants to a 5–2 decision.

Along the way, the Phillies were shut out four times. They lost eight games by one run. And they lost six times by five or more runs.

"We were a bad team," Dallas Green, a relief pitcher with the club understated. "Some guys were too young to do anything about it, and some guys were too old to do anything about it. For the young guys, it was like fourth grade. You learn a lot, but years later, you can't remember much about it."

The losing streak finally ended on August 20 in the second game of a doubleheader at Milwaukee. John Buzhardt and the Phillies captured a 7–4 victory over the Braves. Ironically, Buzhardt was the winning pitcher in the last Phillies win, a 4–3 decision over the San Francisco Giants in the second game of a doubleheader on July 28 at Connie Mack Stadium.

DID YOU KNOW . . . That the Phillies have been holding spring training in Clearwater, Florida, since 1947? Prior to that, they had trained in 20 other locations, the longest being Philadelphia, where they worked out from 1883 to 1900. Only one other team—the Detroit Tigers, in Lakeland, Florida—has held spring training in the same city longer than the Phillies have been in Clearwater.

The night the streak was stopped, the Phillies flew home, and as they were pulling up to the terminal, they could see several hundred fans gathered at the gate.

Peering out the window at the large crowd, pitcher Frank Sullivan issued a warning. "Get off the plane in single file," he advised, "so they can't get us all with one burst."

While the crowd had actually jammed the airport to welcome the team back and to give it some encouragement, Phillies fans took a different view of the team a few years later. That was in 1964, a year that to this day lives in infamy in the minds and hearts of surviving Phils fans.

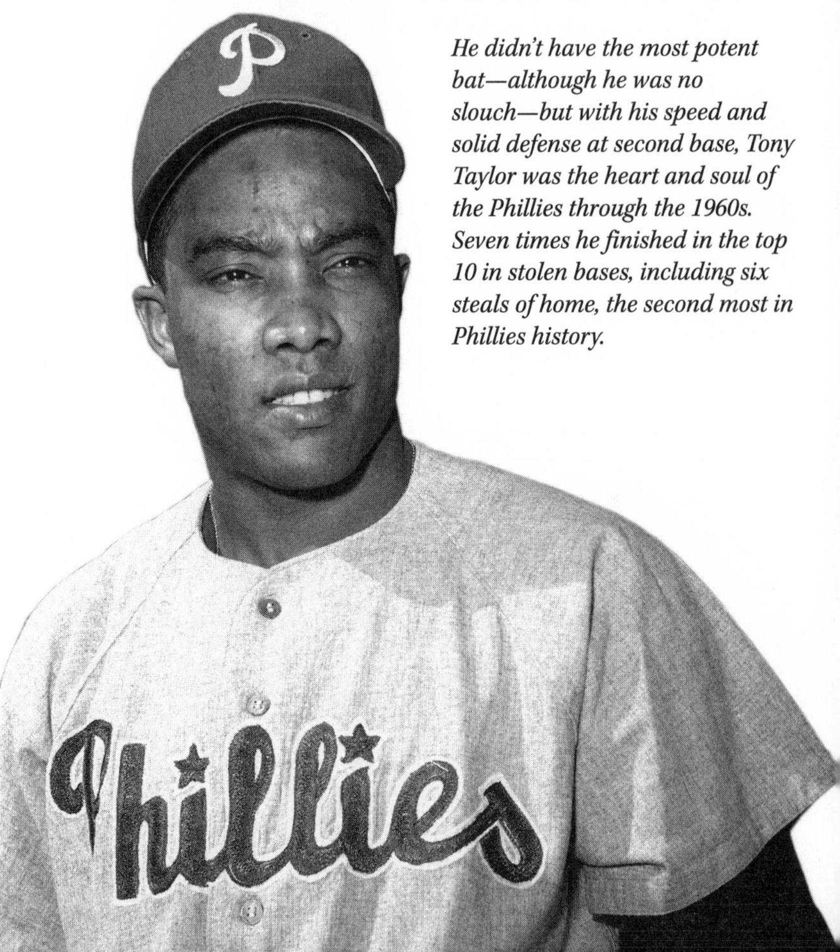

He didn't have the most potent bat—although he was no slouch—but with his speed and solid defense at second base, Tony Taylor was the heart and soul of the Phillies through the 1960s. Seven times he finished in the top 10 in stolen bases, including six steals of home, the second most in Phillies history.

It was the year of the "Great Collapse." The greatest collapse, it could be added, in the history of baseball.

While starting to assemble a team that could appear without embarrassment, the Phillies had climbed to seventh place in 1962, then to fourth the following year. By 1964 the club had acquired standout players such as Johnny Callison, Tony Gonzalez, Wes Covington, Tony Taylor, and Jim Bunning, and the roster also included talented youngsters such as Dick Allen and Short.

It was a team on the move, and that showed right from the start. The Phils won nine of their first 11 games and by the All-Star break had been either in first or second place the whole time. By August, the Phils—who even reeled off three triple plays during the season—were solidly entrenched in first place.

TRIVIA

Who was the first black player to appear in a regular-season game wearing a Phillies uniform?

Answers to the trivia questions are on page 190.

With Bunning, who fired a perfect game, and Short pitching marvelously and Allen and Callison, whose dramatic home run off Dick Radatz won the All-Star Game, leading a band of solid hitters, the Phillies roared into September hotter than a summer heat wave.

"I never saw any other team that was as together as much as that one," said Callison. "Everybody pulled for everybody else."

On the morning of September 21, the Phillies, having won 42 of their last 70 games, had a six-and-one-half-game lead with 12 games left to play. World Series tickets had been printed. But then disaster struck.

In a game against the Cincinnati Reds, Chico Ruiz unbelievably stole home with Frank Robinson at bat and Mahaffey on the mound to give the Reds a 1–0 victory. The collapse had begun.

The Phillies lost nine more games, including one in 12 innings, five by two runs, and one in which Callison hit three home runs. After the seventh loss, catcher Clay Dalrymple told *Philadelphia Evening Bulletin* columnist Sandy Grady, "I haven't seen anybody choke up. We feel absolutely no tension."

Yeah, right. They were swept by the Reds, the Braves, and the St. Louis Cardinals. The final insult came when former Phillies star Curt Simmons, now hurling for the Cards, handed the Phils their 10th straight loss.

By the NUMBERS

17—The number of strikeouts recorded in a 1961 game by Art Mahaffey. That is a club record for both a right-handed pitcher and for a nine-inning game.

"We played so well all season," said Allen. "It was probably one of the best teams I ever played on. But we came up short at the end. That was simply unbearable."

Mauch was later mistakenly accused of starting Bunning and Short every other day. But in fact, Bunning and Short each began three games.

By the time the catastrophe ended, the Phillies had not only given up their seemingly invincible lead, but had tumbled all the way to third place. The fact that they won their last two games and pulled to a second-place tie with Cincinnati, just one game behind St. Louis, was of no consolation.

"Everything we did was right until the last 12 games," Callison recalled. "At the end, we hit a streak that we couldn't get out of. Balls took funny bounces. We lost in funny ways. And we got beat by funny people. It was the worst disappointment I ever had."

The same could be said for everyone else in the employ of the Phillies. And to many fans, the disappointment is vividly recalled to this day.

It was, after all, a collapse almost beyond belief. And, despite high hopes that the team could bounce back the following year, it never happened. The Phillies soon returned to the lower levels of the National League, finishing in the first division only once more the rest of the miserable decade.

The Little General

Seldom over the years have the Phillies been led by a manager who could be described as ordinary. Of the 51 men who have piloted the club with widely varying degrees of success, most have been at least slightly off the norm.

Gene Mauch was a perfect example. Called, appropriately, the "Little General"—even though he stood 5'10"—Mauch was an unyielding tyrant who was as brilliant as he was controversial and who skippered the Phillies for parts of nine years. During the period from 1960 to 1968, Mauch managed in more games (1,332), won more games (646), and lost more games (684)—he had two ties—than any other pilot of the Phillies.

Despite a won-lost percentage of .486, Mauch is generally considered the best manager the Phillies ever had. He directed the team with a kind of creative touch that most managers only wish they could have. His mind worked constantly. He was usually thinking two or three innings ahead, and he maneuvered his team with relentless diligence.

Some said he over-maneuvered. He often did. And he often outsmarted himself, making moves that backfired. But Mauch was a genius at running a game. He had a mind like the proverbial steel trap and a memory to match. He was also intense, caustic, foul-mouthed, confrontational, and arrogant, with a temper that could rage like an August hurricane. And he backed down from no one, not the least of whom were his players, most of whom disliked him intensely, opponents who hated him even more and whom he rode mercilessly, and umpires, quite a few often suggesting that he take an early shower and many of whom did not know the rulebook as well as Mauch.

Mauch, who studied the game with zealous fervor during a nine-year playing career in which he was mostly a utility infielder with six different teams, is the only Phillies manager to lead the team to six straight winning seasons. Of course, he was in command when the 1961 Phillies set a major league record with 23 consecutive losses and in 1964 when the team staged the greatest collapse in baseball history.

Unfortunately, much of Mauch's legacy involves those two teams. He said that the 1961 season, in which they lost 107 games, "was a nightmare." The 1964 campaign was even worse.

That year, the Phillies had a six-and-one-half-game lead with 12 games left to play and blew what was a sure pennant when they lost 10 straight games. "For the first 150 games of the season, we played as per-

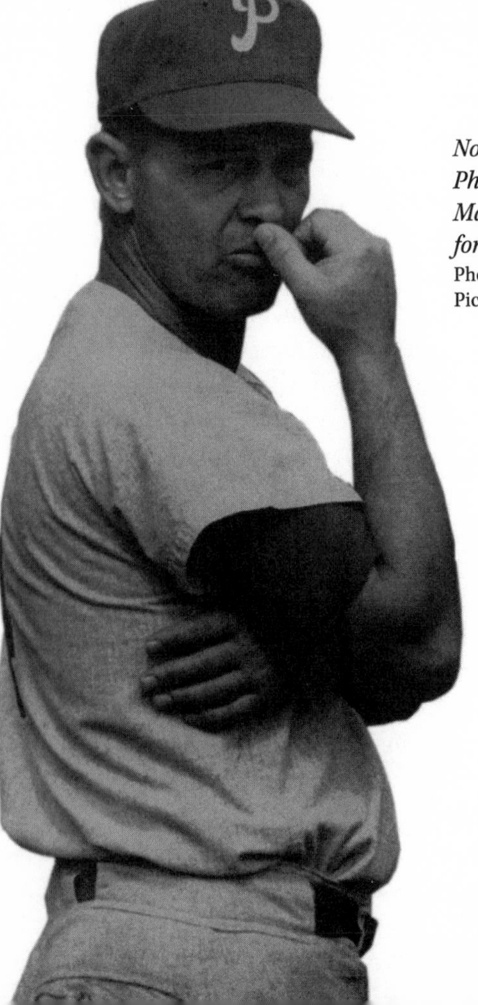

No one won more games as a Phillies manager than Gene Mauch, who captured 646 victories for the Phillies from 1960 to 1968. Photo courtesy of Time Life Pictures/Getty Images.

By the NUMBERS **10**—The number of consecutive hits Ed Delahanty slugged in 1897. The feat, which ties a major league record, came with the aid of nine straight hits in a doubleheader.

fectly as I have ever seen a team play," he said. "Then I took a couple of dumb pills and we couldn't turn the corner."

Mauch unfairly took most of the heat for the team's collapse. But he had plenty of company, including a decimated pitching staff and a team of heavy hitters who stopped hitting.

Many years after that devastating year, Mauch was asked what he remembered about it. "Every f*cking pitch," he sneered.

But despite that disaster and in view of the many contenders, pretenders, and tail-enders who ran the club, the bottom line is that Mauch was the best of a diverse batch of Phillies managers. He had his battles—most notably with slugger Dick Allen. He once said that Robin Roberts threw "like Dolly Madison." Another time he said that Ferguson Jenkins threw like "Betsy Ross."

Certainly, Mauch was not the most jovial guy, especially after a loss. Once, after a painful 1–0 defeat in Houston—in which the Phillies were beaten in the ninth inning on a game-winning hit by rookie Joe Morgan, whom Mauch said looked like "a Little Leaguer"—the manager stormed into the clubhouse and overturned the table holding the players' postgame meal. Food spilled all over the floor, and Mauch fired spareribs around the clubhouse, some of it staining players' clothing. "That was the day that the spareribs went haywire," he said years later.

Another time, ungentle Gene whacked Jerry Grote across the arms as the New York Mets catcher reached into the Phillies' dugout in an attempt to catch a foul pop. The action prompted a new rule that required members of the opposing team to get out of the way if a defensive player needed room to make a play.

On one occasion, the author was asking Mauch questions after a game when his pen went dry. Later, he wondered which had been worse: the embarrassment of having an inkless pen or the withering stare that a scornful Mauch gave him.

Every so often, Mauch revealed a mostly hidden sense of humor. Asked by a writer if a particular player in a batting slump was having problems with high fastballs, Mauch said, "Nope. His problem is with fast highballs."

TOP TEN

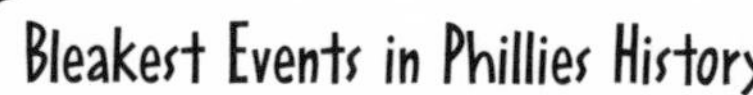

1. Twelve people are killed and 232 injured when a balcony crumbles at Baker Bowl, pitching fans onto the street below, 1903.
2. Team loses 10 straight games to blow a six-and-one-half-game lead with 12 games to play in the worst collapse in baseball history, 1964.
3. Grover Cleveland Alexander is traded at the peak of his career for two players who appear in a combined total of 46 games with the Phillies, 1917.
4. Joe Carter's walk-off home run sends the Phillies down to a crushing defeat in the final game of the World Series, 1993.
5. Ace pitcher Charlie Ferguson dies of typhoid fever at the age of 25 after winning 99 games in four years, 1888.
6. A stunning string of futility occurs when the Phillies set an NL record with their fifth straight season of 100 or more losses, 1942.
7. Phillies set a major league record with 23 losses in a row, 1961.
8. Dodgers rally to beat Phillies in ninth inning of third game of LCS when manager Danny Ozark fails to make a key defensive change, 1977.
9. National League office takes over the bankrupt team and ousts owner Gerry Nugent, 1942.
10. Phillies presidents Horace Fogel (1912)and William Cox (1943) are banned for life from baseball for various indiscretions.

Frank Bilovsky covered the Phillies for the long-departed *Evening Bulletin*. "I learned more about baseball in two minutes with Mauch than I did in two weeks with anybody else," he said. Once, Bilovsky asked Mauch to name the greatest play he ever saw Willie Mays make. Mauch paused, as he always did before answering a question, then said, "You ought to know. You were there that night."

Mauch's encyclopedic memory was again demonstrated many years later when some writers showed him a series of trivia questions involving Phillies history. Mauch answered 80 percent of the questions correctly, astonishing the writers with his knowledge of the history of a team he had managed long ago.

The Phillies were playing in Colt Stadium in Houston one terrifically hot afternoon, and as players returned to the dugout after each inning, many of them complained loudly about the heat and the bugs. Finally, Mauch had had enough of the bickering. "I'm sick of you griping about the insects," he screamed. "They have to play in this heat, too."

But Mauch could manage. He was innovative—he was the first pilot to move the bullpen to the side opposite the dugout so he could keep an eye on what was happening there. And he was the first manager to make the double switch standard procedure. A master strategist, he jockeyed his lineup, he bluffed, he cajoled, he plotted, and he never gave in.

"If I was ever going to have a managers clinic, Gene Mauch would be the guy I would have conduct it," said four-time pennant-winning pilot Dick Williams. Another pretty successful skipper, Sparky Anderson, who won five pennants and a couple World Series, said, "I would like to spend one year as a coach under Gene Mauch."

TRIVIA

Which were the best and worst decades in Phillies history?

Answers to the trivia questions are on page 190.

While he was with the Phillies, Mauch had three first-division finishes, a second-place tie in 1964, and fourth-place endings in 1963 and 1966. After he was fired by the Phillies during the 1968 season, he went on to pilot the California Angels, Minnesota Twins, and Montreal Expos, finally ending a 26-year managerial career in 1987. The 11th-winningest major league manager of all time, Mauch came close to winning American League pennants in 1982 and 1986 with the Angels, but both times suffered devastating defeats in the ALCS.

"Being with the Phillies was a wonderful experience," said Mauch. "I loved the team, and Philadelphia was a great, great town."

And while he was there, "Number Four," as he was also called, carved a niche as the Phillies' finest manager.

A Perfect Father's Day

On Father's Day in 1964, Phillies pitcher Jim Bunning, who by then had sired seven of his nine children, gave himself the perfect gift. It was a perfect game.

Coming on June 21 in the first game of a doubleheader against the New York Mets at Shea Stadium, it was not only the first perfect game during the regular season in the major leagues since 1922, but the first one in modern National League history. It was also the first no-hitter for a Phillies pitcher in 58 years.

Bunning, who had pitched a no-hitter in 1958 with the Detroit Tigers, was in his first year with the Phils, having been traded from the Tigers the previous winter. A nine-year veteran on his way to the first of three straight 19-win seasons, he had been acquired to lead a young Phillies pitching staff.

Although the 1964 season would turn out to be the year of the Great Collapse for the Phillies, there was no inkling of that disaster just yet. At the time, the Phillies were locked in a battle for first place as they faced a Mets team that was in just its third year of existence.

There were 32,026 people in the stands, including Jim's wife, Mary, who had driven to the game with the couple's oldest daughter, Barbara, and the wife of Phillies outfielder Danny Cater from their home in Cherry Hill, New Jersey. The weather was hot and humid—the temperature eventually reaching 92 degrees—as Bunning began his warm-ups.

As he threw, Bunning figured it was just another day. "I felt nothing spectacular warming up before the game," he said. "I felt no different from any other day. Actually, it's not important if you have or don't have good stuff when you're warming up."

Jim Bunning, here pitching against the Giants in 1964, pitched a perfect game against the Mets in the same season and became the first pitcher since Cy Young to win more than 100 games and strike out 1,000 batters in each league.

Maybe Bunning didn't feel any different than usual. But others did. "We knew when he was warming up that this was something special," said Phillies manager Gene Mauch. "The way he was throwing, so live, and as high as he was. Not high with his pitches. High himself."

When the game started, Tracy Stallard, who in 1961 had thrown the pitch that Roger Maris hit for his 61st home run, was on the mound for the Mets. The Phillies touched Stallard for single runs in the first and second innings, the runs scoring on Dick Allen's single and Gus Triandos' double.

Meanwhile, Bunning was sizzling. "He had everything," recalled second baseman Tony Taylor. "His breaking ball was excellent. His fastball was outstanding. His stuff was unbelievable. You could see it from the first inning."

The Mets, a last-place team made up largely of castoffs, struggled right from the start. New York leadoff hitter Jim Hickman fouled off the first two pitches, both hanging sliders. "You had your chance," Bunning uncharacteristically yelled at him. "You won't get any more like that."

By the NUMBERS

9—Number of no-hitters thrown by Phillies pitchers. They include Charlie Ferguson (1885), Red Donahue (1898), Chick Fraser (1903), Johnny Lush (1906), Jim Bunning (1964), Rick Wise (1971), Terry Mulholland (1990), Tommy Greene (1991), and Kevin Millwood (2003).

After Hickman struck out, Bunning mowed through the Mets' lineup with ease. There wasn't a tough chance for a Phillies fielder until the fifth inning when Jesse Gonder lined a ball between first and second. The ball looked like a sure hit, but Taylor dashed madly to his left, amazingly knocked the ball down, ran and picked it up, and threw out Gonder at first.

"With a faster runner, we could have had a problem," Taylor admitted later. Instead, his spectacular play saved the streak for Bunning. It would be the only tough chance for the Phillies defense in the entire game.

The Phillies added four more runs in the sixth inning, two of them scoring on Bunning's bases-loaded double and one each on a home run by Johnny Callison and a single by Triandos.

As the game progressed, though, and it became more and more apparent that Bunning had a chance for at least a no-hitter, Phillies players, following the ageless superstition of not mentioning such a feat, got quieter and quieter. All, that is, except Bunning.

"You don't get the feeling about a no-hitter until after it's an official game," he said. "But after Taylor's play on Gonder, I started to feel good about the game. Things were pretty much going my way."

By the seventh inning, Bunning was the only one in a Phillies uniform making any noise. "Nine more outs," he proclaimed. "Dive for the ball. Don't let anything fall in."

Bunning's teammates, who by then were being told by the pitcher where to position themselves in the field, were horrified. "Six more outs," he shouted as the home eighth began. "I know I'm going for it. I'll give it my best." Then, "three outs to go," he yelled in the ninth.

"Some baseball superstitions are hokey," Bunning said later. "I don't believe in that kind of thing. So I talked incessantly about it. I was a one-man cheerleader.

"I wasn't talking perfect game," he added. "I was talking no-hitter. I had been through one. But I was talking on the bench to relax my teammates. Most of them had never been through one."

In the ninth, Bunning retired former Phillie Charlie Smith on a foul pop and then struck out George Altman, who during the at-bat had hit a pitch over the fence but foul. The last batter was pinch-hitter John Stephenson. Bunning went to a 2–2 count before striking him out.

The perfect game and a 6–0 Phillies win were now in the books. And Bunning and his ecstatic teammates danced happily off the field, celebrating in the clubhouse as they awaited the start of the second game, which the Phils also won, 8–2, behind Rick Wise.

Bunning had thrown just 90 pitches, 69 for strikes. He went to 2–0 and 3–2 counts each twice. He struck out 10 with only four balls being hit out of the infield.

Catcher Triandos, who was behind the plate for most of Bunning's games after coming with him in a trade with the Tigers, said that he had had an easy day behind the plate. "Guys like Jim who are good pitchers are not hard to catch because they are always around the plate," he said. "And they always have good stuff. Bunning was always sharp."

That night, Bunning, a future Hall of Famer, appeared on *The Ed Sullivan Show*, earning $1,000 and knocking that day's U.S. Open winner, Ken Venturi, into the background. Later, hoping to celebrate over dinner, the Bunnings went to Toots Shor's restaurant, only to find the well-known eatery closed.

The Bunnings wound up toasting the perfect Father's Day gift on the way home at a Howard Johnson's on the New Jersey Turnpike.

DID YOU KNOW . . . That the last time a major league pitcher completed both games of a doubleheader was in 1927 when the Phillies' Jack Scott beat the Cincinnati Reds, 3–1, before losing 3–0?

Tape-Measure Homers and Controversial Acts

The Phillies' first African American superstar was a wonderfully talented athlete with the sleek body of a racehorse, muscles that rippled, and wrists like coiled springs. Particularly when he was at the plate, you knew he was something special, and more often than not, that view was confirmed by the hits that rocketed off his bat.

Originally called Richie, then Rich, the man eventually known as Dick Allen was by any name as exciting a player as anyone who ever wore a Phillies uniform. And although controversy seemed to follow him through much of his career, he remains to this day extremely popular with Phillies fans.

Over the years, Phillies rosters have never been overly populated with top-rate African Americans. Matter of fact, a good case can be made that Allen was not only the club's first black superstar, but that he was also its last up to this point.

Allen's numbers speak for themselves. In two stints with the Phillies—one from 1963 to 1969, the other from 1975 to 1976—he hit .291 with 204 home runs and 655 RBIs. Overall, during a 15-year career that included stops at St. Louis, Los Angeles, Chicago (AL), and Oakland, he had a career batting average of .292 with 351 home runs and 1,119 RBIs. There are people in the Hall of Fame who don't have those kinds of numbers.

Dick, originally signed for a $70,000 bonus out of Wampum (Pennsylvania) High School, where he was a third-team all-state basketball player, was National League Rookie of the Year in 1964, hitting .318 with 29 home runs, 91 RBIs, and a league-leading 125 runs.

"I don't think I ever enjoyed watching a first-year player as much as I did Allen," manager Gene Mauch said. "I loved watching him play. I have also never seen a more enthusiastic, more talented offensive player in my life. And I have never seen anybody endear himself, without trying, to his teammates with such great élan as Richie did."

Later, Allen was the American League's Most Valuable Player in 1972. He won home-run titles in 1972 and 1974 and led the league in runs scored in 1964 and in RBIs in 1972. Six times he hit more than 30 home runs, and three times he passed the 100 mark in RBIs.

Despite his superb numbers, Allen, whose brothers Hank and Ron also played in the big leagues, is often remembered for two things: his tape-measure home runs and controversy.

Swinging a 40-ounce bat, an instrument that is virtually unheard of today, he once smashed a home run that flew over a billboard high atop the roof in left-center field at Connie Mack Stadium. The ball was estimated to have traveled 529 feet.

Another time, he drilled a ball over the center-field wall at Connie Mack, the ball jetting between the flagpole and the upper deck. No other ball ever left the park in that particular spot.

Allen, mostly a third baseman in his early days with the Phillies, but later converted to first base because of the one glitch in his game—fielding—hit many other balls over the towering left-field roof at Connie

TOP TEN

Most Home Runs in One Season by a Phillies Hitter

	Name	Year	Home Runs
1.	Mike Schmidt	1980	48
2.	Jim Thome	2003	47
3.	Mike Schmidt	1979	45
4.	Chuck Klein	1930	43
5.	Jim Thome	2004	42
6.	Cy Williams	1923	41
7.	Chuck Klein	1930	40t
	Dick Allen	1966	40t
	Mike Schmidt	1983	40t
10.	Greg Luzinski	1983	39

DID YOU KNOW . . . That the Phillies have finished in either second or third place 29 times since the team began in 1883? They've also wound up in last place 31 times.

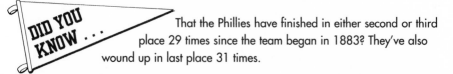

Mack. Although that gave him top billing with the old Philadelphia Athletics slugger Jimmie Foxx in that category, Dick was never overly thrilled with the notoriety that his tape-measure blasts gave him.

"I like to think that there are other things in the game that I could do besides hit the long ball," he lamented. "But people don't see that I was an actual ballplayer. I could bunt, I could steal a base. They always think, tape measure, tape measure, tape measure."

Another condition that followed Allen, who during one stretch in 1966 hit 10 home runs in 19 games, was his penchant for controversy. His problems may have all begun when the Phillies unwisely assigned him to Little Rock, Arkansas—then in the running as the bigotry capital of the world—in his final minor league season in 1963. Dick was subjected to unmerciful abuse by the city's low-life racists.

After becoming one of the stars on the ill-fated 1964 Phillies collapsers, Allen's difficulties were illuminated by his celebrated fight in 1965 with teammate Frank Thomas during batting practice. Thomas had been razzing Dick rather hard. When Allen suggested a fight, Thomas hit him with a bat. That night, Thomas hit a pinch-hit home run, but afterward was released. Fans booed Dick the rest of the season.

"Thomas hit Richie in the back," Mauch remembered. "I was furious. Thomas was totally in the wrong, and I sided with Richie. I saw to it that Thomas was gone."

Allen reached a point where he was often tardy for games. He said he was at the park, but was hanging out with the grounds crew. They, policemen, parking lot attendants, and assorted vendors were among his chosen circle of friends. Once, though, he did miss a train that was taking the team to New York. When he failed to appear for the game, he was suspended for 26 days.

In a widely quoted line, coach George Myatt made the claim that "God Almighty Hisself couldn't handle that man."

In 1967 Allen had to be rushed to a hospital with severe cuts after he said he put his hand through a headlight while pushing an old car near his home. The accident ended his season.

Slugger Dick Allen bats during the 1975 season, the first year of his second stint with the ballclub. Allen belted 204 home runs in a Phillies uniform. Photo courtesy of MLB Photos via Getty Images.

8—Number of Phillies players who were named Rookie of the Year. The honorees (including those from both *The Sporting News* and the Baseball Writers' Association of America) are Del Ennis (1946), Richie Ashburn (1948), Jack Sanford (1957), Ed Bouchee (1957), Dick Allen (1964), Lonnie Smith (1980), Juan Samuel (1984), and Scott Rolen (1997).

Dick endured suspensions, battles with managers, and disappearances. In 1969 he wrote words such as *boo* and *mom* and *Oct. 2* (the date he would be able to leave the Phillies) with his spikes in the dirt around first base. And in his second trip back, he sat alone in the dugout as his teammates celebrated in the clubhouse after the Phils had won the 1976 division title.

In the 1960s, as his problems mounted and the patience of management, including Mauch, and fans decreased, Allen's withdrawal had begun. "But a lot of things weren't told," he said. "They couldn't be told. I was put on the spot back then a lot of times. It seemed everything I did was magnified."

Allen loved his freedom. He loved the horses he owned and rode in Philadelphia's Fairmont Park. But he never loved playing on artificial grass. "If a horse can't eat it," he once said, "I don't want to play on it."

Over the years, Dick's erratic behavior faded from his life. He was at peace with himself and with the rest of the world. He became one of the most likeable fellows you'd ever want to meet. And he took a community-relations job with the Phillies.

"I guess I was always kind of a Jesse James without a gun," Allen said, looking back. "But I matured. I'd like to let bygones be bygones. I like to think now that I had a swell career, both in Philadelphia and elsewhere.

"It was better the second time in Philadelphia than the first," said Dick, who got a standing ovation when introduced in his first at-bat back in 1975. "The first time, I left with a lot of bitterness. I said I'd never return. Then I did. I guess it goes to show that a lot of times we say things that we really don't know how they're going to turn out."

This Trade Was for Real

If you counted them up, bad trades that the Phillies made over the years would surely outnumber good ones.

After all, this is a team that dealt away a couple of young players named Ferguson Jenkins and Ryne Sandberg, getting little in return and watching helplessly as they sped to Hall of Fame careers.

Then there was the deal in which the Phils jettisoned Grover Cleveland Alexander at the top of his Hall of Fame career because the team was afraid he would be drafted into military service during World War I. In return, they received two players who appeared in a combined total of 46 games in Phillies uniforms.

This is also the team that sent players such as future Hall of Famers Billy Hamilton and Chuck Klein, future Most Valuable Players Bucky Walters and Dolph Camilli, and stalwarts such as Jack Sanford, Gary Matthews, Curt Schilling, and Scott Rolen to other teams in deals that brought virtually nothing back to Philadelphia.

Ah, but not all has been for naught. Bobby Abreu, Schilling, Johnny Callison, Tug McGraw, Dick Sisler, Garry Maddox, Cy Williams, and Jim Bunning have all come to Philadelphia in lopsided deals that heavily favored the Phillies. So have a number of others.

No deal, however, was any better than the one that brought Steve Carlton to the City of Brotherly Love.

The swap was made on February 25, 1972. It was the last trade made by Phillies general manager John Quinn, who had been wheeling and dealing for the Phils since 1959.

As the story goes, Carlton was in the midst of a salary squabble with the St. Louis Cardinals. Having just become a 20-game winner the year before in his fifth full season in the majors, Carlton was emerging as one of the National League's premier pitchers. All he wanted from the Cards was a $20,000 increase from his $45,000 salary.

Simultaneously, Rick Wise had become the Phillies' top pitcher. He had hurled a no-hitter in 1971 while winning 17 games, his third straight year in double figures, and was among the league leaders in a number of pitching categories. He, too, thought he was entitled to a raise. Wise wanted to double his salary.

Steve Carlton, here winning his 25th game in 1972, won 27 games for the Phillies in a year when they won only 59 as a team. He also had a league-leading 1.97 ERA in 1972. In 15 seasons with the Phillies, he made seven All-Star teams and won four Cy Young Awards.

"I felt I had finally arrived as a big league pitcher," said Wise, who started his first game for the Phillies as an 18-year-old bonus player in the nightcap of a doubleheader in which Jim Bunning hurled his perfect game in 1964. "I was only making $30,000 after seven years in the big leagues. I wanted more money. There were no agents, no trade clauses. It was me against John Quinn."

TRIVIA

What was particularly unusual about the game in which Rick Wise pitched a no-hitter in 1971?

Answers to the trivia questions are on page 190.

While Wise was locked in a salary struggle with Quinn, insisting the Phils double his wages, the general manager happened to be seated that winter next to Rick's wife, Susan, at a banquet. "We're never going to trade Rick Wise," Quinn told her.

A little while later, Cardinals general manager Bing Devine called Quinn. "Has Rick Wise signed?" he wanted to know. "No," Quinn replied. "Well, neither has Carlton," Divine said. "Would you be interested in Carlton?"

Quinn, of course, was. That night, he and then–farm director Paul Owens were bending elbows at a bar at the Phillies' spring-training site in Clearwater, Florida. "I've got a chance to trade Wise for Carlton," Quinn told Owens. "What do you think?"

"Run as fast as you can to the nearest phone" is similar to the way Owens put it.

Quinn talked to Phils owner Bob Carpenter and manager Frank Lucchesi. Then he dialed Devine, and the deal was done. A lefty for a righty; two hurlers entangled in salary spats with their respective teams.

"I want it understood, though," said Quinn, "that we're not trading ballplayers just because they haven't signed. We're trading ballplayers because we think that Carlton is one of the better pitchers in the National League."

The trade was hugely unpopular in Philadelphia. Wise was coming off one of the better years a Phillies pitcher had had in a while and had become a fan favorite, while Carlton was basically an unknown. To most fans, the deal made no sense at all.

The trade was also curious because the Phillies already had left-handers Chris Short and Woodie Fryman in the starting rotation. Why would they want a third southpaw?

TOP TEN

Most Wins for a Phillies Pitcher in One Season

	Name	Year	Wins
1.	Kid Gleason	1890	38
2.	Grover C. Alexander	1916	33
3.	Gus Weyhing	1892	32
4.	Grover C. Alexander	1915	31
5.	Charlie Ferguson	1886	30*t*
	Grover C. Alexander	1917	30*t*
7.	Dan Casey	1887	28*t*
	Charlie Buffinton	1888, 1889	28*t*
	Grover C. Alexander	1911	28*t*
	Robin Roberts	1952	28*t*

"We didn't just trade for a left-hander," Lucchesi said. "We traded for a good left-hander. If I had four Steve Carltons, I'd start them all in the rotation."

Even Wise was perplexed. "It was a weird trade," he said some years later. "There wasn't any reason for it other than the fact that we were both at loggerheads with our respective general managers. I was shocked when it happened."

As is often typical of "weird" trades, Carlton came to Philadelphia and got basically the salary he had sought in St. Louis. Wise went to the Cardinals and received an amount similar to the wage he wanted from the Phillies.

Wise went on to have a fine major league career. He won 188 games and in 1975 helped the Boston Red Sox win the American League pennant. He got the decision in the fabled sixth game of the World Series when Carlton Fisk's twelfth-inning home run won for Boston.

And Steve Carlton? He quit talking to the media after a disagreement with a writer a few years after his arrival, so most of his thoughts are strictly subject to conjecture. Later, at his Hall of Fame induction in 1994, he did say that coming to Philadelphia "was a blessing in disguise. The turning point in my life was coming here. I didn't know what professional baseball could be until then. It gave me a chance to put my ideas into play. It allowed me to practice the art of concentration and to settle into a routine."

Carlton was also a physical fitness fanatic. He sometimes worked out several hours after pitching a game. He could do 1,000 sit-ups with 15-pound weights strapped to his wrists and ankles. And he walked back and forth in a 4' x 12' box containing rice three feet deep. "Whoever put that man together genetically," said Phillies conditioning guru Gus Hoefling, "did one helluva job."

On the mound, Carlton became the best left-handed pitcher in Phillies history. He hurled in 15 seasons with the club, winning more than 20 games five times. A four-time Cy Young Award winner, he is the club's all-time leader in wins with 241. One of just 22 300-game winners, Carlton claimed 329 victories overall, making him the second-winningest left-hander (behind Warren Spahn) in baseball history. He also became one of baseball's all-time strikeout leaders with 4,136 in 741 games.

Carlton was so effective that Pittsburgh Pirates slugger Willie Stargell once said, "Hitting him is like trying to drink coffee with a fork."

Unquestionably, one of the finest years any pitcher in big league history ever had came in Carlton's very first season after the trade. The 1972 Phillies were terrible, winning just 59 games all season while losing 97 and finishing 37½ games out of first place.

Carlton, however, was the one shining light in this dreary scene. He won 27 games (losing only 10) while at one point setting a club record with 15 consecutive wins. Completing 30 of the 41 games he started, Carlton worked in 346 innings, striking out 310 (all leading the league).

That in itself was enough to make the trade worthwhile. In the ensuing years, Carlton made sure it ranked as the best one the Phillies ever made.

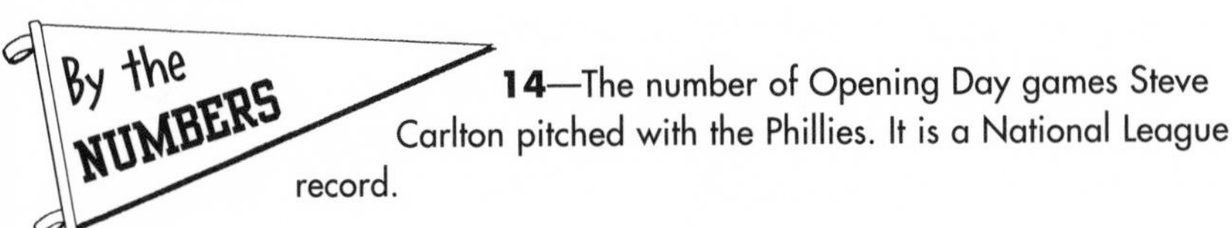

14—The number of Opening Day games Steve Carlton pitched with the Phillies. It is a National League record.

Shootouts in Chicago

There is something about Wrigley Field in Chicago that brings out the best—and sometimes the worst—in teams. Depending on which way the wind is blowing off Lake Michigan, the Friendly Confines can either be a hitter's haven or a hitter's horror.

Like all teams, the Phillies have experienced both sides of the ivy in their games with the Chicago Cubs. They have been exposed to slugfests as well as shutouts. Some of these affairs have been especially heavy in the run-scoring department.

For instance, in 1922 the Phillies dropped a 26–23 decision to the Cubs in the highest scoring game for two teams in major league history. Amazingly, the Phillies trailed 25–6 after four innings. But they roared back and fell just short after crossing the plate 14 times in the last two innings.

Another shootout in Chicago occurred on April 18, 1976, when the Phils edged the Cubs in another slugfest, 18–16. In that gem, Mike Schmidt hit four home runs—joining Ed Delahanty and Chuck Klein as the third Phillies player to perform that feat—to help his club overcome a 12–1 third-inning deficit.

Schmidt had been in a deep slump as the season began and after the first four games was hitting just .167 with nine strikeouts. "You have to relax. Have some fun. With all the talent you have, baseball ought to be fun, so enjoy it," Schmidt's good friend Dick Allen suggested.

Schmidt heeded Allen's advice. After flying out and singling, Schmidt touched Rick Reuschel for a two-run homer in the fourth. In the seventh he smoked a solo homer off Reuschel to cut the Cubs' lead to 13–7. In the eighth in the midst of a five-run uprising, he bagged a three-run blast off Mike Garman, making the score 13–12.

DID YOU KNOW . . . That a father and his son have both played with the Phillies? Infielder Ruben Amaro wore the Phils uniform from 1960 to 1965. His son Ruben Jr. played in the outfield with the club from 1992 to 1993 and again from 1996 to 1998. Amaro Sr. went on to become a longtime coach and manager in the Phillies organization, while the younger Amaro is the team's assistant general manager.

Bob Boone's homer in the ninth tied it, and Larry Bowa tripled home the go-ahead run and scored later in the inning, giving the Phillies a 15–13 lead. The Cubs rallied to send the game into extra innings. Then Schmidt's fourth consecutive homer, a feat that was last accomplished in 1894 by Bobby Lowe of the Boston Braves, cleared the ivy with Allen aboard. The blow came off another Reuschel—Rick's brother Paul. That put the Phillies up for good.

"I couldn't believe what was happening to me," Schmidt recalled. "But I decided to think about that later and concentrate on winning. I was sure after the third homer that we were going to win."

As for his fourth home run, Schmidt said he "was nice and relaxed" and just trying to make contact. "Maybe get a single and move Dick to third where he could score on a fly ball," he said. "Reuschel tried to come inside on me, and I had what I thought was my best swing of the day."

While the first two shootouts defied the imagination, the third one was even more improbable. It happened on May 17, 1979. The Phillies won 23–22 in a game that featured 50 hits, including 11 home runs, 10 doubles, and two triples. Along the way, the Phillies blew a 21–9 lead.

Dave Kingman slammed three home runs and drove in six runs to lead the Cubs' 26-hit barrage. Larry Bowa had five hits—all by the sixth inning—and Schmidt and Boone each clubbed two homers. Boone drove in five runs, while Schmidt, Pete Rose, and Garry Maddox collected four RBIs apiece as the Phils, who batted around three times, collected 24 hits.

By the NUMBERS **13**—The most runs by a Phillies team in one inning. The outburst came in 2003 in the fourth inning of a 13–1 victory over the Cincinnati Reds.

The Phils had copped a 13–0 decision the previous day, which gave the team's starting pitcher, Randy Lerch, cause for concern. "Don't forget to get me some runs," he urged teammates.

A 20- to 30-mile-per-hour wind whipped toward left field as the game began. Hitters licked their chops while pitchers fought off anxiety attacks. Neither Lerch nor Cubs starter Dennis Lamp lasted through the first inning.

Like most sluggers, Mike Schmidt loved to play at Wrigley Field when the wind was blowing out. His dramatic tenth-inning home run off of Bruce Sutter sealed one of the wildest in Phillies history, a 23–22 win over the Cubs. Photo courtesy of MLB Photos via Getty Images.

IF ONLY . . . The Athletics had never left town. We'll never know for sure, but one thing is certain: during the season, there'd be a game in town almost every day.

Schmidt and Boone both hit three-run homers, and Lerch added a solo shot to rocket the Phillies to a 7–0 lead in the first. In the bottom half, however, Kingman laced a three-run home run as the Cubs came back with six runs.

Garry Maddox doubled to start the inning, then stroked a three-run blast to lead an eight-run Phillies salvo in the third, and they had two more runs in the following inning. A two-run homer by Kingman and a solo clout by Steve Ontiveros in the bottom of the fourth brought the Cubs back to a 17–9 deficit.

The Phillies stretched their lead to 21–9 in the top of the fifth, but Chicago exploded for seven runs in the bottom of the inning with the help of Bill Buckner's grand slam and Jerry Martin's two-run homer. And the Cubs weren't done. They scored three more runs in the sixth, with Kingman slugging his third home run of the game. Then, after the Phils scored a lone run, Chicago added three more in the eighth. The score was now 22–22.

In the ninth, for only the second time in the game, neither team scored in an inning. Phils reliever Rawly Eastwick became the game's first pitcher to retire the side in order.

Now, once again, as the battle raged into the tenth inning, it was Schmidt to the forefront. Schmidt, who had the unusual distinction of committing two errors in the game—one leading to three unearned runs—came to the plate with two outs and Cubs' crack reliever Bruce Sutter on the mound.

Mike worked a 3–2 count before Sutter came in with his patented split-fingered fastball. Schmidt jettisoned it clean over the left-field bleachers and out onto Waveland Avenue. The titanic blast gave the Phillies a 23–22 lead.

"I hit the same pitch that I swing and miss at all season," Schmidt said.

Eastwick again retired the Cubs one-two-three in the bottom of the tenth to complete one of the weirdest games the Phillies ever played.

The Pope

Paul Owens and ex-Phillies catcher and coach Andy Seminick were engaged in a rather animated exchange regarding the fine art of sliding. Nothing unusual about two baseball lifers discussing one of the elements of the game.

Except it was 3:00 in the morning. And the conversation was taking place in a hotel lobby.

Suddenly, Owens arose from his chair, raced across the room. . .and slid into a couch. "That's how you slide," said the Phillies general manager.

Whether he was safe or out doesn't matter. The point is, there was never anything orthodox about Owens. Quite possibly, that is why he was so successful. Owens never did anything with the lackluster approach favored by so many of his peers. He abhorred the status quo. He hated to be typecast.

That was nothing Owens ever had to worry about. After all, this was a guy who once challenged a whole team to a fight. He was a guy who, because he couldn't stomach what was happening on the field, came down out of the front office on two different occasions during the season to manage the team after firing the managers, one a fan favorite, the other a pilot who had the club in first place. He was tough, he was shrewd, and he was bold. He was never afraid to stick his neck out.

These are all qualities that made Owens—the Pope, as he was universally called because he bore a facial resemblance to Pope Paul VI—not only the best general manager the Phillies ever had, but the most influential person in the club's long history.

During a reign as GM from 1972 to 1983, Owens made 47 trades. He built a farm system that ranked as one of the best in the major leagues. And he led the Phillies into and through what is regarded as the club's golden era, a period when the team went to two World Series and five National League Championship Series.

"Paul Owens," said Larry Bowa, "meant more to the Phillies organization than anyone who's ever been there—the Hall of Famers, all of them. He was one of a kind—a great man."

No one should be more cognizant of Owens' abilities than Bowa. As a junior college shortstop in California, he was completely ignored in the big league draft. But Phillies scout Eddie Bockman liked the skinny kid. At the time, Owens was the Phillies' farm director, a position he held from 1965 to 1972.

Bockman asked Owens to view some films of Bowa. They spread a bed sheet on the wall of a motel room, ran the film, and before long, Owens was also convinced the kid could play. Owens signed him for a $1,500 bonus, and Bowa became the best shortstop the Phillies ever had.

Whether it was as farm director or general manager, Owens could spot talent with uncanny proficiency. Many of his trades reflected that ability. Such was the case when he swapped popular and capable first baseman Willie Montanez for center fielder Garry Maddox. The deal was loudly criticized at the time, but it became one of the best the Phillies ever made.

TOP TEN

Coaches Who Spent the Most Years with the Phillies

	Name	Years	Seasons
1.	John Vukovich	1988–2004	17
2.	Mike Ryan	1980–1995	16
3.	Benny Bengough	1946–1959	14
4.	Billy DeMars	1969–1981	13
5.	Bobby Wine	1972–1983	12
6.	Cy Perkins	1946–1954	9t
	George Myatt	1964–1972	9t
	Ray Rippelmeyer	1970–1978	9t
	Larry Bowa	1988–1996	9t
10.	Hans Lobert	1934–1941	8t
	Denis Menke	1989–1996	8t
	Ramon Henderson	1998–2005	8t

Owens also made deals that brought the Phillies Tug McGraw, Dave Cash, Manny Trillo, Jim Lonborg, Bake McBride, Dick Ruthven, Gary Matthews, Von Hayes, and John Denny. He helped to sign Pete Rose as a free agent. And he raised through the Phillies' farm system Mike Schmidt, Greg Luzinski, Bob Boone, Bowa, and many others. Overall, he sold, bought, signed, or traded hundreds of players while building a franchise that grew to become one of the top clubs in the National League.

Just like the Phillies' emergence from the depths of the National League, Owens' rise to the top had been a long, hard struggle. A veteran of World War II who had fought in the Battle of the Bulge, Owens had married a French girl who spoke no English after his discharge, then earned a degree from St. Bonaventure College. While launching what he thought would be a lifelong career as a teacher, Owens got a tryout in 1951 with Olean, an upstate New York club in the low minors.

When Owens reported for the tryout, it was pouring rain. The Olean general manager told him to go into town and have lunch, then come back to the ballpark. On his way out, Owens, thinking he'd be sitting in the stands, bought a ticket to the game for 75¢.

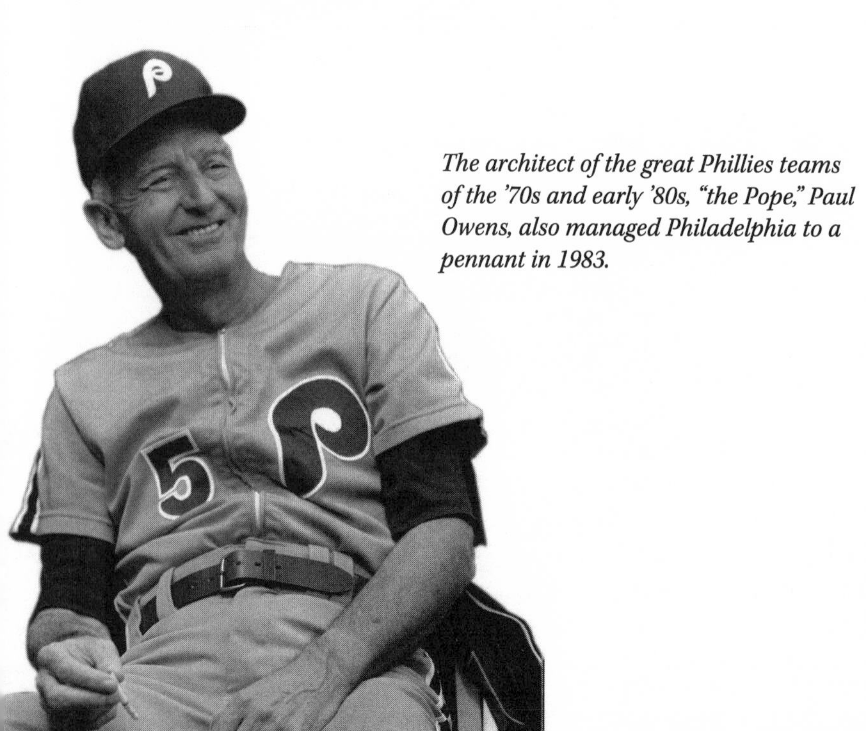

The architect of the great Phillies teams of the '70s and early '80s, "the Pope," Paul Owens, also managed Philadelphia to a pennant in 1983.

DID YOU KNOW . . .

That the Phillies never had a full-time general manager until Herb Pennock held the job from 1943 to 1948? Since then, the club has employed just seven more GMs, including Roy Hamey (1954–1959), John Quinn (1959–1972), Paul Owens (1972–1983), Woody Woodward (1987–1988), Lee Thomas (1988–1997), Ed Wade (1997–2005), and Pat Gillick (2005–present). Between 1948 and 1954 and again from 1983 until 1987, the Phillies had no general manager. Bob Carpenter handled that function the first time, and a committee known as the Gang of Six headed by Bill Giles performed the GM duties the second time.

After arriving back at the park, however, Owens was told to suit up because he was going to start at first base. The new player promptly lashed two hits. "I was probably the only guy in pro baseball who had to pay to play in his first game," Owens said.

Owens hit .407 with 17 home runs and 101 RBIs in 111 games and was named both Rookie of the Year and Most Valuable Player. After the season, he returned to his job as a teacher.

But Owens was no kid, and his playing career was short lived. By 1954 Owens had given up playing and teaching and had become a manager in the Phillies' farm system. Eventually, he became a scout, then in 1965, he was hired as the Phillies' farm director.

"When I took over, we were really bad," Owens said. "We had a helluva rebuilding job to do."

One of his first orders of business was to evaluate the team's 20 scouts. He then fired half of them. "Some of those guys were my friends," he said. "But this was a business, and to be frank, the Phillies had been terrible for far too long. Why? Because we weren't signing big league players."

Soon, that practice had changed. The Phillies started to sign some good young players, and the farm system became increasingly productive. But the parent club was still floundering.

In 1972 Owens was named general manager, succeeding John Quinn. Thirty-seven days after he took the job, and with the Phillies buried in last place, Owens fired popular manager Frank Lucchesi and made himself the skipper.

"I went down there to find out some things about the players," Owens said. "I wanted to find out who wanted to play and who didn't. The ones who didn't weren't going to stay around."

TRIVIA

Who were the last brothers who played with the Phillies?

Answers to the trivia questions are on page 190.

Although the Phillies finished last, winning just 59 games—27 of them by newly acquired Steve Carlton—Owens had the information he sought. Soon the trades began as the Pope returned to his full-time duties as GM.

Within two years, the Phillies had begun their ascent. By 1976 they won the first of three straight NL East Division titles. Then, in 1980, with the help of a legendary clubhouse tirade by Owens in which he challenged the whole team to a fight, the Phils won the team's first and only World Series.

But the Pope was not done yet. In midseason 1983, with the Phillies clinging to a slim lead but playing well below their perceived capability, Owens fired manager Pat Corrales and put himself back in the dugout. This time, the Phils went all the way to the top, winning the National League pennant before losing to the Baltimore Orioles in the World Series.

During the season, Owens had once again demonstrated his foresight and courage. He acquired Joe Lefebvre, Willie Hernandez, and Sixto Lezcano in trades. Each played a major role in the Phillies' season. Then, after becoming manager, he benched Rose late in the campaign, replacing him with rookie Len Matuszek. And he gave more playing time to a slumping Joe Morgan, who, it turned out, became one of the key players in the Phils' stretch drive.

"Sure, there was self-satisfaction," Owens said in response to a question about his own sense of worth. "I don't think we'd have won if I hadn't gone down there. No way we were going to win the way we were going. But the only thing that counts is the bottom line. How I did it or what I did doesn't matter. All I knew is, there were 24 other teams that sat and watched us in the World Series."

Owens managed one more year (a fourth-place finish) before retiring from full-time duty with the Phillies. Not ready to leave the game entirely, he became a special advisor to club president Bill Giles, evaluating minor league players. Later, he served as an aide to general manager Ed Wade.

When he died in 2003, Owens was still working part-time with the Phillies. He had served the club for nearly 50 years, most of them with extraordinary success.

No Era Was Any Better

When a ballclub wins just 59 games in a single season, there is an obvious message: it's time for a massive overhaul.

That message came crashing to the surface after the Phillies posted a pathetic 59–97 record during the 1972 season. If it hadn't been for the presence of Steve Carlton and his 27 wins, the team's sorry record would surely have been much worse.

Actually, since the late 1950s the Phillies had been pretty terrible. Take away the disastrous season of 1964 when they almost won the pennant, the Phillies had left the second division only two other times. By 1972 they had lost more than 90 games in three of the last four years.

Names such as Joe Verbanic, Al Raffo, Lowell Palmer, Rich Barry, Del Bates, Joe Lis, and Pete Koegel had made brief appearances in Phillies uniforms and were never heard from again. Washed up veterans such as Bob Buhl, Bo Belinsky, Lew Burdette, Jackie Brandt, Bobby DelGreco, Phil Linz, and Roger Freed also dotted the lineups on occasion while contributing virtually nothing.

In 1971 the Phillies had moved into a new ballpark called Veterans Stadium, located in South Philadelphia far from their old Connie Mack Stadium home at the other end of the city. They had hired a new announcer by the name of Harry Kalas, who three decades later would enter the broadcasters' wing of the Hall of Fame. And vice president Bill Giles had begun to demonstrate his genius as a promoter with a series of attention-grabbing attractions before and during games.

It was Giles who plotted the memorable closing of Connie Mack Stadium, among other things giving away wooden slats from unused chairs. Fans who hadn't brought tools used the slats to bang apart the old ballpark. "I even saw a guy walking down the street with a toilet seat," said Giles, who watched in amazement as fans ripped up virtually everything that wasn't bolted down and stormed the field after the final out, tearing up grass and anything else they could pry loose.

Giles also planned the events at the opening of the Vet. The highlight was catcher Mike Ryan's grab of the first ball after it was dropped from a helicopter hovering some 150 feet above the field. Ryan battled wind currents to make the catch.

The 1971 team drew a then-club-record 1.5 million fans to the stadium, but the Phillies lost 95 games under manager Frank Lucchesi. "Skipper," as he called himself, was still at the helm in 1972, still employing the philosophy he had used during more than 25 years as a pilot in the Phillies' minor league system. "There's only 18 inches between a pat on the back and a kick in the butt," was the affable skipper's mantra.

Lucchesi didn't finish the '72 season. Newly named general manager Paul Owens fired him and appointed himself as the Phillies' new skipper so he could get a close look at who could play and who couldn't. Then, after the season had ended, owner Bob Carpenter stepped down as president and handed the job to his son, Ruly. Owens and Ruly had previously worked together for seven years and had an excellent relationship.

Ruly had been an invaluable aide to Owens in rebuilding the club's farm system. Now, the two would join forces to rebuild the parent club.

"One month after I got the job as farm director," Owens recalled, "I said, 'Cripes, it's worse than I thought.'" To Owens and the young Carpenter, the job of rebuilding the parent club appeared to be even harder.

By the time they were done, though, the Phillies had evolved into one of the top teams in the major leagues. And for one memorable decade, they enjoyed the most successful period in the club's mostly inglorious history. It was truly the Phillies' golden era.

Between 1974 and 1983, the Phillies won five East Division titles, two National League pennants, and one World Series. The team finished lower than third only once and twice posted a team-record 101 wins.

The era began with Owens replacing himself with Danny Ozark, a longtime coach with the Los Angeles

TRIVIA

Which player appeared in the most games in one season for the Phillies?

Answers to the trivia questions are on page 190.

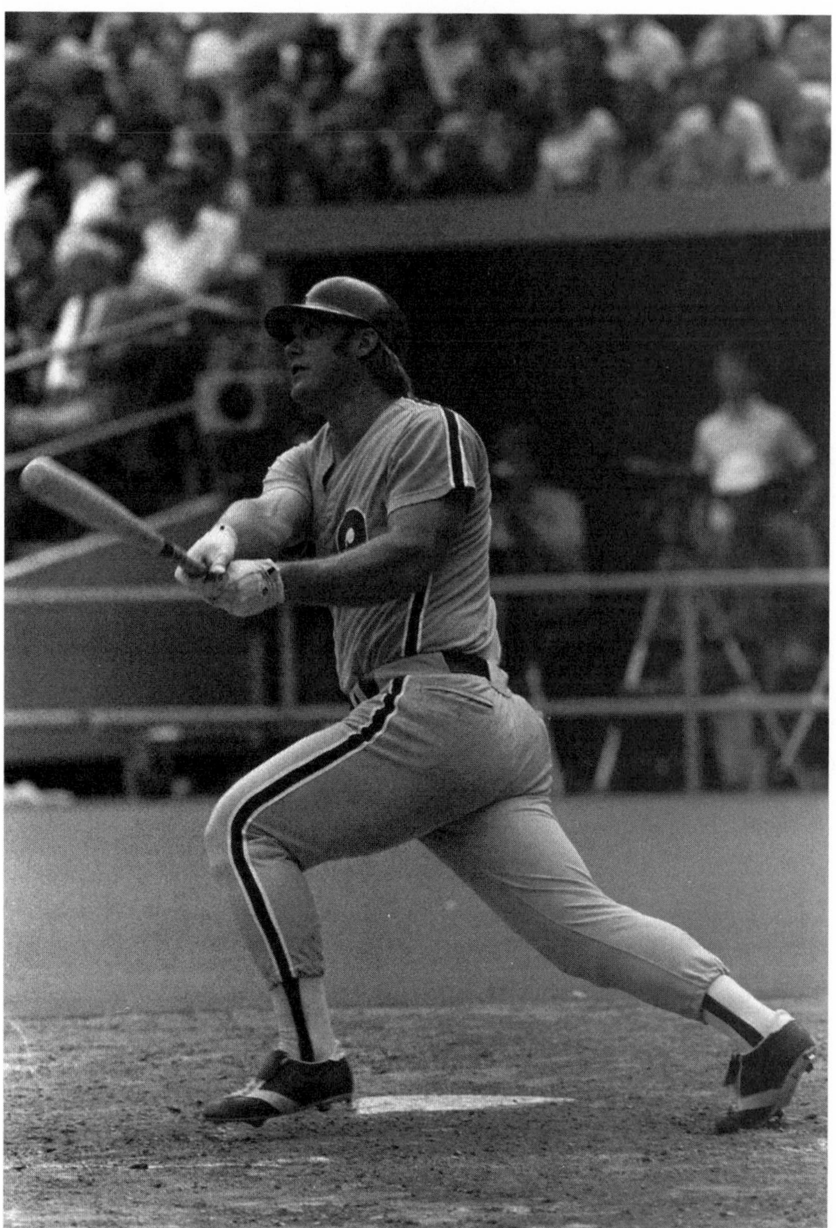

Stocky and awkward in the field, Greg Luzinski, "the Bull," here hitting a three-run homer to help the Phillies beat the Pirates to clinch the 1978 division title, combined with Mike Schmidt to average nearly 66 home runs from 1975 to 1980. He's fourth on the all-time Phillies home-run list.

By the NUMBERS

6—Number of Cy Young Awards that have been won by Phillies pitchers. Steve Carlton took home four of them—in 1972, 1977, 1980, and 1982—while John Denny got the prize in 1983 and Steve Bedrosian won the trophy in 1987.

Dodgers, but a man with no managerial experience. Ozark was a kindly gentleman, but sometimes his temper could explode. He also had a way with words.

Once, while engaged in a discussion with Associated Press writer Ralph Bernstein, Ozark said, "You know I'm a fascist." "You're a what?" said the stunned writer. "Not the Italian kind," Ozark responded. "The other kind. Somebody who says one thing and means something else."

Ozark was somewhat less facetious when it came to running a ball-club. Although the Phillies finished sixth in 1973, he drove the club to third- and second-place spots over the next two years.

Along the way, Owens was accumulating good players. In one of his best early deals, he acquired Dave Cash, a spirited second baseman who had put in some good years with the Pittsburgh Pirates.

One night during his first spring training with the Phils, Cash went to the dog track. An expert handicapper, he carried a considerable chunk of money that teammates had given him to bet on the greyhounds. When Cash arrived at the clubhouse the next day, teammates asked if they'd won anything. "Yes, we did," Cash replied.

With that, a slogan was born.

Somewhere along the way, it was changed to "Yes, We Can." And it became the rallying cry for the Phillies as they embarked on their journey to the top.

Cash, who led the league with well over 600 at-bats in three straight seasons, including 699 in 1975, was the spark plug. But others obtained in trades, particularly Garry Maddox, Jay Johnstone, Jim Lonborg, Tug McGraw, Ron Reed, and Dick Allen, also became heavy contributors, while joining a steady flow of youngsters from the farm system that included Larry Bowa, Bob Boone, Greg Luzinski, Mike Schmidt, and Larry Christenson.

With Carlton reigning as the bellwether of the starting rotation, the Phillies made brief runs at first place in 1974 and 1975. But there was nothing brief about their perch at the top in 1976. Adding Jim

Kaat to the rotation, the Phils won 50 of their first 70 games, and held a 15½-game lead in late August. But then trouble appeared. The club lost 12 of 13 games, and in slightly more than three weeks, their lead had been cut to three games.

Memories of the 1964 Phillies reared their ugly heads. The team, the fans, the press battled panic attacks. That's ridiculous, advised McGraw, "None of us were here in 1964."

The Phillies eventually pulled themselves back together, winning 13 of their final 16 games to clinch the division title. The Phils wound up with 101 wins and finished nine games ahead of the second-place Pirates.

Although the Phils had won their first title of any kind since 1950, the joyride didn't last long. In the League Championship Series, they lost three straight to the Big Red Machine, also known as the Cincinnati Reds. In a touch of irony, the Reds were managed by Sparky Anderson, a former second baseman whose only year as a big league player came in 1959 with the Phillies.

In 1977 the Phillies, having added Richie Hebner and Ted Sizemore, started slowly and by mid-June were eight games off the lead. But Owens pulled another of his magic deals out of the hat, landing Bake McBride in a trade with the St. Louis Cardinals. With McBride playing a key role, the Phils went 70–33 the rest of the way to win the division title, this time by five games over the Pirates. Again, the team won 101 games.

Many thought it was the best club the Phillies ever had. The team had a standout starting eight, a forceful pitching staff, and as good a bench as there was in the big leagues.

But it again fared poorly in the playoffs against the Los Angeles Dodgers. After winning the first game, the Phils lost three straight, one being the infamous Black Friday defeat.

DID YOU KNOW . . . That no one today goes back any further with the Phillies than Maje McDonnell? McDonnell first joined the club as a batting practice pitcher in 1947. He was on the staff when the Whiz Kids won the pennant in 1950, then served as a coach in 1951 and from 1954 to 1957. After that, Maje was a Phillies scout for several years, then left the club, but returned in 1973 in the community-relations department. He's been there ever since, and now in his eighties, still serves in a part-time role.

TOP TEN

Phillies Career Leaders in Saves

	Name	Saves
1.	Jose Mesa	111
2.	Steve Bedrosian	103
3.	Mitch Williams	102
4.	Tug McGraw	94
5.	Ron Reed	90
6.	Ricky Botallico	78
7.	Turk Farrell	65
8.	Jack Baldschun	59*t*
	Billy Wagner	59*t*
10.	Al Holland	55

The Phils won again in 1978, finishing one and one-half games ahead of Pittsburgh. Once more, though, it was the same old story in the playoffs. Again, the Dodgers won in four games. The winning run in the fourth game was set up when Maddox, an eight-time Gold Glove winner, dropped an easy fly ball hit by Dusty Baker.

"The ball was right in my glove," said Maddox afterward. "It was not a tough play. It was just a routine line drive."

Feeling that the Phillies needed someone to light a fire under his mostly laid-back crew, Giles negotiated a deal during the off-season that brought Pete Rose to Philadelphia as a free agent. But while Rose hit .331, the Phils tumbled to fourth place, finishing 14 games out of first. Ozark was fired late in the season and replaced by Dallas Green.

All was forgotten in 1980 when the Phillies captured their first National League pennant in 30 years and the only World Series the team ever won. It was a season that erased all the bad memories and all the bad years that had plagued the Phillies for so long. "Tonight," said Bowa after the final game, "we put some ghosts to rest."

In the strike-shortened season of 1981, it was decided to declare first- and second-half winners. The Phillies won the early crown, then met Montreal in a best-of-five playoff. George Vukovich's tenth-inning home run gave the Phils a 6–5 victory in the fourth game to even the series. In the deciding game, however, Steve Rogers outdueled Carlton for the second time, winning 3–0 and giving the Expos entry into the LCS.

With ex-Phils backup catcher Pat Corrales replacing Green as manager in 1982, the Phillies placed second in the division, three games behind the St. Louis Cardinals.

Then the Wheeze Kids entered the picture. They got that name because the team featured a solid core of older veterans such as Rose, Joe Morgan, Tony Perez, Carlton, McGraw, and several others.

In midseason, Owens, dissatisfied with what he was seeing, fired Corrales, although the team held a slim lead, and again assigned himself to the manager's post. Eventually, the Phils won 11 straight and 14 of 16 games down the stretch in September and clinched the pennant easily, placing six games in front of the Pirates.

The Phils got surprise performances from some unexpected places. John Denny won 19 games and the Cy Young Award, Al Holland was named Fireman of the Year, outfielder Joe Lefebvre hit .310, and unheralded rookie Len Matuszek came on strongly at the end after Owens pulled Rose off of first base.

Los Angeles again provided the opposition in the playoffs. And with Gary Matthews hitting .429 and belting home runs in three games, the Phillies took three out of four games to win the pennant. Matthews' three-run homer propelled the Phils to a 7–2 verdict in the final game and won for him the series MVP award.

Back to the fall classic for the second time in four years, the World Series was anticlimatic. Denny and the Phils beat the Baltimore Orioles, 2–1, in the opener. But then the Orioles won four straight.

The 1983 season concluded what had been a marvelous decade for the Phillies. It had been a decade like no other the team had ever experienced.

Late Bloomer Becomes a Hall of Famer

By the time he finished high school, Mike Schmidt had undergone two knee operations because of injuries from playing football. In baseball, he was a switch-hitting shortstop, a good player, but with no particular power.

Scouts waving lucrative contracts were not wearing out a path to his doorstep. In fact, the interest in the young Dayton, Ohio, youth was so minimal that he enrolled at Ohio University, where he set his sights on becoming an architect.

In high school, Schmidt had been a power forward in basketball and a quarterback in football. But at Ohio U., he concentrated on baseball. After hitting .260 as a freshman, Ohio coach Bobby Wren convinced Mike to give up switch-hitting. That's when a Hall of Fame career started to take off.

"I liked him the first time I saw him," said the late Phillies superscout Tony Lucadello. "I could see that he was an excellent athlete and a better-than-average prospect. I felt, though, that Mike would be a late bloomer. At times, he did things that truly amazed me. At other times, he did not play well."

At first, Lucadello, who during a storied career saw some 50 of the players he signed reach the big leagues, was the sole believer. Alone, he followed Schmidt through high school, college, and summer ball. Eventually, however, other scouts picked up the trail. That forced Lucadello to change his tactics.

"When scouts see another scout at a game," he told Kevin Kerrane, "they usually know who he's there to look at. If they see him again and again at one team's games, they know the scout really likes the player. And if the scout has a good track record, some of the other scouts are going to turn the player's name in as a top choice."

DID YOU KNOW . . . That high-wire artist Karl Wallenda twice walked across the top of Veterans Stadium? The Great Wallenda's tightrope walk was performed in 1972 and 1976 and was estimated to have been 900 feet across and 150 feet high.

So Lucadello turned to the fine art of espionage. He stayed away from other scouts. Instead of sitting behind home plate, as the others always did, he moved constantly around the perimeters of the field. "Sometimes, I watched from behind trees or around the corners of buildings," he said. "I even went to a few games in disguise."

Meanwhile, Schmidt was hitting hundreds of balls each day, attempting to develop his talent as a right-handed batter. He hit .310 as the regular shortstop in his sophomore season. After hitting .313 as a junior and leading Ohio to fourth place in the College World Series, Schmidt was named first-team All-American.

Ohio finally awarded him a full scholarship. In his senior year, Schmidt hit .330 with 10 home runs and 45 RBIs, again earning All-American honors. By then, Lucadello, still staying one step ahead of the other scouts, had brought Phillies farm director Paul Owens into the loop. Owens came to Ohio to watch Schmidt play.

"I was so impressed with him that I moved him up on our draft list," Owens recalled years later.

That spring, after Schmidt had graduated with a degree in business administration, the Phillies took a big chance. Although other teams, particularly the California Angels and Minnesota Twins, were interested in Mike, the Phils figured that they would steer clear of him in the first round of the 1971 draft because of his gimpy knees.

They were right. With Schmidt still available, the Phillies selected him in the second round, right after George Brett had been chosen by the Kansas City Royals. In the first round, the Phillies picked pitcher Roy Thomas, who it turned out never appeared in a single game with the Phils and won just 20 games in his entire major league career.

The Phillies anted up a $35,000 bonus—which Mike used to buy a new Corvette—brought him to Philadelphia, gave him a uniform and a locker, and figured they'd let him sit on the bench for a few days and get the feel of pro baseball before they sent him to the minors.

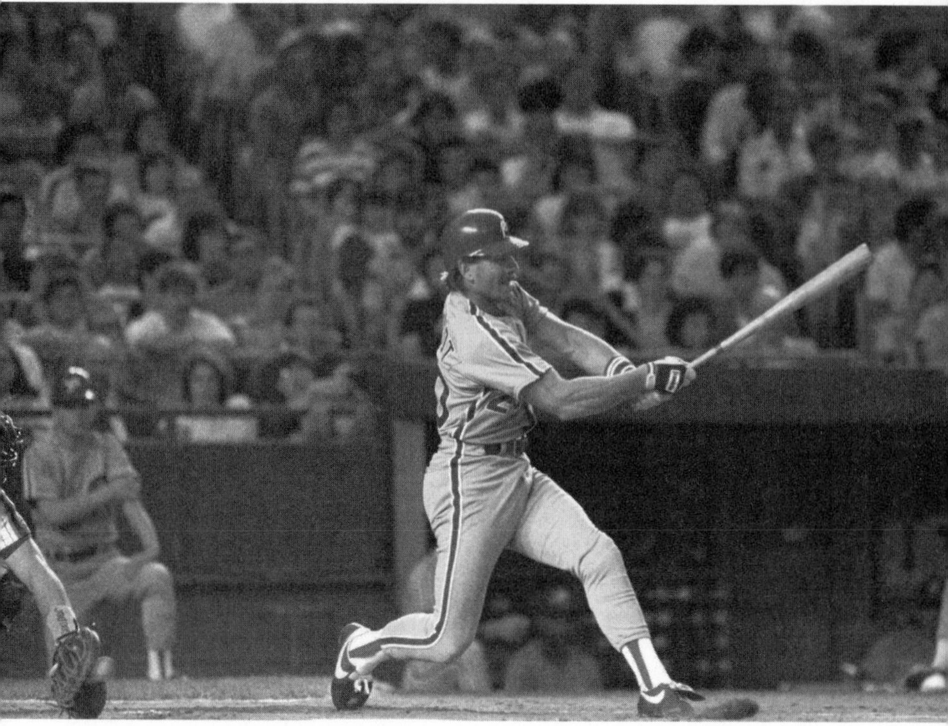

The greatest Phillie of all time, Mike Schmidt won three National League MVPs, led the league in home runs eight times, and hit 548 career home runs in 18 seasons with the Phillies. He also won 10 Gold Gloves at third.

The next night, the Phillies had an exhibition game with their Double A farm club at Reading. When regular shortstop Larry Bowa became too sick to play, Schmidt's name was placed in the lineup. In the eighth inning, facing Mike Fremuth, he hit his first professional home run, a game-winner over the left-field wall.

As planned, Schmidt stayed in Reading, where he learned some of the mental aspects of the game under hard-nosed manager Jim Bunning. Although he struggled at the plate, hitting just .211 with eight home runs in 74 games, Mike moved up to Triple A at Eugene, Oregon, the following year. By then his days as a shortstop were over. Schmidt played both second and third bases during the season while hitting .291 with 26 homers and 91 RBIs.

"I feel he can be a real fine player," said manager Andy Seminick. "He's aggressive and will hit with power. And I think third base is his best position."

Future Hall of Fame manager Tom Lasorda, then piloting the Los Angeles Dodgers' farm club at Albuquerque, was especially impressed with Schmidt's defensive prowess. "I couldn't believe my eyes the first time I saw him," he said. "I thought they had sent Brooks Robinson out there in a disguise. He made some of the doggonedest plays I ever saw."

When the Eugene season ended, Schmidt got a September call-up to the big team. He made his major league debut on September 12, 1971. A few days later, he hit his first big league homer, a three-run blast off Balor Moore that gave the Phils a 3–1 victory over the Montreal Expos.

And that is how Mike Schmidt began a pro career during which he became the finest all-around third baseman ever to play the game and eventually a first-ballot Hall of Famer.

Schmidt's success didn't come immediately, though. He was a bust in his first full season in 1973, hitting just .196. Although he managed 18 home runs, his strikeout rate was alarming. In 132 games, he whiffed 136 times in 367 at-bats.

Not helping the situation was Schmidt's relationship with Phils manager Danny Ozark. "He called me Dutch because he figured I was a big, dumb kid," Schmidt said.

But, said Owens, "Danny and I didn't give up on him because we could see that he had a great deal of potential. When you see the kind of power he displayed and the kind of wrists he had, and add in a guy who could field and run and throw as well as Mike could, you knew you had some kind of player. And each year he got a little better."

Did he ever. In his second season, Schmidt not only upped his batting average all the way to .282, he led all major leaguers in home runs with 36, thereby becoming the first Phillies player since Chuck Klein in 1933 to lead the National League in that category.

By the NUMBERS

10—The number of Phillies pitchers who have started in an All-Star Game. Robin Roberts leads the way with five. Curt Simmons had two, and Steve Carlton, Terry Mulholland, and Curt Schilling each had one.

TOP TEN

Players with the Most Years Spent with the Phillies

	Name	Years
1.	Mike Schmidt	18
2.	Granny Hamner	16
3.	Chuck Klein	15*t*
	Tony Taylor	15*t*
	Steve Carlton	15*t*
6.	Jack Clements	14*t*
	Darren Daulton	14*t*
	Robin Roberts	14*t*
	Chris Short	14*t*
10.	Ed Delahanty	13*t*
	Red Dooin	13*t*
	Cy Williams	13*t*
	Willie Jones	13*t*
	Curt Simmons	13*t*

In the ensuing years, Schmidt won six more home-run titles outright and tied for one other. Only Babe Ruth, with nine, won more home-run crowns.

Led by a career-high 48 four-baggers in 1980, Schmidt hit more than 30 homers in a season 13 times, three times going over 40. By the time his career was over, he had hit 548 home runs, which currently ranks 11th on the all-time list.

The man often referred to as Michael Jack hit the magic 500 number with a shot April 18, 1987, in the ninth inning against the Pittsburgh Pirates' Don Robinson. It gave the Phillies an 8–6 triumph.

"It was," he said at the time, "without question the most exciting moment of my career."

Schmidt is one of only 13 big leaguers to hit four home runs in one game. He hit countless other memorable homers, including the game-winning homer in the tenth inning of a memorable 23–22 Phillies victory over the Chicago Cubs in 1979. In 1980 his two-run homer on the next-to-last day of the season beat Montreal, 6–4, in the eleventh inning to give the Phils the East Division championship. And his round-tripper in the fifth game of the 1980 World Series led the Phils to a 4–3 victory over Kansas City.

During more than 17 years in the big leagues in these days of free agency, he was one of those almost nonexistent players to perform his entire career with one team. Schmidt hit more homers than any third baseman in baseball history, batted .267, drove in 1,595 runs, and scored 1,506. He tops the Phillies' all-time list in 12 batting categories.

Schmidt led the National League in slugging percentage five times and in RBIs four times. But he wasn't just a hitter. He won 10 Gold Gloves. In 1986 he made only six errors at third base all season. And he stole bases in double figures eight times, reaching a career high of 29 in 1975.

Schmidt was the National League's Most Valuable Player in 1980 when he hit .286 with career highs in home runs (48) and RBIs (121). He repeated the honor in 1981 and 1986. He was also MVP in the 1980 World Series. He earned berths on 12 All-Star teams, eight as a starter.

When he retired early in the 1989 season, Schmidt acknowledged what had been for him a most satisfying career. "Some 18 years ago," he said, "I left Dayton, Ohio, with two very bad knees and a dream to become a major league baseball player. I thank God that the dream came true."

Black Friday

It has often been said that the 1977 Phillies were one of the two greatest teams in the long life of the ballclub. And maybe they were.

After all, this was a team that tied a club record for most wins (101) in one season. At one point, it set a modern club record with 13 consecutive victories. It captured the club's second straight National League East Division title by five games after taking over the lead in early August.

The '77 Phils, under easygoing manager Danny Ozark, were staffed by some of the top players in the National League. Mike Schmidt played third base, Larry Bowa was at shortstop, Ted Sizemore at second, and Richie Hebner at first. Greg Luzinski was in left field, Garry Maddox in center, Bake McBride in right, and Bob Boone was behind the plate. On the mound, the Phils had starters such as Steve Carlton, Larry Christenson, and Jim Lonborg, and a bullpen featuring Tug McGraw, Ron Reed, and Gene Garber. The bench was manned by a strong crew led by Jay Johnstone, Tim McCarver, Tommy Hutton, Jerry Martin, and Dave Johnson.

General manager Paul Owens had gone to great lengths to put that team together. A promising contingent of players such as Schmidt, Bowa, Luzinski, Boone, and Christenson had come up through the Phillies' farm system. To that group, Owens had added through trades and free agency Maddox, McBride, Hebner, Sizemore, Lonborg, McGraw, and assorted others. When Owens acquired McBride in June 1977, he had seemingly landed the last key ingredient of what would now be a powerful team.

It was a team that was expected to send the Phillies to their first World Series since 1950, a team that was stamped for greatness. But one thing got in the way: Black Friday.

Black Friday ranks right near the top as one of the Phillies' greatest disasters. It's there with the Whiz Kids' total capitulation in the 1950

By the NUMBERS

15—The number of men who have been president of the Phillies since the team originated in 1883. The ones serving the longest terms include Al Reach (1883–1902), William Baker (1913–1930), Gerry Nugent (1932–1942), Bob Carpenter (1943–1972), Ruly Carpenter (1972–1981), Bill Giles (1981–1997), and David Montgomery (1997–present).

World Series, with the 1964 collapse, and with Joe Carter's home run in 1993. It marks a day in infamy that to this moment bears deep scars in the mostly somber world of Philliedom.

"It was," said Owens, "probably the worst day of my career."

Until Black Friday reared its ugly head, the Phillies had been on a highly prosperous roll. They had won the division title by nine games in 1976 before getting swept by the Cincinnati Reds in the National League Championship Series. That team had won 101 games.

Big things were expected of the 1977 team. And although the season had begun disappointingly—the Phils losing six of their first seven games and still roosting in fourth place by mid-June—the team, following McBride's arrival, had moved up to second by the end of the month.

The Phillies were still two games behind the front-running Chicago Cubs as August began. But on August 3, Carlton's six-hit, 8–1 win over the San Diego Padres launched the 13-game winning streak, the most consecutive wins for a Phillies team since 1892. The streak ended on August 17, but by then the Phillies had taken over first place. And as the end of the month approached, they had won 19 of 20 games.

Despite a five-game losing streak in September, the Phils romped home with the division crown. Next up was the NLCS against the Los Angeles Dodgers.

The Dodgers had cruised to an easy title in the West Division, finishing 10 games ahead of second-place Cincinnati. They, too, had a star-studded lineup that featured position players Steve Garvey, Davey Lopes, Ron Cey, Dusty Baker, and Reggie Smith and pitchers Tommy John, Don Sutton, Rick Rhoden, and Burt Hooton.

The series began with two games at Dodger Stadium. With Carlton on the mound in the opener, Luzinski's two-run homer in the first got the Phils started. The Phillies then built a 5–1 lead only to give it up as Cey cracked a grand-slam homer. A run-scoring single by Schmidt—his only

RBI of the series—regained the lead in the ninth, and the Phils wound up with a 7–5 victory.

"All we need in Los Angeles is a split," claimed Luzinski. "We're practically unbeatable at home. I can't see any way we'll lose two out of three at the Vet."

Bowa and others expressed the same sentiment, the shortstop analyzing that "with the crowd on our side the Dodgers don't have a chance."

The Dodgers obliged the forecasters by prolonging their expected agony with a 7–1 triumph in Game 2. Baker's fourth-inning grand slam off Lonborg, and the arm of Sutton, who surrendered just a third-inning home run to McBride, keyed the victory.

Larry Bowa, here celebrating the Phillies' division title in 1977 before the infamous Black Friday in the NLCS, was a gifted but tempestuous shortstop who gave the Phillies excellent strength up the middle of the diamond.

The series then moved on to Philadelphia with Christenson facing Hooton in what became one of the most bizarre games ever played at Veterans Stadium. It was Friday, October 7.

The Dodgers took a 2–0 lead in the second, only to give it up as the Phillies scored three runs in the bottom half of the inning. As Bowa had predicted, the fans played a major role in the rally.

With the bases loaded, Hooton complained vehemently after he thought he'd struck out Christenson. The crowd loudly booed the pitcher, who then walked Christenson. The booing got louder and Hooton more rattled as he walked McBride. Then, with most of the crowd of 63,719 standing and booing practically loud enough to be heard all the way to Manyunk, Hooton walked Bowa to force in the third run. By this time Hooton was totally unnerved and had to be taken out.

The Phillies still led, 5–3, as the ninth inning began. They seemingly had the game wrapped up as Garber retired the first two Dodgers batters. But 41-year-old pinch-hitter Vic Davalillo, who'd been in the Mexican League earlier in the season, bunted for a hit. That brought 39-year-old Manny Mota to the plate.

Mota quickly fell behind in the count, 0–2. But as he did, he turned to Lopes in the on-deck circle and smiled. "I knew then that he was going to hit one for us," Lopes said afterward. He was right. Mota drilled an arcing shot to deep left.

Normally in the late innings, Ozark inserted Martin, a defensive whiz, in left. But in such a pivotal game, he had decided to stay with Luzinski, later offering the excuse that he wanted Greg's bat in the lineup should L.A. tie the score.

But Luzinski, a poor fielder at best, was no match for this ball. As he retreated to the wall, the ball clunked off his outstretched glove. Davalillo scored easily, and when Sizemore bobbled an off-line relay, Mota took third. Lopes then smashed a vicious shot that bounced off Schmidt's glove and caromed to Bowa, who alertly picked up the ball and fired to first. As

TRIVIA

Can you name the Phillies players who have been the winning pitchers in All-Star Games?

Answers to the trivia questions are on page 190.

DID YOU KNOW . . . That the Phillies top farm club from 1948 to 1950 was a team called the Toronto Maple Leafs? Their top minor league team from 1951 to 1953 was one known as the Baltimore Orioles. How ironic is it that these two International League teams should grow up to become major league clubs that beat the Phillies in their last two World Series appearances?

Mota crossed the plate, umpire Bruce Froemming blew the call, ruling Lopes safe.

"I couldn't believe it," screeched Hebner later. "He didn't beat the throw to first." Bowa agreed. "He [Froemming] didn't think I could throw it over there, so he called him safe."

It didn't matter. Froemming's terrible call, confirmed by TV replays, stood. Totally rattled, Garber then threw a wild pickoff attempt to first that allowed Lopes to go to second. Bill Russell followed with a single through Garber's legs that scored Lopes. That gave the Dodgers the winning run and a 6–5 victory.

Black Friday had arrived. In one hellishly painful inning, the Phils had lost a game they should have won. "That game stands out to me more than any game I ever played," Bowa told Sam Carchidi of the *Philadelphia Inquirer* many years later. And it was all because of a bad decision by the manager.

"I messed up," Ozark bravely admitted some 16 years later. "I should have taken Greg out."

For the broken-hearted Phillies, the series was for all practical purposes over. The next night it poured rain throughout the game while commissioner Bowie Kuhn and National League president Chub Feeney sat obliviously in their box seats, refusing to call a halt to play. Allowing just seven hits, John went the distance to pitch the Dodgers to both a 4–1 win over the Phils and Carlton and the National League pennant.

For a season that had started with such high hopes, the finish was nothing less than an excruciating disappointment and disaster—thanks to the infamous day known as Black Friday.

An Unforgettable Series

What would be the chances of beating Nolan Ryan when he had a 5–2 lead in the eighth inning? None. Zilch. Forget it. Get the hot water ready in the showers.

That was about the gist of things when the Phillies came to bat in the top of the eighth in the final game of the 1980 League Championship Series against the Houston Astros at the Astrodome. With the Series tied at 2–2, the game was for all the marbles. And it looked like the Phillies were about to cash in their aggies.

Once again, the Phillies appeared ready to follow in the footsteps of their 1976, 1977, and 1978 counterparts and surrender yet another chance to go to their first World Series since 1950. It would be another missed opportunity. Another bitter disappointment. One more blot in the infinite view that the Phils can't win the big one.

Sure, this team was probably better than the others. Hadn't it won more playoff games than the team's previous three division winners? But now it was about to capitulate. There was no joy in Philsville.

The Phils had put up a gallant fight to reach that fifth game. Steve Carlton, with help from Tug McGraw and a two-run homer by Greg Luzinski, had given the team a 3–1 victory in the opener in Philadelphia. Houston, making its first postseason appearance, had won Game 2 with a four-run outburst in the tenth inning to beat the Phils 7–4. Joe Morgan tripled and scored in the eleventh inning to give the Astros a 1–0 victory in the third game. The Phillies had overcome a 2–0 Houston lead to win the fourth game in the tenth when Pete Rose, riding Luzinski's double, scored the winning run while slamming Astros catcher Bruce Bochy with a forearm across the head in what became a 5–3 Phils win.

TRIVIA

How many Most Valuable Player awards have been won during the regular season by Phillies players, and who were the recipients?

Answers to the trivia questions are on page 190.

"There has never been a game to compare with that one," McGraw said. "It was like a motorcycle ride through an art museum. You see the pictures, but afterward, you don't remember what you saw."

Actually, up to that point, the whole series had been like that. But it became more so in the fifth game.

Rookie pitcher Marty Bystrom, owner of a perfect 5–0 record after being called up late in the season, was the Phillies' starter against Ryan, a future Hall of Famer. On paper, it didn't look like much of a match. But Bob Boone's two-run single gave the Phils a 2–1 lead in the second inning. Luzinski couldn't handle Dennis Walling's drive in the sixth, and the batter scored a moment later on Alan Ashby's single to tie the score at 2–2.

Houston then roared ahead with three runs in the seventh against Phils reliever Larry Christenson. Walling singled home one run, another scored on a wild pitch, and the third crossed ahead of Art Howe's triple.

Down 5–2 with the redoubtable Ryan still on the mound, it looked like curtains for the Phillies as the eighth inning began. But the curtains were made of papier-mâché.

Larry Bowa led off with a hit. Boone followed with a ground single off the glove of Ryan. Then Greg Gross laid down a perfect bunt to load the bases.

"I just wanted to get on base," Bowa said later. "If I started it, I knew that the others guys would follow."

Bowa could have made a living as a forecaster. Rose worked the count to 3–2, then walked to force home Bowa. That sent Ryan to the showers. Ace reliever Joe Sambito replaced him and got pinch-hitter Keith Moreland to ground into a fielder's choice, but another run came home. The score was now 5–4.

Ken Forsch took the mound for the Astros to pitch to Mike Schmidt. The strategy worked as Schmidt struck out. Two outs now with pinch-hitter Del Unser, who along with Gross had made immeasurable contributions off the bench all season long, at the plate. Unser singled to right to send the tying run home. Manny Trillo followed with a two-run triple to climax a five-run outburst and send the Phils out to a 7–5 lead.

As Trillo reached third, Phillies third-base coach Lee Elia swung into action. "I grabbed Manny," he explained, "and said, 'I love you, I love you.' I didn't want to kiss him, so I bit him on the arm. Gave him a pretty good bite, too. Manny looked kind of startled."

Proving that nothing ever comes easily for them, the Phillies lost the lead in the bottom of the eighth when McGraw gave up four singles. With

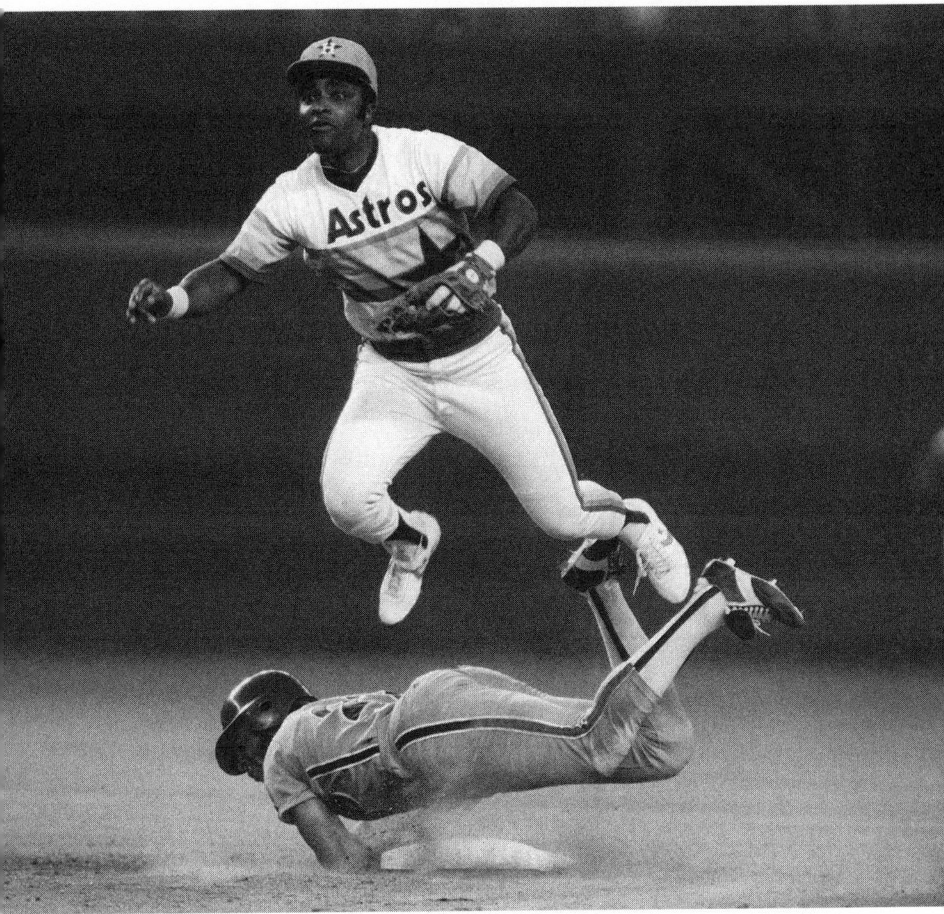

The unforgettable 1980 NLCS against the Astros included numerous hustling plays like this one by Phillies outfielder Lonnie Smith, who slides in hard against Joe Morgan to break up a double play in Game 5, won by the Phillies 8–7 in 10 innings.

ALL-STADIUM TEAM

Veterans Stadium

Position	Player
Left Field	Greg Luzinski
Center Field	Garry Maddox
Right Field	Bobby Abreu
First Base	Pete Rose
Second Base	Manny Trillo
Shortstop	Larry Bowa
Third Base	Mike Schmidt
Catcher	Bob Boone
Right-handed Pitcher	Curt Schilling
Left-handed Pitcher	Steve Carlton
Relief Pitcher	Tug McGraw

two outs, hits by Rafael Landestoy and Jose Cruz each drove in one run to forge a 7–7 deadlock.

After going scoreless in the ninth, the Phillies sent starter Dick Ruthven to the mound. He blanked Houston, and once again, a game went into extra innings.

With one out in the top of the tenth, ultra-reliable Unser doubled. Two batters later, he raced home on a double by Garry Maddox. The Phillies led 8–7. When Ruthven retired the Astros in order in the bottom half, getting Enos Cabell for the final out on a soft fly ball to Maddox, the Phillies owned the National League pennant.

It had been 30 long years since their last flag. And it was only the third pennant the team had ever won. But this one was especially sweet.

"How's that for team character?" roared manager Dallas Green, who had leveled the Phillies with a scathing clubhouse tirade just six weeks earlier. "Tonight, there was so much character on the field, I couldn't believe it. I love it."

No one was happier than Maddox, the brilliant center fielder whose dropped fly had handed the Los Angeles Dodgers the LCS in 1978. "I'm overwhelmed by my own feelings and the feelings I have for all the people who were rooting for us to win this thing," he said.

"If you shine," added Unser, "it's because somebody puts a light on you. We shined in this series because the Astros put a light on us. They pushed us harder than anyone has ever pushed us."

"I'll always remember this series as one in which there were no losers," said Astros manager Bill Virdon.

Many have called it "the greatest postseason playoff" since the games were initiated in 1969. "It was probably the finest ever played," said commissioner Bowie Kuhn. "I don't see how anything can top it."

All but one game was decided by two runs or less. Four of the five games went into extra innings. It was truly a series for the ages.

By the NUMBERS

117—Outfielder Greg Gross blasted that many pinch-hits during his career with the Phillies. The total is a club record, exceeding by 65 the runner-up (Tony Taylor) in that category.

After 97 Years, a World Series Winner

The best team the Phillies ever had almost didn't win the division title. It almost didn't win the pennant, either. And it certainly wasn't favored to win the World Series.

This was a team, after all, that had six rookies on its final roster. Its manager had been the director of the team's farm system until the previous August. Only one regular (Bake McBride) hit above .300 for the season. Only one batter (Mike Schmidt) hit more than 20 home runs. Ten different pitchers started games during the season, including a career reliever. Only three hurlers (Steve Carlton, Dick Ruthven, and Bob Walk) won in double figures. The top reliever (Tug McGraw) lugged a sore arm around much of the season.

The 1980 Phillies were also a team with an odd mix of personalities. There was super-cool Schmidt; Carlton, the Silent Sphinx, who never talked to the media; the exuberant Pete Rose with the Prince Valiant haircut; the gregarious clubhouse humorist McGraw; the volatile Larry Bowa; quiet and gentlemanly Garry Maddox; grumpy McBride; Walk, nicknamed Whirlybird; a guy who once forgot to take his glove to the mound, the cantankerous former pro basketball player Ron Reed; studious Bob Boone; pensive Manny Trillo; and a sometimes moody and somber Greg Luzinski.

Nevertheless, despite the disparity, the team won the East Division, the National League pennant, and the World Series, the first win in the fall classic in the club's 97 years of existence. No Philadelphia sports team ever had a finer, more exciting season—or was ever more unconventional.

"Hemingway would struggle over this one," wrote the astute columnist Frank Dolson in the *Philadelphia Inquirer*. "Shakespeare would grope for words to describe it and give up in despair. Grantland Rice would be in over his head. I don't have a chance."

DID YOU KNOW . . . That in the entire 33-year history of Veterans Stadium only 93 home runs were hit into the upper deck? Willie Stargell hit the first one in 1971, and Jim Thome clubbed the last one in 2003.

At the beginning of the season, most people didn't think the Phillies had a chance, either. Dallas Green had relinquished his minor league duties to replace Danny Ozark as manager on August 31 the previous year. But neither that nor the addition of Rose as a free agent had kept the Phillies from finishing a meek fourth.

After a lackluster spring training, the 1980 Phillies got off to a mediocre start. Then they climbed atop the East Division standings for two days in May. Soon afterward, number-three starter Larry Christenson was lost for the season following elbow surgery, and the team began to drift downward. It briefly captured a half-game lead in mid-July, but by then McGraw was on the sidelines with tendinitis. The Phils quickly fell out of the lead.

It was not a pretty sight. There was bickering and unrest in the clubhouse. Players criticized each other and the manager. The manager claimed the clubhouse had a country club atmosphere. And in the second week of August, the Phils were swept in four games by the Pittsburgh Pirates, dropping all the way to third place, six games out of first.

The four losses proved to be one of the turning points in the season. Between games of the Sunday doubleheader in that series, Green took action. Using virtually every obscenity known to mankind, he tore into the team with a withering outburst, even citing certain players by name. Green's normally loud voice, which was often heard blasting players, was even louder than usual. His tirade could be heard through the steel doors between the clubhouse and the corridor at Three Rivers Stadium.

"I lit into them pretty good," remembered Green in an interview with Sam Carchidi of the *Philadelphia Inquirer*. "They were talking the talk but not walking the walk. I accused them all of being too cool. That was part of the agenda. Everyone wanted to be Mr. Cool like Mike Schmidt."

During the second game, Green and reliever Reed nearly staged a fistfight in the dugout. Then, shortly after the Phils left Pittsburgh, the manager sent starters Luzinski, Maddox, and Boone to the bench. Although they sat only briefly, all three expressed their extreme displeasure. In fact, it appeared that there wasn't a happy face in the clubhouse.

TRIVIA

Who from the Phillies had a connection with each of the club's pennant winners in 1950, 1980, 1983, and 1995?

Answers to the trivia questions are on page 190.

Tirades had become common with this club. But on September 1, the most effective outburst all season took place in the Phillies' clubhouse.

This time it was general manager Paul Owens' turn. Before a game in San Francisco, Owens, in an uncharacteristic and unexpected explosion, lashed into his players over what he felt were their selfish and lackadaisical performances. "You guys played the first five months for yourselves," he roared. "You've gone your own different ways. Dallas has been trying to get this across to you, and now I'm telling you, and I know I'm also speaking for [team president] Ruly Carpenter. The man's right, and you better stop your goddamn pouting. The last month is Ruly's and mine."

During the outburst, Owens, then in his late fifties, offered to fight any player who disagreed with him. He had no takers. "I was as mad as I've ever been," Owens confided later. "I was screaming, and my hands were trembling. I told them they had all the ability they needed. But I felt they were slipping, although I put it a little more strongly than that."

Owens' tirade worked. With Green continuing to emphasize his "we not I" message, the Phillies quickly vaulted back into first place. They tumbled off the perch briefly, but wound up posting a 23–11 record in September and winning 19 of their last 25 games.

During the stretch drive, there was still room for one more tirade. Trailing the Expos at the time by one-half game, the Phillies were locked in a 3–3 tie with the Chicago Cubs at Veterans Stadium when the visitors scored twice in the top of the fifteenth inning. The fans booed about as loudly as Philly fans can boo. But the Phils came back to win with three runs in the bottom of the inning.

Afterward, Bowa, the feisty often-snarling shortstop, was livid. Bowa, who already had engaged in several screaming matches with Green, lit into the boo birds. "Those f*cking front-runners," he screeched, "are the worst fans in baseball."

On the final weekend of the season, the Phillies went into Montreal for a three-game series in a virtual tie for first with the Expos. Schmidt shook off the flu to hit a home run and sacrifice fly, and Ruthven pitched masterfully as the Phils took a 2–1 decision on Friday night.

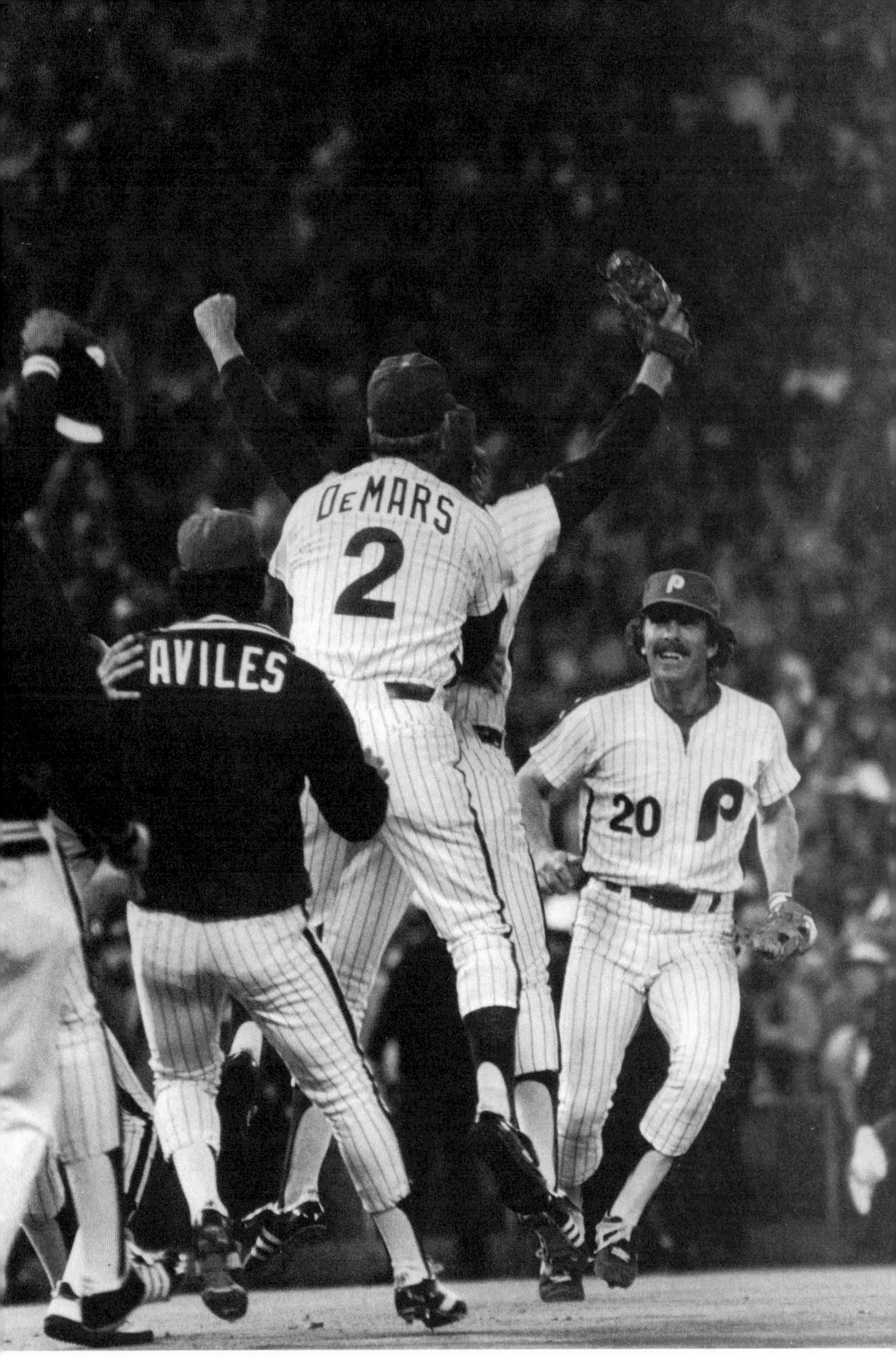

Mike Schmidt (20), Tug McGraw (arms raised), and Coach Billy DeMars celebrate the Phillies' first championship, won in six games over the Kansas City Royals.

Greatest Moments in Phillies History

1. The only World Series victory in team history is clinched in the sixth game against Kansas City at Veterans Stadium, 1980.
2. Whiz Kids beat the Brooklyn Dodgers to win the National League pennant on the last day of the season, 1950.
3. Phillies capture their first National League pennant in 30 years with victory over Houston in the LCS, 1980.
4. One of the most popular teams in Phillies history beats the Atlanta Braves for the National League pennant, 1993.
5. Win over the Los Angeles Dodgers in the LCS gives the Phillies their second NL pennant in four years, 1983.
6. Phillies win their first National League pennant with a victory over the Boston Braves, 1915.
7. Playing in their first major league game, the Phillies launch a franchise that will become one of the oldest in baseball, 1883.
8. Jim Bunning pitches the only perfect game in Phillies history, beating the New York Mets at Shea Stadium, 1964.
9. The greatest trade in Phillies history is made when the club acquires Steve Carlton in a deal for Rick Wise, 1972.
10. Richie Ashburn and Mike Schmidt are inducted into the Hall of Fame as a record crowd of 28,000 attends the ceremony, 1995.

The following afternoon, there was a three-hour rain delay before play began. Then the game went into extra innings. Finally in the eleventh, Schmidt cracked a two-run homer to give the Phillies a 6–4 victory. The division crown, their fourth in five years, belonged to the Phillies.

The tirades and the tantrums had played a key role. But so had some strong individual performances. Schmidt won the home-run (48) and RBI

(121) titles, McBride hit .309 with 87 RBIs, Rose hustled and sparked the club while hitting .282, Trillo fielded brilliantly at second and batted .292, rookie Lonnie Smith hit .339 in a part-time role, and Greg Gross and Del Unser repeatedly came up with major pinch-hits. Carlton won 24, Ruthven 17, and McGraw pitched terrific relief down the stretch. Rookies Bob Walk and Marty Bystrom won 11 and five games, respectively, after a late-season call-up.

In the playoffs, the Phillies beat the Houston Astros for only their third National League pennant, 3–2, in what has often been described as the greatest playoff series ever held. The Phils had to overcome a 5–2 Houston lead with Nolan Ryan on the mound for the Astros to win the fifth game, 8–7, on Maddox's tenth-inning RBI double.

By then, Philadelphia was going crazy. And the frenzy increased as the World Series began against the Kansas City Royals.

The Royals had won their division title by 14 games, then beaten the New York Yankees—winners of 103 games during the season—in the American League playoffs. Despite a general lack of "name" players, the Royals were a strong team that was heavily favored to win the World Series.

A surprise starter, Walk and the Phillies won the opener, 7–6, with McBride getting three hits and driving in three runs. The Phils won the second contest behind Carlton, 6–4, in a game that attracted nationwide attention because Royals star George Brett had to leave the game because of a painful case of hemorrhoids.

With Brett returning to the lineup, KC won the third game, 4–3. But Brett, who had hit .390 during the season after flirting with .400 much of the way, was not finished being a newsmaker.

In the fourth inning of Game 4 with the Phillies trailing 5–1, hard-throwing reliever Dickie Noles delivered a wicked fastball at Brett's head. The pitch sent the Royals' third baseman sprawling in the dirt. KC manager Jim Frey stormed out of the dugout to protest, and as he did, got into a heated exchange with Rose. Eventually, the fireworks ended, and the Royals went on to a 5–3 victory. But the pitch had further repercussions.

Noles, most observers thought, was throwing at Brett. The pitcher, then a noted brawler and drinker before reforming a few years later, denied the claim. "I have to use both sides of the plate," he said. "I wasn't throwing at him."

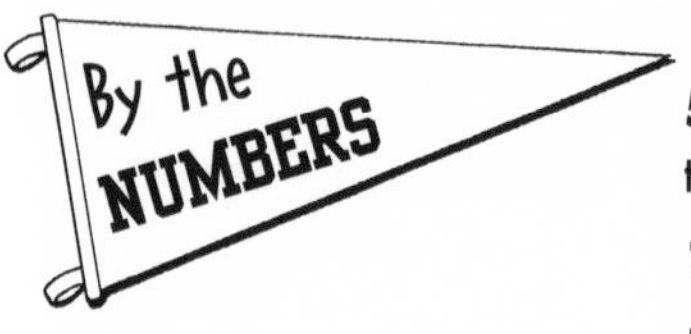

5—The Phillies have retired five numbers worn by their former players. They are the following:

1—Richie Ashburn

14—Jim Bunning

20—Mike Schmidt

32—Steve Carlton

36—Robin Roberts

Years later, Noles—as well as Brett—would say the same thing. And more than one decade after the incident, the two were scheduled to sign autographs together at a Phillies function. "We didn't know each other and hadn't even seen each other since the Series," Noles said. "I was a little nervous. I didn't quite know what to expect."

When Brett showed up with a baseball taped to each side of his face, Noles' uncertainty disappeared.

Nonetheless, the pitch was regarded as the pivotal play in the Series. It was generally conceded that it softened the Royals' resolve and took the momentum away from them. And Brett had temporarily lost his batting touch, or so it seemed.

The Phillies won Game 5, 4–3, as Trillo drove in the winning run with an infield single. The Phillies then earned the clincher with a 4–1 victory behind the pitching of Carlton and McGraw, who escaped bases-loaded jams in both the eighth and ninth innings. Rose caught a foul pop that Boone had bobbled in front of the Phillies' dugout just before McGraw struck out Willie Wilson for the final out.

The victory, coming at 11:29 PM and with policemen, horses, and dogs lining the field, set off the largest celebration in Philadelphia sports history. Fans partied far into the next morning. The following day, some 2 million fans lined Broad Street in downtown Philadelphia to watch the Phils' victory parade.

At John F. Kennedy Stadium, where the parade ended, 100,000 fans packed into the old venue to hear the Phillies one last time. "Take this championship and savor it," Schmidt told the fans. McGraw told New York City to "stick it."

Bowa also spoke. "This is the greatest moment of my life," he said, "and I'm glad to share it with the greatest fans in baseball."

Baseball's Slowest Fastball

If there ever was an athlete who pierced the hardened exterior of Philadelphia's callous sports fans, it was Tug McGraw. With his playful antics and good humor—not to mention his effective pitching—McGraw gained a large and loyal following among the blue bloods, the blue collars, and many of those in between in the city's often cynical, always critical population of sports followers.

Frank Edwin McGraw was as close to a folk hero as Philadelphia ever had. He came to the Phillies in a trade with the New York Mets after the 1974 season, and he stayed in uniform until 1984, winning 49 games for the Phillies and saving another 94. After that, he became a popular television sports reporter, a public relations consultant, and after various other jobs, a leader in the fight against brain cancer, a treacherous illness that took his own life prematurely at the age of 59.

The fun-loving Tug's comments and actions were legendary. Once, when doing a TV interview with the coauthor of a book that weighed more than five pounds, he paraded down the left-field line at Veterans Stadium with the book perched atop his head. It was McGraw's comical way of demonstrating the girth of the book. Another time, the left-handed relief pitcher appeared at a Phillies spring-training game on St. Patrick's Day, wearing a uniform that had been dyed green.

McGraw, who coined the phrase, "You gotta believe," while a key member of the Mets' 1973 NL pennant–winning team, was asked after their momentous victory in the 1969 World Series how he was going to spend his Series share. "Ninety percent I'll spend on good times, women, and Irish whiskey," he said. "The other 10 percent I'll probably waste."

Tug, who supposedly got his nickname from his mother because of the aggressive way he breast-fed, had names for all his pitches. His fastball was the "John Jameson," so named "because I like my Irish Whiskey hard and straight." He called his change-up the "Peggy Lee"—because a hitter would swing and say, "Is that all there is?" His sinker was known as the "Titanic." He threw a "Cutty Sark," which, like the sailboat pictured on the label, sailed. His repertoire also included the "Bo Derek," because "it had a nice little tail on it." And when Tug offered up a home-run pitch, he called it his "Sinatra ball," symbolic of the song, "Fly Me to the Moon."

Always quick with a quip, McGraw was once asked how he compared playing on artificial turf to playing on grass. "I don't know," he said, "I never smoked AstroTurf."

A true lefty, Tug could be self-deprecating. "I have no trouble with the 12 inches between my elbow and my palm," he advised. "It's the seven inches between my ears that are bent."

One day, McGraw was sitting in front of his locker before a game when Phils starter Larry Christenson entered the clubhouse. "Are you pitching today?" Tug asked. "Yes, I am," came the response. "Then, so am I," Tug replied.

Tug's pitching philosophy was simple. "Ten million years from now, when the sun burns out and the Earth is just a frozen snowball hurtling through space," he said, "nobody's going to care whether or not I got this guy out."

One guy he did get out that Phillies fans will remember as long as they live was Kansas City Royals left fielder Willie Wilson. The deed is considered the greatest moment in Philadelphia sports history and was the climax of the most successful season the Phillies ever had.

The Phillies had won their first National League pennant in 30 years, and had won three of the first five games of the World Series against the Royals. The Series had returned to Veterans Stadium for Game 6 with ace

DID YOU KNOW . . .

That when the Phillies won the 1980 World Series at Veterans Stadium it was the first time in franchise history that a championship had been won at home? In 1915 (at Boston), 1950 (at Brooklyn), 1976 (at Montreal), 1977 (at Chicago), 1978 (at Pittsburgh), and 1980 (at Montreal and LCS at Houston), all pennants or division titles had been captured on the road.

Demonstrative on the mound, Tug McGraw saved 180 games in his career and pitched 10 seasons for the Phillies. He saved Game 5 of the 1980 World Series by striking out the Royals' Jose Cardenal with the bases loaded in the ninth and came back in Game 6 to escape two bases-loaded situations to earn a save in the Series' decisive game.

Steve Carlton on the mound, hoping to clinch the championship for the Phillies.

The Phils had a 4–0 lead in the seventh, but Carlton was wearing down. The call went to the bullpen to get McGraw ready.

Tug had already pitched in three of the five games, winning one, losing one, and saving another, and was dead tired. Calling himself the Tylenol Kid, he said he was taking eight aspirins a day to soothe the pain in his aching arm.

By the time he dragged his weary body to the warm-up rubber in the bullpen, the playing field had been surrounded by Philadelphia policemen. Some were on horses, some had dogs. It was not a pretty sight, but one that the Phillies and the city thought necessary to keep fans from holding a tumultuous, riot-prone celebration on the field should the Phillies win the Series. There were even police dogs in the bullpen.

"When I reached down to pick up my glove to start warming up," McGraw said, "a German Shepherd was resting with his head on my

TOP TEN

Phillies Career Home-Run Leaders

	Name	Home Runs
1.	Mike Schmidt	548
2.	Del Ennis	259
3.	Chuck Klein	243
4.	Greg Luzinski	223
5.	Cy Williams	217
6.	Dick Allen	204
7.	Bobby Abreu	187
8.	Johnny Callison	185
9.	Willie Jones	180
10.	Scott Rolen	150

glove. I went to reach for it, but that was not the smartest thing in the world to do. So I told the cop, 'Hey, I gotta get my glove.' The cop reached down to get my glove, and there was slobber all over it. I don't know what they gave those dogs before the game, but it was stronger than what they gave the players. This dog was drooling all over the place."

The member of Philly's finest quickly reached for a towel to dry the glove. But McGraw intervened. "Don't touch the glove," he pleaded. "That stuff might come in handy later." Added Tug as he told the story, "I was just joking. I never threw a spitter."

Eventually Tug was summoned to the mound in the top of the eighth with two on and nobody out. KC got one run, but McGraw got out of the inning, leaving the bases loaded and the Phils holding a 4–1 lead.

An inning later, Tug was still on the mound as the ring of cops and animals tightened and the pressure intensified. "Over behind the first-base bag is a horse," McGraw said. "After I got the first out, the horse lifts up his tail and takes a big dump. I'm thinking, 'If I don't get out of this inning, that's what I'm going to be.' I'm thinking of the '64 Phillies, the negative fans, and all that other stuff. I have to pull this off. If I don't, I'm going to be Gene Mauch's neighbor next year."

It started to look like that might become a reality as McGraw gave up a walk and two singles to load the bases. That brought Frank White to the plate. He lifted a high foul pop in front of the Phillies' dugout. In one of the most famous scenes in Phillies history, catcher Bob Boone reached out to make the catch, but the ball bounced off his glove. Always ready, first baseman Pete Rose reached under Boone's outstretched glove and caught the ball.

After the out, McGraw glanced toward the dugout. Standing behind manager Dallas Green was a police dog. "He's looking out at the mound and barking like hell," McGraw said. "I see he's with the same cop who tried to dry off my glove in the bullpen, so I figure it's the same dog who drooled on my glove. And I'm thinking to myself, 'That's the canine corps. I need a K. This is a signal from the baseball gods. All I have to do is deliver.'"

Wilson was the next batter for the Royals. At one time, the Phillies had given him a tryout and weighed the possibility of drafting him, but had gone for Lonnie Smith instead. Now he was in a position to reduce or even eliminate the Phillies' lead.

The tension was unbearable. In the stands, long-suffering Phillies fans could hardly breathe. The Phillies had not won a World Series in the 97 years of the club's existence, but now, after all the years of frustration, the championship was oh so close.

McGraw went to a 1–2 count. Then, summoning all that was left in his throbbing arm, he blew a third strike past Wilson to end the game. It was 11:29 PM.

Pandemonium erupted on the field and in the stands. And throughout the Philadelphia area, ecstatic fans poured into the streets to begin a night-long celebration.

In the clubhouse after the game, Tug disclosed that his arm was "killing" him and that he was totally "out of gas." When asked what pitch he had thrown to fan Wilson, McGraw said it was "the slowest fastball ever thrown in the history of baseball."

How did he figure that? "It took 97 years to get there," he said.

By the NUMBERS

22–35—In 12 postseason outings, including special playoffs, NLCS, and World Series, this is the Phillies' overall record.

Let's Play Two

In an era of corporate ownership and bottom lines, baseball doubleheaders have become virtually extinct. They've gone the way of complete games, batters who know how to bunt, and ballparks with no sideshows. They're among the dinosaurs of today's game.

Once in a while, though, one of those rare two-game days that Ernie Banks cherished surfaces. One occurred during the 1993 season, when the Phillies, on their way to the National League pennant, played a doubleheader against the San Diego Padres at Veterans Stadium that gave new meaning to the old phrase, "twin bill."

Unquestionably, it was the strangest doubleheader in which the Phillies ever played. Totally weird. It lasted from one day to the next. And it had a finish that no one could ever have imagined.

Those who were there won't ever forget it. And most of those who weren't there will never forget it, either.

The odd affair that began on July 2 lasted for 12 hours and five minutes. It didn't end until 4:30 AM on July 3 when relief pitcher Mitch Williams, in his only at-bat of the season, drove in the winning run with a single. During the night, there were three rain delays equaling five hours and 54 minutes.

"Have you ever had two hours between each at-bat and faced three different pitchers?" center fielder Lenny Dykstra asked after it was over. That was a nearly perfect summation of the marathon.

The Phillies had just returned from a road trip in which they had lost their final two games. Although in first place, their lead had been sliced to five and one-half games, and there was a fair degree of uneasiness in the clubhouse.

By the NUMBERS

67,064—That's how many people packed Veterans Stadium on October 16, 1983, to see the fifth game of the World Series. It was the largest crowd ever to see a baseball game in Philadelphia.

Sensing a problem with declining morale and half-hearted efforts, Darren Daulton, the Phils' stalwart catcher and unequivocal leader of the team, called a players-only meeting in the clubhouse before the first game. It lasted for 31 minutes. Although no one would reveal afterward what exactly had been said, it was known that Daulton gave the team a rather strongly worded pep talk in which he urged his teammates to upgrade their level of intensity and their work ethic.

But by the time the players were ready to take the field and apply that message, it had started to rain. The scheduled 4:35 PM start had to be pushed back, and the ground crew scurried to cover the playing surface.

An announced crowd of 54,617 packed the stands. Originally, the fans were in a festive mood. But that mood was quickly damped as the rain, heavy at times, continued.

Eventually, the game was started. With the help of Fred McGriff's two-run homer, the Padres quickly built a 5–1 lead. Before the game could be completed, however, it rained again. Then it rained some more. And it rained and rained. Twice more, play was stopped, and the field had to be covered. The 16 groundskeepers even pulled out the tarp a fourth time, but it turned out to be a false alarm, as the rain stopped before the field was covered.

As the night wore on, one might have justifiably asked why such a game was not canceled. But no answer was forthcoming. And the game sloshed toward completion.

At midnight, ushers in the stands were told they could go home. Twenty supervisors were kept on the job. And by then, groundskeeper Mark "Froggy" Carfagno was sporting his fifth shirt of the night, the first four having become too wet to wear.

The game finally ended with a 5–2 victory for San Diego. It was just past 1:00 AM. The contest had used only two hours and 34 minutes of actual playing time. But the three rain delays had pushed the game into

TOP TEN

Cities with Longest Minor-League Affiliations with Phillies

	City	Years	Length
1.	Reading, Pa.	1967–present	39 years
2.	Spartanburg, S.C.	1963–1994	32 years
3.	Clearwater, Fla.	1986–present	20 years
4.	Batavia, N.Y.	1967, 1988–present	19 years
5.	Scranton/ Wilkes-Barre, Pa.	1989–present	17 years
6.	Schenectady, N.Y.	1946–1950, 1951–1957	12 years *t*
	Peninsula, Va.	1970–1971, 1976–1985	12 years *t*
8.	Bakersfield, Calif.	1956, 1958–1967	11 years
9.	Eugene, Ore.	1964–1968, 1969–1973	10 years
10.	Bend, Ore.	1979–1987	9 years *t*
	Terre Haute, Ind.	1946–1954	9 years *t*
	Utica, N.Y.	1944–1950, 1986–1987	9 years *t*
	Wilmington, Del.	1944–1952	9 years *t*

the bewitching hours of the night. "At my age, this is past my bedtime," advised Phils manager Jim Fregosi.

The fans agreed. Most of them had long since departed, leaving a hard-core group of about 6,000 remaining in the stands. Among the departees was Mitch Williams' family. "My father went to sleep in my truck in the parking lot," he disclosed. "My mother went home to bed."

Incredibly, it was decreed that the second game would be played. "I couldn't believe it," said outfielder Pete Incaviglia when told of the decision. "I had no clue that they'd play it."

Umpire Dana DeMuth, the crew chief, explained later the unlikely rationale. "There are no curfews," he said. "It was scheduled as a doubleheader, and our job was to get it in. There are no rules, no guidelines for canceling a game just because it's late or because there's been bad weather. So we treated this just like any other game."

Except it wasn't like any other game. The first pitch was delivered at 1:26 AM. In the dugouts, coffee urns had replaced the water buckets. And San Diego had moved out to a 5–0 lead by the top of the fourth.

As the game progressed, the size of the tiny crowd still in the stands began to increase. People just getting out of work and those with peculiar sleeping habits had heard about the bizarre event taking place at Broad and Pattison, and they flocked to the stadium to see history in the making. As the game continued, the crowd got bigger as hundreds of night owls converged on the ballpark. They were told to sit wherever they wanted.

At 3:00 AM, a group of loud fun-lovers started the wave. A little later, broadcaster Richie Ashburn, calling it the "shank of the night," leaned out of the booth to lead some cheers.

After Ricky Jordan's three-run homer in the fifth reduced their deficit to 5–4, the Phillies tied the score in the eighth. Then, with two outs in the bottom of the ninth, pitcher Tommy Greene, no speed demon but pinch-running out of necessity for Mariano Duncan, was thrown out at home while trying to score from third on a wild pitch. And the long night was extended even farther.

Williams, in his second inning of relief, retired the Padres in the top of the tenth. In the bottom half, Incaviglia walked and went to second on a single by Jim Eisenreich. With no outs and Williams due up, it was the spot for a pinch-hitter. Not only did the Phillies have none left, they were out of relievers. Williams had to bat.

Williams had not been to the plate all season. In fact, he had previously batted only 15 times in his career. But with no options left, Williams grabbed a bat and—miracle of miracles—slapped a single. Incaviglia, no world-class sprinter, raced home from second with the winning run.

Phillies 6, Padres 5. The clock read 4:40 AM. It was the latest any major league game had ever finished, far surpassing the old record of 3:35 AM set in 1985 when the New York Mets defeated the Atlanta Braves, 16–13, in 19 innings.

TRIVIA

Who had the only unassisted triple play in Phillies history?

Answers to the trivia questions are on page 190.

Although the actual playing time of the two games was five hours and 36 minutes, the twin bill had lasted 12 hours and five minutes. "I would like to think this sets a record that will never be broken," Ashburn said to what few listeners he may have still had.

As the players tumbled into the clubhouse, fans shouted, "We want Mitch." The batting hero, who never came to the plate again the rest of the season but who set a team record that year with 43 saves, emerged from the clubhouse, clamored up the dugout steps, and waved to the boisterous crowd. "I've never seen anything like this and probably never will," he said in a gross understatement.

As the Phillies filed out of the clubhouse to which they would soon return for a game that night, second baseman Mickey Morandini had a parting comment. "See you today," he said.

Gypsies, Tramps, and Thieves

During the long history of the Phillies, it can safely be said that the franchise never had a team quite like the one that took the field in 1993.

This was a team that had finished last in the National League's East Division the previous year and wasn't expected to do a whole lot better in '93. The squad was made up mostly of hard-boiled veterans who had previously played for teams that had enjoyed limited success. It was managed by a guy with a huge ego whose temperament ranged from fiery to curt to amiable.

Jim Fregosi could often be seen ambling around the clubhouse, chatting and joking with players, even playing cards with them on occasion. "The job is to relate to players and get the best out of them," he said. "The day of managing where you say, 'This is how it's done and this is how it's going to be' is done with. Players have to respect you, and they have to trust you. I don't have a lot of team meetings. But I do have a lot of meetings on an individual basis."

Most of the team had arrived in Philadelphia through trades engineered by general manager Lee Thomas. Because many of them performed with the rough-and-tumble style of old-time players, the team was often called a throwback to an earlier generation.

"We're a throwback, all right," said first baseman John Kruk. "Thrown back by other organizations."

The clubhouse was often called a nuthouse. Relief pitcher Mitch Williams said it was populated by "a bunch of misfits." "We lead the league in characters," added pitcher Terry Mulholland.

In Atlanta, a newspaper warned residents "to hide the women and children" when the Phillies arrived. A Toronto rag described the Phillies

TOP TEN

The Phillies' Most Significant Free-Agent Signings (with Years They Were Signed)

	Name	Year
1.	Pete Rose	1978
2.	Jim Thome	2002
3.	Jim Eisenreich	1993
4.	Mariano Duncan	1991
5.	Gregg Jefferies	1995
6.	Jose Mesa	2000
7.	Richie Hebner	1976
8.	Pete Incaviglia	1992
9.	David Bell	2002
10.	Lance Parrish	1987

as "a motley crew of hairy, beer-soused brutes." Someone else called the Phils "long-haired, slack-jawed, pot-bellied, and snarly-lipped."

To these descriptions, outfielder Pete Incaviglia had a terse response. "This ain't no f*cking beauty show," he roared. "It's baseball. All that other stuff don't mean a thing."

The back of the Phillies' clubhouse was lined with the lockers of catcher Darren Daulton, outfielder Lenny Dykstra, third baseman Dave Hollins, and Kruk, Incaviglia, and Williams. "The Ghetto," some called it. Nevertheless, these were the leaders of the team—all grizzled veterans. Daulton presided from a lounge chair crammed into his locker.

It was Daulton who gave the team its most descriptive name. "We're just a bunch of gypsies, tramps, and thieves," said the team's undisputed leader.

The '93 Phillies, though, were not just a bunch of raucous crazies, standup comics, and scruffy beer-guzzlers. They could play the game. They were intense, highly motivated. They had guts, desire, and talent. They were hell-bent on winning. And they played brilliantly together as a team.

"People look at this team and think we have a bunch of loose cannons," Fregosi said. "But that's simply not true. If crazy is running out ground balls, playing hard, and getting the uniform dirty, then, yeah, they're crazy."

The Phillies, though, were not really a team of wild men. The club had an ample supply of quiet, clean-cut, diligent players who shaved every day, didn't guzzle beer in the clubhouse, and refrained from spewing profanities or spitting on the carpet.

Because of the players' perceived blue-collar demeanor and special personalities, Phillies fans loved them. In fact, the '93 Phillies surely rank as one of the most popular clubs the team ever had. Until the team opened its first season in new Citizens Bank Park in 2004, the '93 club was the only Phillies team ever to draw more than 3 million fans in a single season.

The fans, who fashioned eight sellouts at Veterans Stadium while exceeding 50,000 at 16 different games, were duly rewarded. With a team that included just six players who came up through the Phils' farm system, the Phillies became only the third major league team since 1900 to go from last place one year to first the next.

The Phillies led their division for all but one day of the entire season. But it wasn't easy. The Montreal Expos stayed closely on their tails through most of the season, not wilting until the very end.

"This was a team that never quit, that never died," said Dykstra. And almost every time it won, a different player led the team to victory, whether it was one of the boys from the Ghetto, the quietly elegant Jim Eisenreich, the talkative Curt Schilling, the diligent Mickey Morandini, the refreshing Mariano Duncan, the sometimes cantankerous Danny Jackson, the innocent and wide-eyed Kevin Stocker, the amiable Milt Thompson, the quiet country boy Tommy Greene, or the ebullient Wes Chamberlain.

They all had nicknames: Dude (Dykstra), Bubba (Daulton), Jethro (Greene), Mikey (Hollins), Jake (Kruk), Wild Thing (Williams), Batty (Kim Batiste), Andy (Larry Andersen), and Shill (Schilling), Mul (Mulholland), Stocks (Stocker), Inky (Incaviglia), and Eisey (Eisenreich). And all played important roles in the Phillies climb to the top.

DID YOU KNOW . . . That in two of the four years that he managed the Phillies, Larry Bowa's teams had identical 86–76 records? (Bowa's 2004 team also went 86–76, but Gary Varsho managed the last two games.) Mayo Smith had two 77–77 seasons, Gene Mauch had two 87–75 clubs, and Danny Ozark's team twice went 101–61.

Lenny Dykstra once led the league in hits and another time tied for the lead. He was named to three All-Star teams and played a scrappy brand of baseball that endeared him to Phillies fans in the early '90s.

It was a climb to the top that started early in the season. After winning their first three games at Houston, including their first Opening Day win since 1984, the Phillies returned home where the largest Opening Day crowd in Philadelphia baseball history up to that point—60,985—gathered for the first game. Although the Phils lost to the Chicago Cubs 11–7, they went on to post a 17–5 record in April, a club record. As May began, they were in first place for the first time on that date since 1964.

In early May, the record stretched to 23–7, making it the best start in club history. "We expect to win every time we take the field," said Larry Andersen, who was also a member of the club's previous pennant winner in 1983. "This group today is the best I've ever been associated with."

In late May, the Phillies thrashed the Colorado Rockies 18–1. By mid-June, the team had a 45–17 record and an 11½-game lead. Soon afterward, though, the Phils went into a tailspin, losing 14 of 20 games. The lead plummeted to a mere three games.

In the midst of that slump, the Phils and San Diego Padres performed in one of the weirdest doubleheaders ever played. Held at Veterans Stadium, there were three rain delays equaling five hours and 54 minutes, which forced the conclusion of the first game back to 1:00 AM. The second game lasted 10 innings and finally ended at 4:40 AM, the latest a major league game was ever completed.

Just five days later, the Phillies had to go 20 innings to beat the Los Angeles Dodgers 7–6, in what was the second-longest game in Phillies history.

By late August, the Phillies had pushed their lead back as high as 11 games. And everybody on the team was contributing, not the least of whom was the courageous Eisenreich, the exquisite right fielder who suffered from Tourette's syndrome.

"I didn't know until January whether I would even be playing again," he said. "But I thought someone would want me. I'm just an average player," added the guy who would hit more than .300 in each of his four seasons with the Phillies. "It's just a joy to be able to play."

Eisey was occasionally the butt of some good-natured clubhouse comedy. "Compared to what most of us have on this team," said Schilling when first told about Eisenreich's illness, "that's like having a common cold."

In early September, Montreal got hot and won 17 of 20 games. But even though the Phils' lead shriveled to as low as four games, they held on, and on September 28, riding Duncan's grand slam—the eighth of the season for the team—the division title was clinched with a 10–7 victory over the Pittsburgh Pirates.

The Phillies continued to show how good they were in the National League Championship Series against the Atlanta Braves. After winning the first game, 4–3, in 10 innings on an RBI single by Batiste, whose error an inning earlier had set up the Braves' tying run, the Phils were thrashed 14–3 and 9–4 in the next two games. They then won three straight behind strong pitching by Jackson, Schilling, and Greene and Dykstra's electrifying tenth-inning home run in Game 5. A 6–3 victory over Hall of Fame–bound Greg Maddux in the sixth game gave the Phillies the National League pennant.

In the World Series against the Toronto Blue Jays, the Phillies fell behind two games to one. Then came one of the most memorable games in World Series history. In an incredible battle in which the two teams combined for 32 hits—two of them home runs by Dykstra—the Phils blew 12–7 and 14–9 leads, finally losing, 15–14, as the Blue Jays scored six runs in the eighth inning. The four-hour, 14-minute marathon was the longest nine-inning game ever played in a World Series.

Showing their fierce determination, the Phillies bounced back to win Game 5, 2–0, as Schilling fired a brilliant five-hitter. "I wanted the ball," said Schilling afterward. "If you don't want the ball in these situations, why show up?"

The win was the final bright note of the season for the Phillies. After trailing, 5–1, in Game 6, the Phils fought back with a five-run seventh, only to lose, 8–6, on Joe Carter's three-run, walk-off homer off Mitch Williams. The Series was over, ruined by one of the most memorable home runs in baseball history.

Nevertheless, it had been one of the most glorious years the Phillies ever put together.

By the NUMBERS

6—Of the players who were on the 1993 Phillies roster through most of the season, only six of them came up through the club's farm system. They were Kim Batiste, Darren Daulton, Tyler Green, Ricky Jordan, Mickey Morandini, and Kevin Stocker.

Schmidt, Ashburn Fans Take Over Cooperstown

Over the years, the Phillies have been involved in many memorable events. One came on a hot, stifling summer day far from any big league field.

It was the day Richie Ashburn and Mike Schmidt were inducted into the Baseball Hall of Fame in Cooperstown, New York. The date was July 30, 1995.

Ashburn was voted in by the Veterans Committee some 27 years after he had first become eligible for induction. Schmidt was a first-ballot selection of the Baseball Writers' Association of America. Their entry into the Hall marked the first time two players from the same team had been inducted together since 1985.

At the time of the induction, the Phillies were on a hot streak. Steve Carlton had entered the baseball shrine one year earlier. And Jim Bunning would be taken in 1996.

The induction of Ashburn and Schmidt raised to 33 the number of people who at one time or another served with the Phillies. Along with the two new inductees, however, only seven of those players, including Grover Cleveland Alexander, Carlton, Ed Delahanty, Chuck Klein, and Robin Roberts, entered the Hall based mostly on their records with the Phillies.

But this induction was unlike the others. It was one in which Philadelphians amply demonstrated that they do have warm hearts after all. It was a true lovefest. And it was a day in which Philly fans nearly busted Cooperstown apart at the seams.

Hundreds of carloads and a record 171 buses carrying Phillies fans had streamed into the tiny upstate New York village in a display of hero-worshipping that seldom rises above the discontent so prevalent among

By the NUMBERS

7—The Phillies' record for most home runs in one game. It happened in 1998 against the New York Mets when Rico Brogna, Kevin Sefcik, and Bobby Estalella each homered twice, and Marlon Anderson hit a pinch-hit four-bagger in his first major league plate appearance.

Philadelphia's cynical sports lovers. The hamlet was so jammed, in fact, that neither the museum, the streets, the stores, the restaurants, the hotels, nor any other commercial establishment could hold them all. Retail sales reached an all-time high. Some fans were even forced to camp out or to find hotel space as far as 50 miles away.

And when the ceremony took place in 90-degree weather, Phillies fans, the players' families, plus numerous Phillies executives and former players flocked to Clark Sports Center in record numbers. A crowd that included Ashburn's 91-year-old mother, Toots, and more than 100 of his friends and family from Nebraska and was estimated at between 25,000 and 28,000 filled every available spot in the area in front of the stage where the ceremony took place. It was the largest crowd that had ever attended a Cooperstown induction ceremony, far exceeding the previous mark of 20,000 in attendance for Brooks Robinson's induction in 1983.

Red, red, red, everywhere the eye could focus, there was nothing but a sea of red, as Phillies fans, hundreds of whom had placed lawn chairs at the site of the event the night before, wore the team's primary color on virtually every piece of clothing but their underwear—and maybe some even did that. Perhaps never in the history of mankind has there ever been such a massive display of the color red in one place.

It was such a partisan Phillies crowd that team president Bill Giles was prompted to call it "a great day for Phillies fans and a great day for the city of Philadelphia." To that, then Philadelphia mayor Ed Rendell added that the turnout "proves that we have the best fans in the world."

Ashburn, who at the time was in his 32nd season as a Phillies broadcaster and his 50th year in baseball, was one of the most popular figures the team ever had. Along with recognizing his former Whiz Kids manager Eddie Sawyer, he said, "I can't believe the turnout. It's so wonderful to see this many people. This is awesome, just awesome. Fans, you have made this the greatest day of my life."

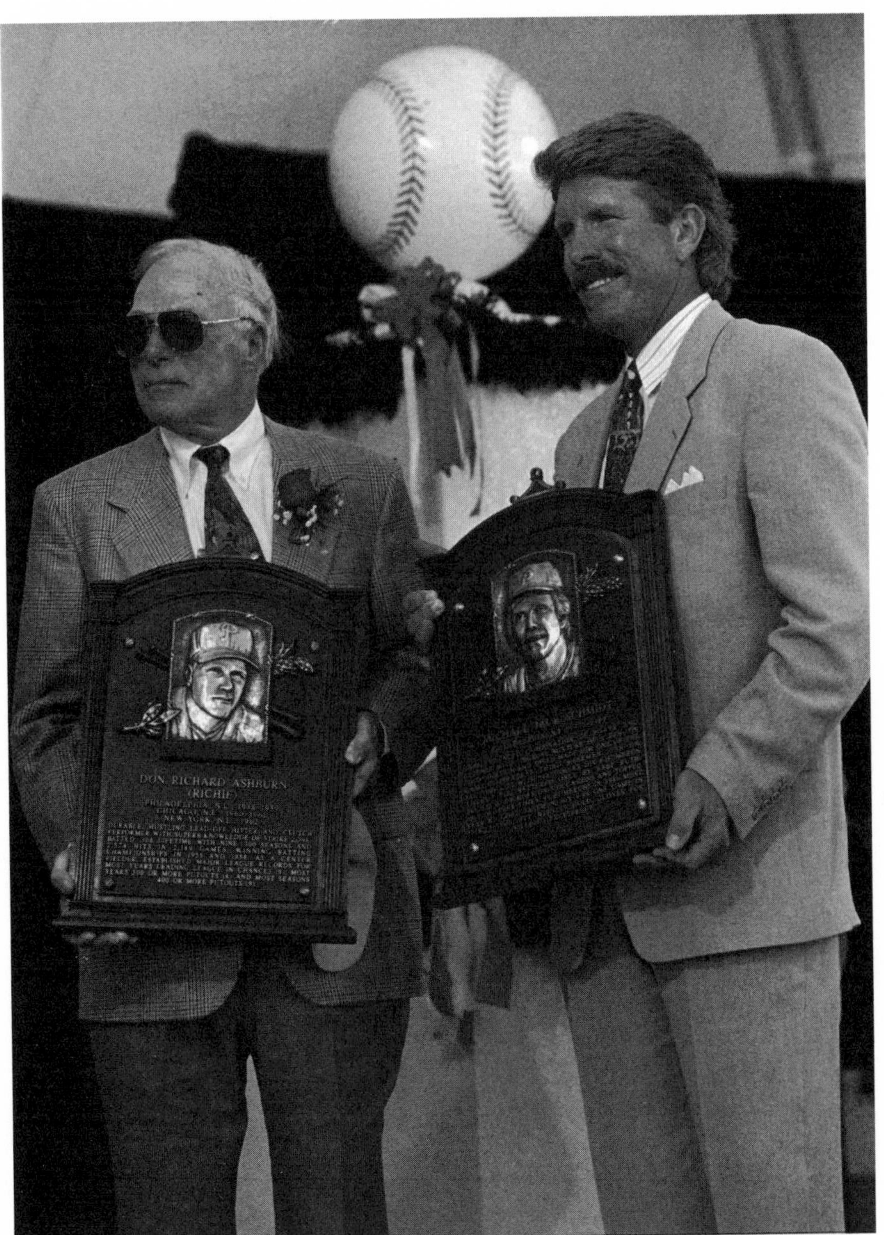

Phillies legends Richie Ashburn and Mike Schmidt were inducted into the Hall of Fame on the same day, July 30, 1995.

TOP TEN

Phillies All-Time Stolen-Base Leaders

	Name	Stolen Bases
1.	Billy Hamilton	508
2.	Ed Delahanty	411
3.	Sherry Magee	387
4.	Jim Fogarty	289
5.	Larry Bowa	288
6.	Juan Samuel	249
7.	Bobby Abreu	234
8.	Roy Thomas	228
9.	Von Hayes	202
10.	Richie Ashburn	199

Schmidt also took note of the multitudes. "You have stretched the Philadelphia city limits all the way to Cooperstown," he said. "It's unbelievable." Later, the ex–third baseman said, "From the podium, all you could see was a sea of red hats. It was just like Woodstock."

During his career, Schmidt was often criticized by local fans. He used the occasion to extend an olive branch. "My relationship with Philadelphia fans has always been misunderstood," he said. "Can we put that to rest today? I and my family sure hope we can. Sure, there were tough nights and tough games at Veterans Stadium. You've got to realize that that's the nature of the sport we play."

Schmidt, the eighth third baseman inducted and whose 944 votes were to that point the highest total ever garnered, said he also remembered the cheers, the curtain calls, and all the other good moments at the ballpark. "I know you cared," he said. "And for that, I thank you."

Much to their credit, both Schmidt and to a lesser extent Ashburn avoided the usual platitudes and hollow remarks. They used their speeches to urge positive changes in baseball, which at the time was buried under an avalanche of serious problems and not far removed from a disastrous strike that had pushed back the start of the season. Each made a number of meaningful points, sometimes with evangelical fervor.

Returning to the subject of fans, Ashburn, the former center fielder, emphasized their importance. "The greatest part about this day is the fans," he said. "I hope that baseball will pay attention a little bit to what has happened here today. There's a message here. You hear so many things about what's wrong with baseball. You people aren't here because they're having fireworks. You're not here because they gave something away. You're here for baseball, and I think that's the message you send—that maybe we ought to get some things straightened out.

"The owners, the players, the guys like us who are the veterans," he added, "we're all in this together. We're in it together with the fans. Listen to the fans."

Schmidt also noted the importance of the fans. "No other sport has fans attached to such a significant and rich history as baseball," he said. "No other sport has fans that depend on it to entertain them through the long, hot summer. Those who are currently enjoying the fruits of the game had best realize that the key to the game's survival is that unique bond that this game has with its fans."

Schmidt paid special tribute to three teammates he said had gone out of their ways to help him during his career—Bob Boone, Dick Allen, and Pete Rose. In addition, he called for the reinstatement of Rose, although a number of Hall of Famers on the stage seemed to resent the suggestion. He criticized the current state of baseball and the uncaring attitudes of the game's players. And he had encouraging words for youth. "Never stop chasing that dream," he said. "Your dreams are your best motivators. Believe in your dreams."

Dreams, he might have added, were what made this day...the dreams of his, the dreams of Ashburn's, the dreams of the legions of fans who came to watch two hometown heroes reach baseball's ultimate dream.

It was a day that ranked as one of the greatest in Philadelphia sports.

DID YOU KNOW . . . That when Pat Burrell (117), Chase Utley (105), and Bobby Abreu (102) all drove in more than 100 runs in 2005, they became the first Phillies trio to perform that feat since 1932 when Don Hurst (143), Chuck Klein (137), and Pinky Whitney (124) did it?

Thome Meets the Press

Sports teams in Philadelphia have never been reluctant to hold press conferences. With a large and varied number of media types clamoring for news, press conferences in the city are a regular part of the business of providing information for public consumption.

Naturally, not all media confabs have been successful. Some have promoted fiction, others have focused on spinning, and still others have lacked either substance or clarity. But then there are those that do what they're supposed to do, which is to supply usable information to the assembled reporters.

That's where the press conference the Phillies held on December 3, 2002, enters the picture. The event was held to introduce newly signed free agent Jim Thome.

To say it was an extraordinary affair is to put it mildly. It was, one might say, quite possibly the granddaddy of all Philadelphia press conferences.

The Phillies, of course, have had many huge press conferences. One was when the signing of Pete Rose was announced. Another was when Mike Schmidt declared his retirement. Yet another was when the club hired Larry Bowa as manager.

"But I think the one with Thome was bigger than the others," said Phillies vice president of public relations, Larry Shenk. "We expected a big event, and we certainly got it."

More than 100 representatives of news organizations were there. And not a one left early or went away without a major story.

One day earlier, Thome, a down-to-earth guy who possesses none of the distasteful attitudes or behavior so prevalent among most of today's modern superstars, had signed the most lucrative contract ever parceled out by the Phillies. It called for a reported $85 million spread over six years, plus a signing bonus of $10 million.

The money alone gave the event historical significance. Add to that the fact that the Phils had signed one of the biggest names in baseball, and it made the day even more noteworthy. Not since the club signed Rose in 1979 had the acquisition of a new player attracted so much attention.

Several years later, Thome remembered the day with particular fondness. "There are so many words to describe it," he said. "It was awesome. It was overwhelming. It was exciting. It was a fresh start with a new organization, and it was just a very special time.

"For me," he added, "it was not only a fun day, it was one of the highlights of my career. It's something I'll always, always remember."

Signed as a free agent during the off-season in 2002, first baseman Jim Thome hit 89 home runs his first two seasons before injuries shelved him for much of 2005.

The day had been preceded by a succession of events involving the Phillies' pursuit of the slugging first baseman. The club had begun its courtship with Thome soon after the end of the 2002 season. With money freed up by the departure of Scott Rolen and the move to the new Citizens Bank Park scheduled for 2004, the Phils had made a commitment to lure front-line players to the fold.

Pitcher Tom Glavine was one of them. So was third baseman David Bell. But Thome was viewed as the big prize. And an all-out effort to lure him away from the Cleveland Indians was foremost in the Phillies' plans.

General manager Ed Wade headed the effort. With the blessing of team president David Montgomery, Wade and assistant general manager Ruben Amaro pursued Thome with unyielding persistence. They had repeated conversations with Thome. They met with his agent, Pat Rooney. They spent most of their waking hours vigorously tracking their prey.

TOP TEN

Longest Phillies Hitting Streaks

	Name	Year	Hitting Streak
1.	Jimmy Rollins	2005	36
2.	Ed Delahanty	1899	31
3.	Billy Hamilton	1894	27
4.	Chuck Klein	1930	26t
	Chuck Klein	1930	26t*
6.	Willie Montanez	1974	24
7.	Goldie Rapp	1921	23t
	Johnny Moore	1934	23t
	Richie Ashburn	1948	23t
	Pete Rose	1979	23t
	Lonnie Smith	1981	23t
	Lenny Dykstra	1990	23t

*Klein had two 26-game hitting streaks in 1930.

All the while, the media was giving the story top coverage. And Phillies fans were working themselves into a frenzy as they contemplated Thome's big bat in the lineup.

TRIVIA

Who had the first four-hit game at Citizens Bank Park?

Answers to the trivia questions are on page 190.

In early November, the 32-year-old Thome visited Philadelphia. Having never been to the city before, he was anxious to see places where he might live. He also wanted to see some of the sites. One was the steps that Rocky (played by Sylvester Stallone) had climbed at the Philadelphia Museum of Art. Thome climbed the steps, duplicating the feat shown in his favorite movie.

The Phillies took Thome to view the site of their forthcoming ballpark. Riding in a limo on the way out, the assembled entourage passed a group of electricians holding signs urging Thome to sign with the Phils. "He saw them, and said, 'We gotta stop and acknowledge them,'" Amaro said. When the limo stopped, Thome jumped out, ran over to the tradesmen, and shook their hands in a genuine display of good will.

After eating a cheesesteak, Thome went to a Flyers game. He was introduced during the game, receiving a thunderous ovation. The next day, he returned home to Cleveland to ponder.

Thome was also being pursued by a number of other teams, not the least of which were the Indians, as well as the Baltimore Orioles, Chicago Cubs, and Los Angeles Dodgers. To meet the challenge, the Phillies were not only offering more money, but they were also getting help from unexpected sources.

At the urging of Phillies manager Larry Bowa, Rose, Thome's boyhood idol, called the big batsman to tell him what a great sports town Philadelphia is. Bell, a former teammate of Thome's who by then had signed with the Phillies, called to urge Jim to come east. Other Phils called, too, including Pat Burrell. Even Tug McGraw's son Tim, Thome's favorite country music singer, called.

Meanwhile, Thome put in a call to Rolen, who had turned down a $90-million-contract offer from the Phillies, thereby forcing the club to trade him. What, Thome asked the ex–Phils third baseman, was his opinion of his contemplated move? "I have to give Scott a lot of credit," Jim said later. "He never said one bad thing about the Phillies."

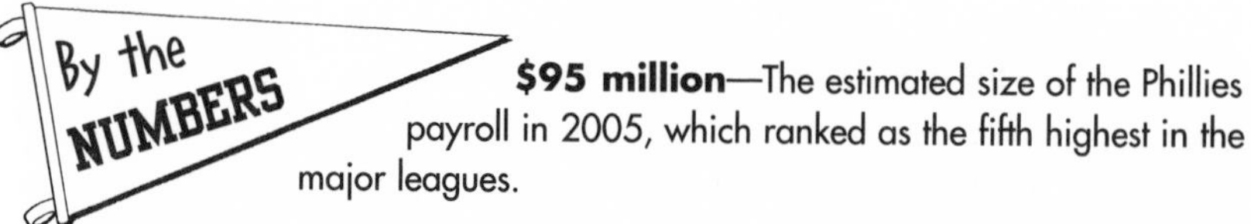

$95 million—The estimated size of the Phillies payroll in 2005, which ranked as the fifth highest in the major leagues.

Finally, after long weeks of thought and consultations with his wife, Andrea, Thome made his decision. He was coming to Philadelphia.

The media was alerted; the press conference was set. And on the day after he had settled on a decision, the Peoria, Illinois, native made his first appearance as a Phillie in a temporary building that the team was using for such occasions on the site of the new ballpark.

Those who were there won't soon forget the excitement that dominated the atmosphere. It was a press conference to beat all press conferences, and even the notoriously hard-bitten Philadelphia press was at least temporarily caught up in the epic moment.

"This is certainly a big day for the city of Philadelphia to be able to add a player not only of the ability of Jim Thome, but of his character," said Wade. "We've taken a huge step forward, both on the field and in the clubhouse."

"The bottom line is, I want to challenge myself and win," Thome told the assembled multitudes. "The money Philly offered is tremendous. But if it was just about money, I would have stayed in Cleveland.

"Everyone knows my ties to Cleveland," he added. "I love the organization. But as a player, you always want to give yourself the best chance to win. I felt this was the place to be. It was a very, very difficult decision. I spent a lot of sleepless nights thinking about it. I went back and forth a bunch of times."

Thome revealed that his only fight in baseball had been with then–Boston Red Sox pitcher Rheal Cormier, now one of his new teammates. During a game at Fenway Park, Cormier had thrown a retaliation pitch that hit Thome in the rump. In accordance with the unwritten hitter's handbook, Thome was obliged to charge the mound, an act that precipitated a brawl between teams and resulted in the ejection of the two main combatants.

A few hours later, as Jim and Andrea stood outside the park awaiting a cab, who should drive by but Cormier. He stopped and offered to drive them back to the hotel. "I charged the mound, and he gave me a ride home," laughed the new Phillies cleanup hitter.

One of the highlights—and certainly the warmest and most touching moment—of the press conference came when Thome began talking about Andrea, a Cleveland native and former television personality who at the time was eight months pregnant with the couple's first child.

"My wife is my rock," said Thome, tears filling his eyes. After a few more descriptive phrases, he was too emotional to continue and left the podium. Ten minutes later, his composure having returned, Thome reentered the room. "I hate it when these allergies kick in like that," he joked in a deft move to lighten the moment.

Ninety minutes after it began, the press conference was over. By then, the Phillies' phones had been engulfed in a torrent of calls from fans wishing to purchase season tickets. Within the next few days, more than 1,200 new season tickets had been sold, and the whole town was buzzing about the Phillies' new superstar.

"I've never seen the city get so excited over a player coming in," said Bowa.

The excitement, of course, was justified. In his first at-bat in a spring-training game, Thome hit a home run. He tripled on the first pitch in his first at-bat of the regular season. And he homered on the first pitch in his first at-bat at Veterans Stadium.

In his first season in Philadelphia, Thome drove in 131 runs and led the National League in home runs with 47, just one short of Mike Schmidt's club record. The following season, he blasted 42 homers with 105 RBIs, at one point socking his 400th career home run.

Injuries sidelined Thome through much of the 2005 season, and during the winter he was traded to the Chicago White Sox. No matter what, though, the press conference that had trumpeted his arrival in Philadelphia will forever rank high on the list of special Phillies moments.

Phillies' Finest 50

During 123 years, you'd expect the Phillies to have a substantial number of top players. And you'd be right.

Over the years, the Phillies may not always have had good teams. But they've always had at least some good players. A few teams such as the 1950 and 1980 Phils were downright full of them.

Accordingly, the following commentary ranks the top 50 Phillies of all time and lists the highlights of their careers. Because of the vast difference in qualifications, pitchers and position players are listed separately. Although some players were not long-term Phillies, their records were too exceptional to overlook, and they were included on this list. Only a player's performance with the Phils was considered and discussed here.

One other point: although players from early times and ones from the modern era are virtually impossible to compare—the difference between elephants and squirrels is not nearly as great—they have been lumped into one group. That somewhat skews the rankings. So be it.

Position Players

1. Mike Schmidt, 3B, 1972–1989

Only Babe Ruth won more home-run titles than Schmidt, who captured seven and tied for another. He ranks 11th on baseball's all-time home-run list with 548. Arguably the best all-around third baseman in baseball history, Schmidt hit four home runs in one game, drove in more than 100 runs nine times, won 10 Gold Gloves, and was selected to play in 12 All-Star Games, earning the starting berth nine straight times. He was voted National League MVP three times and World Series MVP in 1980. He is the club's all-time leader in 12 offensive categories. Schmidt was voted into the Hall of Fame in 1995.

2. Ed Delahanty, LF, 2B, 1B, 1888–1889, 1891–1901

The best all-around Phillies hitter of all time, Delahanty has the fourth-highest batting average (.346) in major league history. He hit above .400 three times and over .300 on seven other occasions. With the Phillies, Delahanty won one batting title, one home-run crown, and three RBI championships. In 1896 he became only the second major leaguer to hit four home runs in one game. He once had 10 straight hits and also had six hits in one game. He entered the Hall of Fame in 1945.

3. Richie Ashburn, CF, 1948–1959

A two-time National League batting champion and a three-time league leader in hits, Ashburn had a lifetime batting average of .308 with 2,574 career hits. He is the Phillies' all-time leader in hits, while going over .300 eight times. One of baseball's finest defensive center fielders, he led the National League in putouts nine times, four times making 500 or more putouts in a season (both NL records). One of the most popular Phillies players of all time, Ashburn was inducted into the Hall of Fame in 1995.

4. Chuck Klein, RF, 1928–1933, 1936–1939, 1940–1944

Another Hall of Famer (1980), Klein led the league in home runs four times and won the Triple Crown in 1933. He was also NL MVP in 1932. He led the league in RBIs twice and in runs scored and slugging percentage each three times. Another Phillie who homered four times in one game, Klein had his best year in 1930, when he hit .386 with 40 home runs, 170 RBIs, and 158 runs. He hit .320 for his career. A top fielder, he still holds the NL record for an outfielder with 44 assists in one season.

5. Billy Hamilton, CF, 1890–1895

An outstanding hitter and base stealer, Hamilton won two batting titles and over one three-year stretch with the Phillies hit .380, .404, and .389. He holds the all-time record with 192 runs scored in 1894. During a 14-year major league career, he compiled the eighth-highest batting average (.344) of all time. He stole more than 100 bases twice and is the third highest base stealer in baseball history. He made the Hall of Fame in 1961.

6. Sam Thompson, RF, 1889–1898

Baseball's first true power hitter, Thompson was the first National Leaguer to hit 20 home runs in one season (1889) and the first to slug 200 hits in one season (1887) when he blasted 203 safeties for Detroit, also compiling 222 for the Phils in 1893. A Hall of Fame member since 1974, Thompson won two home-run crowns and an RBI title with the Phillies. He collected more than 100 RBIs seven times, including 165 in 1895. Five times he hit above .300, including .407 in 1894. Thompson was also an excellent base stealer and defensive player.

7. Nap Lajoie, 1B, 2B, 1896–1900

Although he had a distinguished career elsewhere, Lajoie gave the Phillies five glittering seasons at the start of his career. A member in 1937 of the second group elected to the Hall of Fame, Lajoie never batted less than .324 as a regular with the Phillies. In 1897 and 1898, he had 197 hits and 127 RBIs both years. He also led the National League in RBIs, doubles, and slugging percentage each once. After leaving the Phillies, he set an all-time American League record with a .426 batting average in 1901.

8. Gavvy Cravath, RF, 1912–1920

Often called the Babe Ruth of his time, Cravath led the National League in home runs six times and RBIs twice. His 24 homers in 1915 were a major league record until Ruth hit 29 in 1919. Cravath's 115 RBIs and .285 batting average added to his homer total to make him the key slugger on the Phillies' first pennant winner. In 1913 he hit .341 with 19 homers and 128 RBIs. Ironically, Cravath didn't start his major league career as a regular until he was 31.

9. Sherry Magee, LF, 1904–1914

The 1910 batting champion with a .331 average, Magee was the Phillies' first outstanding hitter of the 20th century. He hit over .300 five times and three times led the NL in RBIs, reaching a high of 123 in 1910. Also an outstanding base runner, Magee stole no fewer than 38 bases during a six-year period from 1905 to 1910. His high was 55 in 1906.

10. Cy Williams, LF, 1918–1930

Easily the Phillies' finest hitter of the 1920s, Williams won four home-run titles, including three with the Phils. In 1923 he crushed an unbelievable 41 homers. He homered in double figures nine straight times and hit above .300 six times over a seven-year period (1920–1926). He had a career-high .345 batting average in 1926 after hitting .331 the year before.

11. Del Ennis, LF, RF, 1946–1956

One of the great RBI men in Phillies history, Ennis drove in more than 100 runs six times while blasting home runs in double figures 11 times. The main power hitter on the 1950 Whiz Kids, he led the league that year in RBIs with 126 and batted .311 with 31 home runs. He was Rookie of the Year in 1946 when he hit .313, his first of three times above .300.

12. Dick Allen, 3B, 1B, LF, 1963–1969, 1975–1976

As good a power hitter as the Phillies ever had, Allen hit from 20 to 40 homers a season in each of his first six years with the club. Some of his homers were among the longest ever hit at Connie Mack Stadium. His best year came in 1966, when he hit .317 with 40 home runs, 110 RBIs, and 112 runs scored. Allen hit over .300 four times. He was Rookie of the Year in 1964.

13. Larry Bowa, SS, 1970–1981

The finest shortstop ever to wear a Phillies uniform and one of the best in National League history, Bowa once held the major league record for highest fielding percentage by a shortstop. In one season (1972) he made just nine errors in 150 games. He led the NL in fielding percentage six times. His highest batting average was .305, in 1975. He also stole more than 20 bases nine times.

14. Greg Luzinski, LF, 1970–1980

One of the top hitters during the Phillies' Golden Era, Luzinski hit 29 or more home runs four times, including a high of 39 in 1977. That year, he also hit .309 with 130 RBIs. He hit above .300 and collected more than 100 RBIs three times each. In four appearances in the All-Star Game, Luzinski was a starter three times. His two-run homer won Game 1 in the 1980 LCS.

15. Bobby Abreu, RF, 1998–present

Abreu has hit above .300 six times, including a high of .335 in 1999. Also an outstanding power hitter, he has homered in double figures in all eight years, reaching 31 in 2001. That year, he became the first Phillie to hit 30 homers and steal 30 bases in the same season. He is only the third player in ML history to have seven straight 20-homer, 20–stolen base seasons and just the fourth to draw 100 or more walks seven straight years.

16. Pinky Whitney, 3B, 1928–1933, 1936–1939

While ranking as one of the club's finest third baseman of all time, Whitney was an outstanding clutch hitter who drove in more than 100 runs and hit above .300 each four times. Twice he had more than 200 hits, once lashing 207 in 1930, a year in which he hit .342 with 117 RBIs. He drove in 124 in 1932. His .982 fielding average in 1937 is the best by a Phillies third baseman.

17. Garry Maddox, CF, 1975–1986

One of the great defensive center fielders of all time, Maddox won more games with his glove than most Phillies have with their bats. He earned eight Gold Gloves, third most for an outfielder in NL history. A fine hitter, too, he batted as high as .330 in 1976. Maddox homered in double figures four times. His double drove in the winning run in the final game of the 1980 LCS.

18. Elmer Flick, RF, 1898–1901

Although Flick played in just four seasons with the Phillies, all of them were spectacular. He hit .302, .342, .367, and .333. In 1900 he led the league in RBIs with 110 and was second in batting average, slugging average, total bases, and home runs; third in triples; and fourth in hits and doubles. He led the league with 297 total bases. He also averaged nearly 30 stolen bases a season. In 1963 he was elected to the Hall of Fame.

19. Johnny Callison, RF, 1960–1969

The only player to appear as a regular for the Phillies throughout the 1960s, Callison was the heart of the club's offense. He scored 90 or more runs five times, hit 23 or more home runs four times, and collected more than 100 RBIs twice. He hit .300 in 1962 and .274 with 31 homers and 104 RBIs in 1964. Perhaps his most famous hit was his game-winning, three-run homer in the '64 All-Star Game.

20. Granny Hamner, SS, 2B, 1944–1959

A clutch hitter and the team sparkplug and captain on the Whiz Kids, Hamner broke in with the Phillies at the age of 17. He never hit higher than .299 as a regular, but he was as solid a player as the team ever had. He hit 21 homers and drove in 92 in 1953. Hamner made the All-Star team in 1953 as a shortstop and the following year made it as a second baseman.

21. Roy Thomas, CF, 1899–1908, 1910–1911

Thomas was one of the great leadoff batters of all time. He led the NL in walks seven times, reaching a high of 115 in 1899 and 1900. He went over 100 five other times. Thomas hit over .300 five times, his high being .325 as a rookie, a year when he scored 137 runs. Primarily a singles hitter, he was also an accomplished base stealer, his high being 42, and an excellent defensive player.

22. Jimmie Wilson, C, 1923–1928, 1934–1938

Not only was Wilson an outstanding hitter, but his ability to handle pitchers and his fine defensive work made him arguably the top catcher in Phillies history. His best batting average was .328 in 1925. He was the starting catcher in the 1935 All-Star Game after returning to the Phils as a player/manager. Wilson was credited with turning third baseman Bucky Walters into a pitcher.

23. Dick Bartell, SS, 1931–1934

Bartell was the NL shortstop in the first All-Star Game (1933). A fiery competitor, he was repeatedly among the league leaders in fielding. Also a standout hitter, he had .308 and .310 years with the Phillies. He was also a skilled base stealer and drawer of walks. Bartell was the Phillies captain. In 1933 he became the first major leaguer to hit four straight doubles in one game.

24. Pete Rose, 1B, 1979–1983

Rose's biggest contribution to the Phillies was that he showed them how to hustle. He played a major role in the team's first World Series winner with his spirited style. Few will ever forget the pop-up he caught after it jumped out of Bob Boone's glove in the final game. Rose also set the all-time NL hit record while with the Phillies in 1981. That year he batted .325. He carried a .331 mark in 1979.

25. Lefty O'Doul, LF, 1929–1930

Despite having played only two years with the Phillies, O'Doul is impossible to keep off the list of top 50 because of his two fabulous seasons. He hit .398 one year and .383 the next. His league-leading .398 was just one hit short of .400. That year, he set an NL record (since tied) with 254 hits and another mark by reaching base 334 times. He also collected 32 home runs, 122 RBIs, and 152 runs.

26. Tony Taylor, 2B, 3B, 1B, 1960–1971, 1974–1976

One of the steadiest players ever to wear a Phillies uniform, Taylor played in more games at second base than any other Phillie. A fine fielder, a solid hitter, and a swift base runner, he had superb all-around skills that made him invaluable. His best year was in 1970, when he hit .301. Taylor collected both his 1,000th and 2,000th hits while playing with the Phillies.

27. Jim Thome, 1B, 2003–2005

Another owner of two banner seasons, Thome led the National League in home runs in 2003 with 47, just one shy of the Phillies' all-time record. That year, he also drove in 131 runs and scored 111. His 42 homers the following year made him just the second player in history to have back-to-back 40-home-run seasons in different leagues. He also collected 105 RBIs.

28. Fred Luderus, 1B, 1910–1920

Luderus was one of the main cogs on the 1915 pennant-winning Phillies and an offensive force on the team throughout his stay in Philadelphia. In 1915 he hit .315 during the season, second-highest in the NL, and .438 in the World Series. Twice he finished second in the NL in home runs. Although not a skilled fielder, the Phillies' captain played more games at first base than any other Phils player.

29. Bob Boone, C, 1972–1981
A two-time Gold Glove winner and a three-time member of the NL All-Star team, Boone was an outstanding defensive player who, for a while, held the major league record for most games caught in a career. Owner of a whip-like throwing arm and an astute handler of pitchers, he was also a respectable hitter, exceeding .280 three straight times in the late 1970s.

30. Don Hurst, 1B, 1928–1934
One of the Phillies' heaviest-hitting first baseman, Hurst slugged home runs in double figures five straight times, including a high of 31 in 1929 when he batted .304 and drove in 125 runs. In 1932 he led the league with 143 RBIs while placing fifth in the NL in batting with a .339 average. That year, he also had 24 homers and 109 runs. He hit above .300 four times.

31. Scott Rolen, 3B, 1996–2002
A classic five-tool player, Rolen was not only an excellent hitter, but also an outstanding fielder. Named Rookie of the Year in 1997, he won three Gold Gloves. In six full seasons he collected more than 100 RBIs twice, during which time he average 24 homers while reaching a high of 31 in 1998. That year was his finest with a .290 average and 110 RBIs.

32. Dick Sisler, 1B, 1948–1951
Where would the Phillies be without Sisler? Owner of one of baseball's most famous home runs, his tenth-inning swat gave the team the pennant in 1950 on the last day of the season. Sisler was a fine hitter who went .274, .289, .296, and .287 with the Phils. In 1950 he lashed eight straight hits. When the Phillies needed a left fielder after the return of Eddie Waitkus, Sisler ably filled the position.

33. Johnny Moore, RF, 1934–1937
The Phillies have had few hitters as consistent as Moore. In his four years with the club, he put together seasons of .343, .323, .328, and .319, a record virtually unmatched in the modern Phillies era. Moore led the team in hitting in three of those years. He also homered in double figures three times and twice collected 93 RBIs. Moore skillfully played the tough right-field wall at Baker Bowl.

34. John Kruk, 1B, LF, 1989–1994

On a day-in, day-out basis, Kruk was the Phillies' best hitter while he played for the club. He hit above .300 four times, going as high as .331 and .323. In 1993 Kruk hit .316 with 14 home runs and 85 RBIs. He was second in the NL in on-base percentage twice. He finished in the top 10 in hitting twice. Often overlooked was Kruk's glove. He had a career fielding average of .994.

35. Jack Clements, C, 1884–1897

A left-handed catcher, Clements was a fine defensive player and a standout hitter during his long career in Philadelphia. He caught more games than any left-hander in baseball history. One of the first backstops to wear a chest protector, Clements hit over .300 three times as a regular and twice more as a reserve, getting as high as .394 in 88 games in 1895. He drove in more than 70 runs five times.

36. Jimmy Rollins, SS, 2000–present

Holder of the Phillies' all-time record for hitting in the most consecutive games (36), Rollins has also been superb with the glove and on the bases. Twice he's stolen more than 40 bases, tying for the NL lead with 46 in 2001. He's never batted fewer than 600 times a season, leading the league twice. He hit a career high of .290 in 2005. A three-time All-Star, he's had a quadruple-double five times and led the NL in triples three times (once tied).

37. Tony Gonzalez, CF, 1960–1968

Gonzalez was a reliable player who could hit, run, field, and throw. He once went 205 straight games without an error. In 1962 he fielded a perfect 1.000. Gonzalez led NL outfielders in fielding three times. He hit .339 in 1967, second best in the NL. That was one of three times he went over .300. While not a power hitter, he had a career-high 20 home runs in 1962.

38. Dolph Camilli, 1B, 1934–1937

The Phillies' premier power hitter of the mid-1930s, Camilli averaged 23 home runs a year with the team, once going as high as 28 in 1936, when he was second in the NL. He hit .316 that year and .339 in 1937, the highest ever for a Phils first baseman. He also scored more than 100 runs twice. Camilli went on to become NL MVP in 1941 with the Brooklyn Dodgers.

39. Andy Seminick, C, 1943–1951, 1955–1957
One of the Phillies' most popular players, Seminick was a rock-ribbed catcher who blocked the plate with fierce determination. He was an expert at handling a pitching staff and was a steadying influence on the 1950 Whiz Kids, when he had his best year with a .288 average and 24 home runs. He homered in double figures in six straight years.

40. Manny Trillo, 2B, 1979–1982
Trillo was the best defensive second baseman the Phillies ever had. In 1982 he set major league records (since broken) for most games (89) and most chances (479) without an error. He was also the MVP in the 1980 LCS when he hit .381 and collected three hits and two RBIs in the deciding game. Trillo hit .292 in 1980 and .287 in 1981. He was named to two All-Star teams, one as a starter.

41. Darren Daulton, C, 1983, 1985–1997
The unchallenged leader of the 1993 Phillies, Daulton was invaluable in driving the club to the pennant. Also an accomplished hitter when he was healthy, Daulton became only the fourth catcher in NL history to lead the NL in RBIs when he chased home 109 in 1992 while also clubbing 27 homers. He had 105 RBIs and 24 home runs in 1993. Daulton was also a first-rate backstop on defense.

Pitchers

1. Robin Roberts, 1948–1961
Of three brilliant Phillies pitchers, Roberts wins out by a slim margin. He won 234 games with the Phillies (and 286 overall) and was a 20-game winner six times in a row. He led the NL in wins four times, in complete games and innings pitched each five times. Most of Roberts' years were spent with weak teams. Nevertheless, he leads the Phillies in most pitching categories. He went 10 gritty innings to get the win in the pennant clincher in 1950 and started an unprecedented five All-Star Games. He once completed 28 straight games. Roberts was Major

League Player of the Year in 1952, when he posted a 28–7 record, and was NL Pitcher of the Year twice. Roberts entered the Hall of Fame in 1976.

2. Steve Carlton, 1972–1986

Carlton was the premier pitcher in baseball in the 1970s and early 1980s while earning four Cy Young Awards and winning more than 20 games five times. His 27 wins on a team that won just 59 all season stands as one of the most remarkable feats in baseball. When he retired, he had the second most strikeouts in baseball history. The tenth-winningest pitcher in baseball, he won 241 games with the Phillies while posting a 3.09 ERA. Carlton was selected to 10 All-Star teams. He won the second and sixth games of the 1980 World Series. A Hall of Fame inductee in 1994 with 329 career wins, he led the NL in strikeouts and innings pitched five times and in wins, games started, and hits each four times.

3. Grover Cleveland Alexander, 1911–1917, 1930

One of the most dominant pitchers of all time, Alexander is tied with the third-most wins in baseball history with 373. Voted into the Hall of Fame in 1938, he won 190 with the Phillies while posting a 2.18 ERA. Alexander won in double figures in all seven of his full seasons with the Phillies. Between 1915 and 1917, he went 31–10, 33–12, and 30–13, all three times posting ERAs less than 2.00, including 1.22 in 1915. In 1916 he tossed 16 shutouts. While pitching with the Phillies, Alexander led the league in innings pitched six times, once working 388⅔ frames, and in wins, complete games, and strikeouts five times. From 1914 to 1917, he never completed fewer than 30 games a season.

4. Jim Bunning, 1964–1967, 1970–1971

Another Hall of Famer, class of 1996, Bunning won 19 three straight years while averaging nearly 300 innings pitched per season. His greatest outing came in 1964 when he hurled a perfect game against the New York Mets, the only time a Phils pitcher has performed that feat and the first perfect game in the NL in 42 years. A tough, no-nonsense competitor, Bunning typically struck out more than 200 batters a season, hitting a high of 268 in 1965. Overall, he won in double figures five times with the

Phillies while collecting 89 victories. Bunning was the starting pitcher when the Phillies opened Veterans Stadium in 1971.

5. Charlie Ferguson, 1884–1887

The Phillies' first superstar, Ferguson won more than 20 games in each of his four seasons with the club, including 30 in 1886. He once won 12 straight games and was the first pitcher in baseball to win two games in one day. Ferguson pitched the Phillies' first no-hitter. Before his untimely death at the age of 25, he completed 165 of the 170 games he started while winning 99. Also a superb hitter, Ferguson often played second base or the outfield when not pitching and had a lifetime batting average of .288.

6. Tug McGraw, 1975–1984

No relief pitcher ever did more for the Phillies than McGraw. He saved 94 games, won 49, and compiled a 3.10 ERA over a 10-year period. His most memorable year was in 1980 when he saved 20 and posted a 1.47 ERA during the regular season, then saved two games in the LCS. In the World Series, he pitched in four of the six games, winning one, losing one, and saving two. His unforgettable strikeout of Willie Wilson for the final out in the last game ranks as the greatest moment in Phillies history.

7. Chris Short, 1959–1972

A hard-throwing left-hander, Short won in double figures five times, topping out with 20 wins in 1966. He won 35 games in the two previous years and 19 in 1968, while posting 132 victories overall with the Phillies. During one six-year stretch, his ERA was under 3.00 five times. Short struck out 18 batters in a 15-inning game. He was a member of two All-Star teams. Short is the second-winningest Phillies southpaw of all time.

8. Curt Simmons, 1947–1950, 1952–1960

Had it not been for military service, injuries, and the Phillies' mistake of letting him go prematurely, Simmons would rank among the club's all-time leaders in virtually every pitching category. As it was, he won 115 for the Phils and was in double figures six times. His best year was in

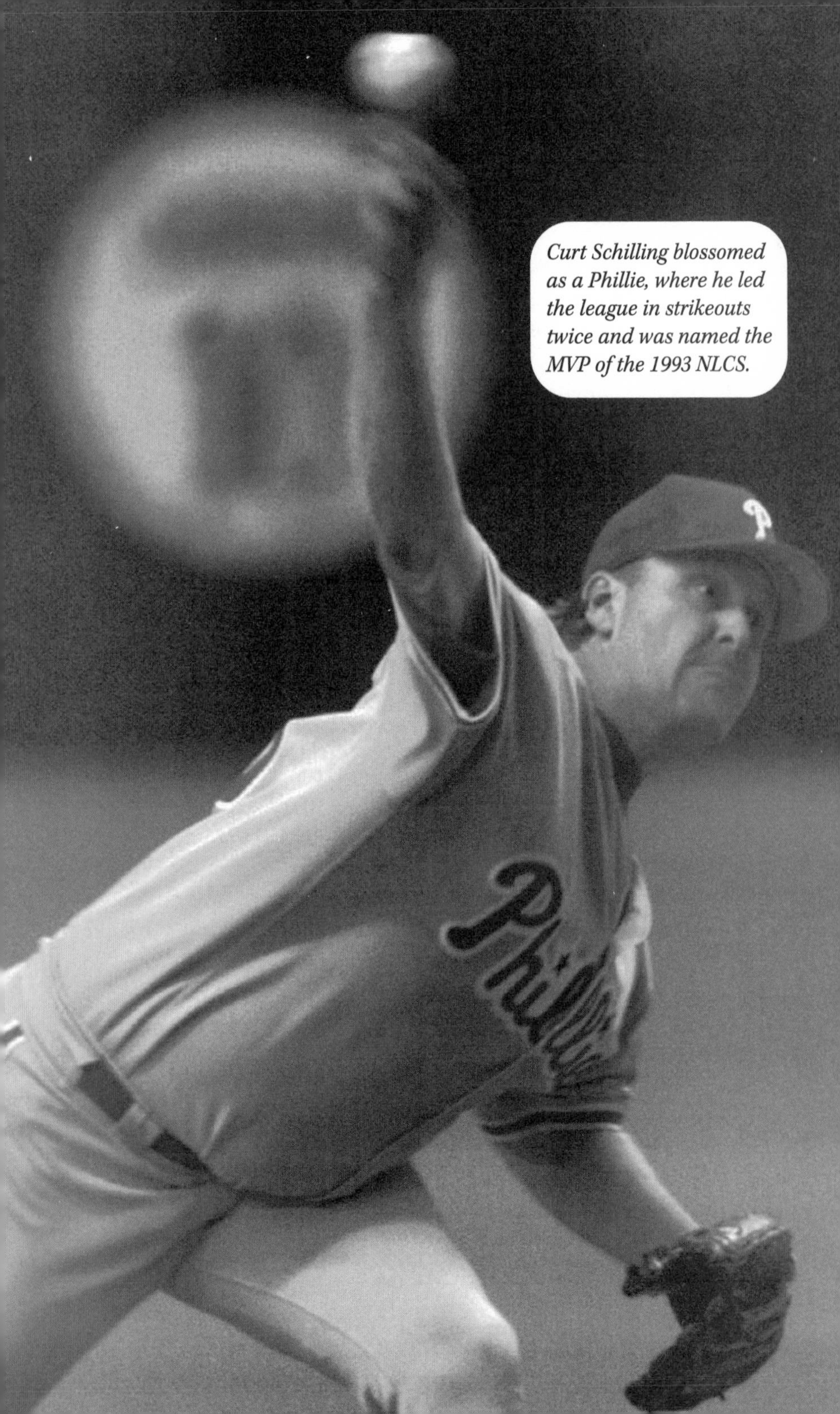

Curt Schilling blossomed as a Phillie, where he led the league in strikeouts twice and was named the MVP of the 1993 NLCS.

1950, when he won 17 before leaving for military duty. A member of three All-Star teams, he was the starting pitcher in the 1952 tilt.

9. Curt Schilling, 1992–2000

Converted to a starter after joining the Phillies, Schilling often battled injuries, but won 101 games while reaching double figures five times. He won 16 in 1993, then in two outings in the LCS, although he didn't get a decision, allowed just 11 hits and three earned runs in 16 innings, and was the series MVP. In the World Series, he hurled a memorable five-hit, 2–0 victory in Game 5. In 1998, he became only the fifth pitcher in big league history to record back-to-back 300-strikeout seasons. A three-time All-Star, he started the 1999 game.

Answers to Trivia Questions

Page 4: Sam Thompson did it with 20 homers in 1889.

Page 9: Miller. Fourteen of them played with the Phillies.

Page 31: Sherry Magee with 19.

Page 42: Eddie Sawyer in 1951, Gene Mauch in 1965, Dallas Green in 1981, Paul Owens in 1984, and Jim Fregosi in 1994.

Page 54: The game was played in 1934 against the Brooklyn Dodgers at Baker Bowl. The Dodgers won, 8–7.

Page 56: Organist Paul Richardson. He missed only a handful of games while manning the keyboard at Veterans Stadium from 1971 to 2003.

Page 67: Ralph "Putsy" Caballero was just 16 years old when he suited up for the first time with the Phillies in 1944.

Page 72: In 1963 shortstop Bobby Wine became the Phillies' first Gold Glove winner.

Page 76: Mike Schmidt hit 10 of the team's 160 walk-off homers.

Page 89: Chico Fernandez played shortstop in the 1957 opener.

Page 95: The best decade was 1890–1899 with a 743–630–15 (.541) record. The worst was 1920–1929 with a 566–962–6 (.370) mark.

Page 107: Wise hit two home runs, the only time a pitcher has ever done that while hurling a no-hitter.

Page 118: Pitchers Dennis (1962–1964) and Dave Bennett (1964).

Page 120: Pete Rose appeared in 163 games in 1979.

Page 135: Ken Raffensberger in 1944, Doug Jones in 1994, and Heathcliff Slocumb in 1995.

Page 138: Six. Chuck Klein in 1931 and 1932, Jim Konstanty in 1950, and Mike Schmidt in 1980, 1981, and 1986.

Page 144: Richie Ashburn. He played on the 1950 team and was a Phillies broadcaster when the team won in 1980, 1983, and 1993.

Page 157: Mickey Morandini performed the feat on September 20, 1992, against the Pittsburgh Pirates.

Page 173: Jim Thome had four hits on April 16, 2004.

Philadelphia Phillies All-Time Roster

Players who have appeared in at least one game with the Phillies.

* Player still active in major league baseball.

A

Ed Abbaticchio (2B)	1897–98
Fred Abbott (C)	1905
Kyle Abbott (P)	1992, 1995
Paul Abbott* (P)	2004
Bobby Abreu* (OF)	1998–2005
Cy Acosta (P)	1975
Bert Adams (C)	1915–19
Bob Adams (P)	1931–32
Buster Adams (OF)	1943–45, 1947
Terry Adams* (P)	2002–03, 2005
Jim Adduci (OF)	1989
Luis Aguayo (SS)	1980–88
Darrel Akerfelds (P)	1990–91
Jack Albright (SS)	1947
Scott Aldred (P)	1999–2000
Grover Alexander (P)	1911–17, 1930
Bob Allen (P)	1937
Bob Allen (SS)	1890–94
Dick Allen (3B, 1B, LF)	1963–69, 1975–76
Ethan Allen (OF)	1934–36
Hezekiah Allen (C)	1884
Bill Almon (SS)	1988
Porfi Altamirano (P)	1982–83
Clemente Alvarez (C)	2000
Ruben Amaro (SS)	1960–65
Ruben Amaro Jr. (OF)	1992–93, 1996–98
Red Ames (P)	1919
Larry Andersen (P)	1983–86, 1993–94
Dave Anderson (P)	1889–90
Harry Anderson (OF)	1957–60
John Anderson (P)	1958
Marlon Anderson* (2B)	1998–2002
Mike Anderson (OF)	1971–75, 1979
Sparky Anderson (2B)	1959
Ed Andrews (OF)	1884–89
Fred Andrews (2B)	1976–77
Stan Andrews (C)	1945
Bill Andrus (3B)	1937
Joe Antolick (C)	1944
John Antonelli (3B)	1945
Alex Arias (SS)	1998–2000
Buzz Arlett (OF)	1931
Morrie Arnovich (OF)	1936–40
Richie Ashburn (OF)	1948–59
Andy Ashby* (P)	1991–92, 2000
Dick Attreau (1B)	1926–27
Bill Atwood (C)	1936–40
Earl Averill (C)	1963
Ramon Aviles (2B)	1979–81
Bob Ayrault (P)	1992–93

B

Wally Backman (2B)	1991–92
Ed Baecht (P)	1926–28
Stan Bahnsen (P)	1982
Doug Bair (P)	1987
Doug Baird (3B)	1919

Floyd Baker (3B)	1954–55
Jack Baldschun (P)	1961–65
Henry Baldwin (SS)	1927
Jay Baller (P)	1982, 1992
Dave Bancroft (SS)	1915–20
Alan Bannister (OF)	1974–75
Salome Barojas (P)	1988
Dick Barrett (P)	1943–45
Tom Barrett (2B)	1988–89
Manuel Barrios (P)	1999–2000
Tony Barron (OF)	1997
Rich Barry (OF)	1969
Shad Barry (OF)	1901–04
Tom Barry (P)	1904
Dick Bartell (SS)	1931–34
Walt Bashore (OF)	1936
Charlie Bastian (SS)	1885–88, 1891
John Bateman (C)	1972
Bud Bates (OF)	1939
Del Bates (C)	1970
Johnny Bates (OF)	1909–10
Kim Batiste (3B)	1991–94
Howard Battle (3B)	1996
Stan Baumgartner (P)	1914–16, 1921–22
Frank Baumholtz (OF)	1956–57
Ernie Beam (P)	1895
Boom-Boom Beck (P)	1939–43
Fred Beck (1B)	1911
Beals Becker (OF)	1913–15
Bob Becker (P)	1897–98
Howie Bedell (OF)	1968
Steve Bedrosian (P)	1986–89
Fred Beebe (P)	1911
Matt Beech (P)	1996–98
Petie Behan (P)	1921–23
Bo Belinsky (P)	1965–66
David Bell* (3B)	2003–05
Juan Bell (2B)	1992–93
Chief Bender (P)	1916–17
Art Benedict (2B)	1883
Ray Benge (P)	1928–32, 1936
Mike Benjamin (SS)	1996
Stan Benjamin (OF)	1939–42
Dave Bennett (P)	1964
Dennis Bennett (P)	1962–64
Gary Bennett* (C)	1995–96, 1998–01
Joe Bennett (3B)	1923
Joel Bennett (P)	1999
Jack Bentley (P)	1926
Rabbit Benton (2B)	1922
Wally Berger (OF)	1940
Jack Berly (P)	1932–33
Bill Bernhard (P)	1899–1000
Joe Berry (C)	1902
Lefty Bertrand (P)	1936
Huck Betts (P)	1920–25
Charlie Bicknell (P)	1948–49
Doug Bird (P)	1979
Jim Bishop (P)	1923–24
Jeff Bittiger (P)	1986
Jim Bivin (P)	1935
Lena Blackburne (SS)	1919
Tim Blackwell (C)	1976–77
Sheriff Blake (P)	1931
Cy Blanton (P)	1940–42
Johnny Blatnik (OF)	1948–50
Buddy Blattner (2B)	1949
Marv Blaylock (1B)	1955–57
Ron Blazier (P)	1996–97
Jimmy Bloodworth (2B)	1950–51
Joe Boever (P)	1990–91
Dan Boitano (P)	1978
Ed Boland (OF)	1934–35
Stew Bolen (P)	1931–32
Jim Bolger (OF)	1959
Jack Bolling (1B)	1939
Rod Booker (SS)	1990–91
Bob Boone (C)	1972–81
John Boozer (P)	1962–64, 1966–69
Toby Borland* (P)	1994–96, 1998
Hank Borowy (P)	1949–50
Rick Bosetti (OF)	1976
Shawn Boskie (P)	1994
Ricky Bottalico* (P)	1994–98, 2001–02

Kent Bottenfield (P)	2000
Ed Bouchee (1B)	1956–60
Larry Bowa (SS)	1970–81
Bob Bowman (OF)	1955–59
Joe Bowman (P)	1935–36
Sumner Bowman (P)	1890
Jason Boyd* (P)	2000
Jack Boyle (C)	1893–98
Jack Boyle (3B)	1912
Gibby Brack (OF)	1938–39
John Brackenridge (P)	1904
Phil Bradley (OF)	1988
King Brady (P)	1905
Bobby Bragan (SS)	1940–42
Art Bramhall (3B)	1935
Bucky Brandon (P)	1971–73
Jackie Brandt (OF)	1966–67
Kitty Bransfield (1B)	1905–11
Cliff Brantley (P)	1991–92
Jeff Brantley (P)	1999–2000
Roy Brashear (1B)	1903
Alonzo Breitenstein (P)	1883
Ad Brennan (P)	1910–13
Rube Bressler (OF)	1932
Ken Brett (P)	1973
Billy Brewer (P)	1997–99
Charlie Brewster (SS)	1943
Fred Brickell (OF)	1930–33
Johnny Briggs (OF)	1964–71
Brad Brink (P)	1992–93
Bill Brinker (3B)	1912
Eude Brito* (P)	2005
Jack Brittin (P)	1950–51
Chris Brock (P)	2000–01
Rico Brogna (1B)	1997–2000
Dan Brouthers (1B)	1896
Buster Brown (P)	1907–09
Lloyd Brown (P)	1940
Ollie Brown (OF)	1974–77
Paul Brown (P)	1961–63, 1968
Willard Brown (1B)	1891
Tommy Brown (SS)	1951–52
Byron Browne (OF)	1970–72
Earl Browne (OF)	1937–38
George Browne (OF)	1901–02, 1912
Mark Brownson (P)	2000
Frank Bruggy (C)	1921
Roy Bruner (P)	1939–41
Warren Brusstar (P)	1977–82
Dick Buckley (C)	1894–95
Charlie Buffinton (P)	1887–89
Bob Buhl (P)	1966–67
Kirk Bullinger* (P)	2000
Eric Bullock (OF)	1989
Jim Bunning (P)	1964–67, 1970–71
Fred Burchell (P)	1903
Lew Burdette (P)	1965
Smoky Burgess (C)	1952–55
Bill Burich (SS)	1942, 1946
Mack Burk (C)	1956, 1958
Elmer Burkart (P)	1936–39
Bobby Burke (P)	1937
Eddie Burke (OF)	1890
Bill Burns (P)	1911
Ed Burns (C)	1913–18
George Burns (OF)	1925
Pat Burrell* (LF)	2000–05
Al Burris (P)	1894
Paul Busby (OF)	1941, 1943
Doc Bushong (C)	1880–82
Joe Buskey (SS)	1926
Mike Buskey (SS)	1977
Max Butcher (P)	1938–39
Charlie Butler (P)	1933
Rob Butler (OF)	1997
John Buzhardt (P)	1960–61
Marlon Byrd* (CF)	2002–05
Paul Byrd* (P)	1998–2001
Bobby Byrne (3B)	1913–17
Marty Bystrom (P)	1980–84

C

Putsy Caballero (2B)	1944–45, 1947–52
Hick Cady (C)	1919

Earl Caldwell (P)	1928
Ralph Caldwell (P)	1904–05
Jeff Calhoun (P)	1987–88
Leo Callahan (OF)	1919
Nixey Callahan (OF)	1894
Johnny Callison (OF)	1960–69
Dolph Camilli (1B)	1934–37
Howie Camnitz (P)	1913
Bill Campbell (P)	1984
Sil Campusano (OF)	1990–91
Milo Candini (P)	1950–51
Mike Cantwell (P)	1919–20
Ralph Capron (OF)	1913
Jose Cardenal (OF)	1978–79
Don Cardwell (P)	1957–60
Jim Carlin (OF)	1941
Hal Carlson (P)	1924–27
Steve Carlton (P)	1972–86
Don Carman (P)	1983–90
Amalio Carreno (P)	1991
Kid Carsey (P)	1892–97
Andy Carter (P)	1994–95
Dan Casey (P)	1886–89
Dave Cash (2B)	1974–76
Ed Cassian (P)	1891
Braulio Castillo (OF)	1991–92
John Castle (OF)	1910
Danny Cater (1B)	1964
Red Causey (P)	1920–21
John Cavanaugh (3B)	1919
Domingo Cedeno (2B)	1999
George Chalmers (P)	1910–16
Wes Chamberlain (OF)	1990–94
Bill Champion (P)	1969–72
Darrin Chapin (P)	1992
Ben Chapman (OF)	1945–46
Travis Chapman* (3B)	2003
Norm Charlton (P)	1995
Endy Chavez* (CF)	2005
Harry Cheek (C)	1910
Bruce Chen* (P)	2000–01
Larry Cheney (P)	1919
Mitch Chetkovich (P)	1945
Rocky Childress (P)	1985–86
Cupid Childs (2B)	1888
Pete Childs (2B)	1902
Pearce Chiles (OF)	1899–1900
Dino Chiozza (SS)	1935
Lou Chiozza (2B)	1934–36
Larry Christenson (P)	1973–83
Bubba Church (P)	1950–52
Ted Cieslak (3B)	1944
Bud Clancy (1B)	1934
Cap Clark (C)	1938
Mel Clark (OF)	1951–55
Ron Clark (3B)	1975
Nig Clarke (C)	1919
Danny Clay (P)	1988
Bill Clay (OF)	1902
Doug Clemens (OF)	1966–68
Wally Clement (OF)	1908–09
Jack Clements (C)	1884–97
Dave Coble (C)	1939
Dick Coffman (P)	1945
David Coggin (P)	2000–02
Alta Cohen (OF)	1933
Jimmie Coker (C)	1958, 1960–62
Dave Cole (P)	1955
Choo Choo Coleman (C)	1961
John Coleman (P)	1883–84
John Coleman (OF)	1890
Hap Collard (P)	1930
Lou Collier* (SS)	2004
Phil Collins (P)	1929–35
Larry Colton (P)	1968
Pat Combs (P)	1989–92
Steve Comer (P)	1983
Jim Command (3B)	1954–55
Mike Compton (C)	1970
Dick Conger (P)	1943
Bob Conley (P)	1958
Gene Conley (P)	1959–60
Bert Conn (P)	1898, 1900–01
Gene Connell (C)	1931

Roger Connor (1B)	1892
Jerry Connors (OF)	1892
Billy Consolo (SS)	1962
Bill Conway (C)	1884
Dennis Cook (P)	1989–90, 2001
Paul Cook (C)	1884
Duff Cooley (OF)	1896–99
Jimmy Cooney (SS)	1927
Claude Cooper (OF)	1916–17
Gene Corbett (1B)	1936–38
Tim Corcoran (1B)	1983–85
Jesus Cordero (P)	2001–02
Rheal Cormier* (P)	2001–05
Pat Corrales (C)	1964–65
Frank Corridon (P)	1904–05, 1907–09
Dick Cotter (C)	1911
Ed Cotter (3B)	1926
Johnny Couch (P)	1923–25
Ernie Courtney (3B)	1905–08
Harry Coveleski (P)	1907–09
Chet Covington (P)	1944
Wes Covington (OF)	1961–65
Billy Cowan (OF)	1967
Joe Cowley (P)	1987
Danny Cox (P)	1991–92
Larry Cox (C)	1973–75
Roger Craig (P)	1966
Gavvy Cravath (OF)	1912–20
Carlos Crawford (P)	1996
Glenn Crawford (OF)	1945–46
Larry Crawford (P)	1937
Felipe Crespo (OF)	2001
Ches Crist (C)	1906
Leo Cristante (P)	1951
Harry Croft (OF)	1899
Lave Cross (3B)	1892–97
Monte Cross (SS)	1898–1901
Bill Crouch (P)	1941
Jim Crowell* (P)	2004
John Crowley (C)	1884
Roy Crumpler (P)	1925
Todd Cruz (SS)	1978
Benny Culp (C)	1942–44
Bill Culp (P)	1910
Ray Culp (P)	1963–66
George Culver (P)	1973–74
Midre Cummings* (OF)	1997
Tony Curry (OF)	1960–61
Cliff Curtis (P)	1911–12
Tony Cusick (C)	1884–87

D

Omar Daal* (P)	2000–01
Babe Dahlgren (1B)	1943
Sam Dailey (P)	1929
Ed Daily (OF)	1885–87
Clay Dalrymple (C)	1960–68
Tony Daniels (2B)	1945
Alvin Dark (SS)	1960
George Darrow (P)	1934
Darren Daulton (C)	1983, 1985–97
Curt Davis (P)	1934–36
Dick Davis (OF)	1981–82
Dixie Davis (P)	1918
Jacke Davis (OF)	1962
Kiddo Davis (OF)	1932, 1934
Mark Davis (P)	1980–81, 1993
Spud Davis (C)	1928–33, 1938–39
Bill Dawley (P)	1988
Bill Day (P)	1889–90
Valerio De Los Santos* (P)	2003
Ivan DeJesus (SS)	1982–84
Wayland Dean (P)	1926–27
Art Decatur (P)	1925–27
Harry Decker (C)	1889–90
Pep Deininger (OF)	1908–09
Bill Deitrick (OF)	1927–28
Jose Dejesus (P)	1990–91
Ed Delahanty (OF)	1888–89, 1891–01
Tom Delahanty (3B)	1894
Jose Deleon (P)	1992–93
Bobby DelGreco (OF)	1960–61, 1965
Eddie Delker (2B)	1932–33
Garton Delsavio (SS)	1943

Al Demaree (P) 1915–16
Don Demeter (OF) 1961–63
Tod Dennehey (OF) 1923
Jerry Denny (3B) 1891
John Denny (P) 1982–85
Mike Depangher (C) 1884
Bob Dernier (OF) 1980–83, 1988–89
Jim Deshaies (P) 1995
Mickey Devine (C) 1918
Jim Devlin (P) 1887
Josh Devore (OF) 1913–14
Bo Diaz (C) 1982–85
Murry Dickson (P) 1954–56
Dutch Dietz (P) 1943
Gordon Dillard (P) 1989
Pickles Dillhoefer (C) 1918
Vince DiMaggio (OF) 1945–46
Kerry Dineen (OF) 1978
Vance Dinges (1B) 1945–46
Ron Diorio (P) 1973–74
Glenn Dishman (P) 1996
Robert Dodd (P) 1998
John Dodge (3B) 1912–13
Cozy Dolan (OF) 1912–13
Joe Dolan (SS) 1899–1901
Deacon Donahue (P) 1943–44
Red Donahue (P) 1898–1901
She Donahue (SS) 1904
Blix Donnelly (P) 1946–50
Alex Donohue (OF) 1891
Jerry Donovan (C) 1906
Red Dooin (C) 1902–14
Mickey Doolan (SS) 1905–13
David Doster (2B) 1996, 1999
Klondike Douglass (1B) 1898–1904
Tommy Dowd (OF) 1897
Ken Dowell (SS) 1987
Tom Downey (SS) 1912
Dave Downs (P) 1972
Tom Dowse (C) 1892
Conny Doyle (OF) 1883
Denny Doyle (2B) 1970–73
Jack Doyle (1B) 1904
Solly Drake (OF) 1959
Karl Drews (P) 1951–54
Monk Dubiel (P) 1948
Rob Ducey (OF) 1999–2001
Brandon Duckworth* (P) 2001–03
Clise Dudley (P) 1931–32
Hugh Duffy (OF) 1904–06
Gus Dugas (OF) 1933
Oscar Dugey (2B) 1915–17
Bill Duggleby (P) 1898, 1901–07
Mariano Duncan (2B) 1992–95
Vern Duncan (OF) 1913
Lee Dunham (1B) 1926
Davey Dunkle (P) 1897–98
Jack Dunn (3B) 1900–01
Ryne Duren (P) 1963–65
George Durning (OF) 1925
Lenny Dykstra (OF) 1989–96

E

Mike Easler (OF) 1987
John Easton (—) 1955, 1959
Rawly Eastwick (P) 1978–79
Tom Edens (P) 1994
Doc Edwards (C) 1970
Jim Eisenreich (OF) 1993–96
Kid Elberfeld (SS) 1898
Hal Elliott (P) 1929–32
Jumbo Elliott (P) 1931–34
Ben Ellis (3B) 1896
Dick Ellsworth (P) 1967
Kevin Elster (SS) 1995
Cal Emery (1B) 1963
Spoke Emery (OF) 1924
Del Ennis (OF) 1946–56
Johnny Enzmann (P) 1920
Don Erickson (P) 1958
Paul Erickson (P) 1948
Duke Esper (P) 1890–92

Nino Espinosa (P)	1979–81
Chuck Essegian (OF)	1958
Jim Essian (C)	1973–75
Bobby Estalella* (C)	1996–99
Johnny Estrada* (C)	2001–02
Nick Etten (1B)	1941–42, 1947
Johnny Evers (2B)	1917
Bob Ewing (P)	1910–11
George Eyrich (P)	1943

F

Rags Faircloth (P)	1919
Ed Fallenstein (P)	1931
Jack Fanning (P)	1894
Ed Farmer (P)	1974, 1982–83
Sid Farrar (1B)	1883–89
Jack Farrell (2B)	1886
Turk Farrell (P)	1956–61, 1967–69
Eddie Feinberg (SS)	1938–39
Harry Felix (P)	1902
Alex Ferguson (P)	1927–29
Bob Ferguson (2B)	1883
Charlie Ferguson (P)	1884–87
Chico Fernandez (SS)	1957–59
Sid Fernandez (P)	1995–96
Don Ferrarese (P)	1961–62
John Fick (P)	1944
Jocko Fields (OF)	1891
Jack Fifield (P)	1897–99
Frank Figgemeier (P)	1894
Nelson Figueroa (P)	2001
Larry File (SS)	1940
Dana Fillingim (P)	1925
Bob Finley (C)	1943–44
Neal Finn (2B)	1933
Happy Finneran (P)	1912–13
Lou Finney (OF)	1947
Steve Fireovid (P)	1984
Newt Fisher (C)	1898
Paul Fittery (P)	1917
Mike Fitzgerald (OF)	1918
Wally Flager (SS)	1945
Patsy Flaherty (P)	1910
Tom Fleming (OF)	1902, 1904
Art Fletcher (SS)	1920, 1922
Darrin Fletcher (C)	1990–91
Frank Fletcher (—)	1914
Paul Fletcher (P)	1993, 1995
Elmer Flick (OF)	1898–1901
Hilly Flitcraft (P)	1942
Kevin Flora (OF)	1995
Ben Flowers (P)	1956
Gavin Floyd* (P)	2004–05
Jim Fogarty (OF)	1884–89
Tom Foley (SS)	1985–86
Lew Fonseca (1B)	1925
Barry Foote (C)	1977–78
P. J. Forbes (2B)	2001
Curt Ford (OF)	1989–90
Hod Ford (SS)	1924
Gary Fortune (P)	1916, 1918
Kevin Foster (P)	1993
Henry Fox (P)	1902
Howie Fox (P)	1952
Terry Fox (P)	1966
Bill Foxen (P)	1908–10
Jimmie Foxx (1B, P)	1945
Julio Franco* (SS)	1982
Tito Francona (OF)	1967
Chick Fraser (P)	1899–1900, 1902–04
Lou Frazier (OF)	1998–99
Ed Freed (OF)	1942
Roger Freed (OF)	1971–72
Marvin Freeman (P)	1986, 1988–90
Gene Freese (3B)	1959
Steve Frey (P)	1995–96
Bernie Friberg (3B)	1925–32
Fred Frink (OF)	1934
Larry Fritz (—)	1975
Ben Froelich (C)	1909
Todd Frohwirth (P)	1987–90
Charlie Frye (P)	1940

Woodie Fryman (P)	1968–72
Charlie Fuchs (P)	1943
Chick Fullis (OF)	1933–34
Aaron Fultz* (P)	2005
Dave Fultz (OF)	1898–99

G

Len Gabrielson (1B)	1939
Bill Gallagher (OF)	1883
Dave Gallagher (OF)	1995
William Gallagher (SS)	1896
Bert Gallia (P)	1920
Oscar Gamble (OF)	1970–72
Bob Gandy (OF)	1916
Ron Gant (OF)	1999–2000
Charlie Ganzel (C)	1885–86
Gene Garber (P)	1974–78
Kiko Garcia (SS)	1983–85
Art Gardiner (P)	1923
Gid Gardner (OF)	1888
Ned Garvin (P)	1896
Geoff Geary* (P)	2003–05
Phil Geier (OF)	1896–97
Al Gerheauser (P)	1943–44
Tony Ghelfi (P)	1983
Jeremy Giambi* (LF)	2002
Charlie Gilbert (OF)	1946–47
Sam Gillen (SS)	1897
Charlie Girard (P)	1910
Buck Gladman (3B)	1883
Doug Glanville (OF)	1998–2002, 2004
Tommy Glaviano (3B)	1953
Whitey Glazner (P)	1923–24
Kid Gleason (2B)	1888–91, 1903–08
Al Glossop (2B)	1942
Bill Glynn (1B)	1949
Billy Goeckel (1B)	1899
Mike Goliat (2B)	1949–51
Wayne Gomes (P)	1997–2001
Chile Gomez (2B)	1935–36
Ruben Gomez (P)	1959–60, 1967
Orlando Gonzalez (1B)	1978
Tony Gonzalez (OF)	1960–68
Wilbur Good (OF)	1916
Glen Gorbous (OF)	1955–57
Howie Gorman (OF)	1937–38
Tom Gorman (P)	1986
Joe Gormley (P)	1891
Nick Goulish (OF)	1944–45
Billy Grabarkewitz (3B)	1973–74
Reggie Grabowski (P)	1932–34
Earl Grace (C)	1936–37
Mike Grace (P)	1995–99
Mike Grady (C)	1894–97
Peaches Graham (C)	1912
Wayne Graham (3B)	1963
Joe Grahe (P)	1999
Eddie Grant (3B)	1907–10
Jim Grant (P)	1923
Lou Grasmick (P)	1948
Don Grate (P)	1945–46
Lew Graulich (C)	1891
John Gray (P)	1958
Dallas Green (P)	1960–64, 1967
Tyler Green (P)	1993, 1995, 1997–98
June Greene (P)	1928–29
Paddy Greene (3B)	1902
Tommy Greene (P)	1990–95
Jim Greengrass (OF)	1955–56
Bob Greenwood (P)	1954–55
Bill Grey (3B)	1890–91
John Grim (C)	1888
Ray Grimes (1B)	1926
Jason Grimsley* (P)	1989–91
Lee Grissom (P)	1941
Dick Groat (SS)	1966–67
Emil Gross (C)	1883
Greg Gross (OF)	1979–88
Kevin Gross (P)	1983–88
Jeff Grotewold (1B)	1992
Ad Gumbert (P)	1896
Tom Gunning (C)	1887
Jackie Gutierrez (SS)	1988

H

Bert Haas (1B)	1948–49
Warren Hacker (P)	1957–58
Harvey Haddix (P)	1956–57
George Haddock (P)	1894
Bud Hafey (OF)	1939
Art Hagan (P)	1883
Don Hahn (OF)	1975
Jim Haislip (P)	1913
Bert Hall (P)	1911
Bob Hall (OF)	1904
Dick Hall (P)	1967–68
Bill Hallahan (P)	1938
Bill Hallman (2B)	1888–89, 1892–97, 1901–03
Billy Hamilton (OF)	1890–95
Earl Hamilton (P)	1924
Jack Hamilton (P)	1962–63
Garvin Hamner (2B)	1945
Granny Hamner (SS, 2B)	1944–59
Ray Hamrick (SS)	1943–44
Josh Hancock* (P)	2003–04
Lee Handley (3B)	1947
Harry Hanebrink (2B)	1959
Andy Hansen (P)	1951–53
Snipe Hansen (P)	1930, 1932–35
Bill Harbidge (OF)	1883
Lou Hardie (C)	1884
Bill Harman (P)	1941
Chuck Harmon (3B)	1957
Terry Harmon (2B)	1967, 1969–77
George Harper (P)	1894
George Harper (OF)	1924–26
Ray Harrell (P)	1939
Bud Harrelson (SS)	1978–79
Mickey Harrington (—)	1963
Gene Harris (P)	1995
Greg Harris (P)	1988–89
Herb Harris (P)	1936
Reggie Harris (P)	1997
Mike Hartley (P)	1991–92
Ray Hartranft (P)	1913
Don Hasenmayer (2B)	1945–46
Mickey Haslin (SS)	1933–36
Billy Hatcher (OF)	1994
Chicken Hawks (1B)	1925
Charlie Hayes (3B)	1989–91, 1995
Von Hayes (OF)	1983–91
Ralph Head (P)	1923
Jim Hearn (P)	1957–59
Cliff Heathcote (OF)	1932
Richie Hebner (1B)	1977–78
Bronson Heflin (P)	1996
Jim Hegan (C)	1958–59
Ken Heintzelman (P)	1947–52
Heinie Heltzel (3B)	1944
Ed Hemingway (2B)	1918
Rollie Hemsley (C)	1946–47
Solly Hemus (SS)	1956–58
Hardie Henderson (P)	1883
Harvey Hendrick (1B)	1934
Butch Henline (C)	1921–26
George Hennessey (P)	1942
Fritz Henrich (OF)	1924
Jim Henry (P)	1939
Ray Herbert (P)	1965–66
Jesus Hernaiz (P)	1974
Roberto Hernandez* (P)	2004
Willie Hernandez (P)	1983
Tom Herr (2B)	1989–90
Pancho Herrera (1B)	1958, 1960–61
John Herrnstein (1B)	1962–66
Ed Heusser (P)	1938, 1948
Kirby Higbe (P)	1939–40
Andy High (3B)	1934
John Hiland (2B)	1885
Tom Hilgendorf (P)	1975
Chuck Hiller (2B)	1967
Pat Hilly (OF)	1914
Charlie Hilsey (P)	1883
A. J. Hinch* (C)	2004
Larry Hisle (OF)	1968–71
Don Hoak (3B)	1963–64
Harry Hoch (P)	1908
Bert Hodge (3B)	1942

Eli Hodkey (P)	1946
George Hodson (P)	1895
Joe Hoerner (P)	1970–72, 1975
Frank Hoerst (P)	1940–42, 1946–47
Bill Hoffman (P)	1939
Brad Hogg (P)	1918–19
Bill Hohman (OF)	1927
Joe Holden (C)	1934–36
Walter Holke (1B)	1923–25
Al Holland (P)	1983–85
Ed Holley (P)	1932–34
Al Hollingsworth (P)	1938–39
Dave Hollins (3B)	1990–95, 2002
Stan Hollmig (OF)	1949–51
Jim Holloway (P)	1929
Mark Holzemer (P)	2000
Buster Hoover (OF)	1884
Marty Hopkins (3B)	1934
Tyler Houston* (3B)	2003
Ryan Howard* (1B)	2004–05
Ken Howell (P)	1989–90
Dan Howley (C)	1913
Bill Hubbell (P)	1920–25
Clarence Huber (3B)	1925–26
Rex Hudler (2B)	1997–98
Charles Hudson (P)	1983–86
Keith Hughes (OF)	1987
Roy Hughes (2B)	1939–40, 1946
Tommy Hughes (P)	1941–42, 1946–47
Billy Hulen (SS)	1896
Rudy Hulswitt (SS)	1902–04
Tom Hume (P)	1986–87
Bert Humphries (P)	1910–11
Johnny Humphries (P)	1946
Brian L. Hunter* (OF)	2001
Brian R. Hunter (1B)	2000
Rich Hunter (P)	1996
Don Hurst (1B)	1928–34
Harry Huston (C)	1906
Jim Hutto (OF)	1970
Tom Hutton (1B)	1972–77

I

Ham Iburg (P)	1902
Doc Imlay (P)	1913
Pete Incaviglia (OF)	1993–94, 1996
Bert Inks (P)	1896
Dane Iorg (OF)	1977
Hal Irelan (2B)	1914
Arthur Irwin (SS)	1886–89, 1894
Orlando Isales (OF)	1980

J

Fred Jacklitsch (C)	1900–02, 1907–10
Danny Jackson (P)	1993–94
Grant Jackson (P)	1965–70
John Jackson (P)	1933
Ken Jackson (SS)	1987
Larry Jackson (P)	1966–68
Mike Jackson (P)	1970
Mike Jackson* (P)	1986–87
Elmer Jacobs (P)	1914, 1918–19
Thomas Jacquez (P)	2000
Art Jahn (OF)	1928
Chris James (3B)	1986–89
Jeff James (P)	1968–69
Stan Javier (OF)	1992
Gregg Jefferies (1B)	1995–98
Irv Jeffries (3B)	1934
Greg Jelks (3B)	1987
Steve Jeltz (SS)	1983–89
Ferguson Jenkins (P)	1965–66
Hughie Jennings (SS)	1901–02
Alex Johnson (OF)	1964–65
Charlie Johnson (OF)	1908
Darrell Johnson (C)	1961
Davey Johnson (2B)	1977–78
Deron Johnson (1B)	1969–73
Jerry Johnson (P)	1968–69
John Johnson (P)	1894
Ken Johnson (P)	1950–51
Si Johnson (P)	1940–43, 1946

Syl Johnson (P)	1934–40
Tom Johnson (P)	1897
Jay Johnstone (OF)	1974–78
Stan Jok (3B)	1954
Alex Jones (P)	1894
Barry Jones (P)	1992
Broadway Jones (P)	1923
Dale Jones (P)	1941
Doug Jones (P)	1994
Nippy Jones (1B)	1952
Ron Jones (OF)	1988–91
Todd Jones* (P)	2004
Willie Jones (3B)	1947–59
Bubber Jonnard (C)	1926–27, 1935
Buck Jordan (1B)	1938
Charlie Jordan (P)	1896
Kevin Jordan (2B)	1995–01
Niles Jordan (P)	1951
Ricardo Jordan (P)	1996
Ricky Jordan (1B)	1988–94
Orville Jorgens (P)	1935–37
Rick Joseph (3B)	1967–70
Oscar Judd (P)	1945–48
Jeff Juden (P)	1994–95
George Jumonville (SS)	1940–41
Eric Junge (P)	2002–03
Al Jurisich (P)	1946–47

K

Jim Kaat (P)	1976–79
Mike Kahoe (C)	1905
Harry Kane (P)	1905–06
Erv Kantlehner (P)	1916
Joe Kappel (OF)	1884
Andy Karl (P)	1943–46
Ryan Karp (P)	1995, 1997
Matt Kata* (2B)	2005
Tony Kaufmann (P)	1927
Ted Kazanski (2B)	1953–58
Chick Keating (SS)	1926
Tim Keefe (P)	1891–93
Ed Keegan (P)	1959, 1962
Jimmie Keenan (P)	1920–21
Harry Keener (P)	1896
Bill Keister (SS)	1903
Hal Kelleher (P)	1935–38
Bill Kelly (1B)	1928
Charlie Kelly (3B)	1883
John Kelly (C)	1883
Mike Kelly (P)	1926
Al Kenders (C)	1961
John Kennedy (3B)	1957
Vern Kennedy (P)	1944–45
Bill Kerksieck (P)	1939
Jim Kern (P)	1984
Bill Killefer (C)	1911–17
Mike Kilroy (P)	1891
Newt Kimball (P)	1943
Wally Kimmick (SS)	1925–26
Lee King (OF)	1921–22
Thornton Kipper (P)	1953–55
Billy Klaus (SS)	1962–63
Chuck Klein (OF)	1928–33, 1936–39, 1940–44
Ted Kleinhans (P)	1934
Red Kleinow (C)	1911
Bill Kling (P)	1891
Johnny Klippstein (P)	1963–64
Otto Knabe (2B)	1907–13
Phil Knell (P)	1892
Alan Knicely (C)	1985
Jack Knight (P)	1925–26
Joe Knight (OF)	1884
George Knothe (2B)	1932
Fritz Knothe (3B)	1933
Darold Knowles (P)	1966
Dick Koecher (P)	1946–48
Pete Koegel (C)	1971–72
Ed Konetchy (1B)	1921
Jim Konstanty (P)	1948–54
Jerry Koosman (P)	1984–85
Joe Koppe (SS)	1959–61
Fred Koster (OF)	1931

Lou Koupal (P)	1929–30
Fabian Kowalik (P)	1936
Ernie Koy (OF)	1942
Joe Kracher (C)	1939
Jack Kraus (P)	1943, 1945
Gary Kroll (P)	1964
Otto Krueger (3B)	1905
Henry Krug (OF)	1902
John Kruk (1B)	1989–94
Mike Krukow (P)	1982
Jack Kucek (P)	1979
Harvey Kuenn (OF)	1966
Bob Kuzava (P)	1955

L

Lerrin Lagrow (P)	1980
Nap Lajoie (2B)	1896–1900
Steve Lake (C)	1989–92
Al Lakeman (C)	1947–48
Wayne Lamaster (P)	1937–38
Gene Lambert (P)	1941–42
Henry Lampe (P)	1895
Don Landrum (OF)	1957
Tom Lanning (P)	1938
Andy Lapihuska (P)	1942–43
Dave Lapoint (P)	1991
Ralph LaPointe (SS)	1947
Dan Larson (P)	1978–81
Billy Lauder (3B)	1898–99
Mike Lavalliere (C)	1984
Jimmy Lavender (P)	1917
Bill Laxton (P)	1970
Freddy Leach (OF)	1923–28
Dan Leahy (SS)	1896
Bevo Lebourveau (OF)	1919–22
Ricky Ledee* (OF)	2002–04
Bill Lee (P)	1943–45
Cliff Lee (OF)	1921–24
Hal Lee (OF)	1931–33
Travis Lee* (1B)	2000–02
Joe Lefebvre (OF)	1983–84, 1986
Greg Legg (2B)	1986–87
Ken Lehman (P)	1961
Clarence Lehr (OF)	1911
Dave Leiper (P)	1996
Mark Leiter (P)	1997–98
Jim Lemon (OF)	1963
Ed Lennon (P)	1928
Izzy Leon (P)	1945
Dutch Leonard (P)	1947–48
Ted Lepcio (2B)	1960
Randy Lerch (P)	1975–80, 1986
Walt Lerian (C)	1928–29
Barry Lersch (P)	1969–73
Roy Leslie (1B)	1922
Charlie Letchas (2B)	1939, 1944, 1946
Jesse Levan (3B)	1947
Ed Levy (OF)	1940
Bert Lewis (P)	1924
Fred Lewis (OF)	1883
Mark Lewis (2B)	1998
Sixto Lezcano (OF)	1983–84
Cory Lidle* (P)	2004–05
Jon Lieber* (P)	2005
Mike Lieberthal* (C)	1994–2005
Johnny Lindell (OF)	1953–54
Jim Lindeman (OF)	1991–92
Doug Lindsey (C)	1991, 1993
Phil Linz (SS)	1966–67
Frank Linzy (P)	1974
Angelo LiPetri (P)	1956, 1958
Tom Lipp (P)	1897
Pedro Liriano* (P)	2005
Joe Lis (1B)	1970–72
Ad Liska (P)	1932–33
Danny Litwhiler (OF)	1940–43
Mickey Livingston (C)	1941–43
Mike Loan (C)	1912
Hans Lobert (3B)	1911–14
Don Lock (OF)	1967–69
Bobby Locke (P)	1962–64
Carlton Loewer (P)	1998–99
Kenny Lofton* (OF)	2005
Jack Lohrke (3B)	1952–53

Bill Lohrman (P)	1934
Jim Lonborg (P)	1973–79
Herman Long (SS)	1904
Tony Longmire (OF)	1993–95
Joe Lonnett (C)	1956–59
Stan Lopata (C)	1948–58
Art Lopatka (P)	1946
Aquilino Lopez* (P)	2005
Marcelino Lopez (P)	1963
Carlton Lord (3B)	1923
Larry Loughlin (P)	1967
Lynn Lovenguth (P)	1955
Jay Loviglio (2B)	1980
Torey Lovullo (2B)	1999
Peanuts Lowrey (OF)	1955
Fred Lucas (OF)	1935
Con Lucid (P)	1895–96
Lou Lucier (P)	1944–45
Fred Luderus (1B)	1910–20
Al Lukens (P)	1894
Tony Lupien (1B)	1944–45
Johnny Lush (P)	1904–07
Greg Luzinski (OF)	1970–80
Sparky Lyle (P)	1980–82
Tom Lynch (OF)	1884–85
Harry Lyons (OF)	1887
Terry Lyons (1B)	1929

M

John Mabry* (OF)	2002
Harvey MacDonald (OF)	1928
Anderson Machado* (SS)	2003
Pete Mackanin (2B)	1978–79
Bunny Madden (C)	1911
Garry Maddox (OF)	1975–86
Mike Maddux (P)	1986–89
Art Madison (2B)	1895
Alex Madrid (P)	1988–89
Ryan Madson* (P)	2003–05
Calvin Maduro (P)	1996–97
Bill Magee (P)	1899, 1902
Sherry Magee (OF)	1904–14
Wendell Magee* (OF)	1996–99
Art Mahaffey (P)	1960–65
Art Mahan (1B)	1940
Frank Mahar (—)	1902
Billy Maharg (3B)	1916
Tom Maher (—)	1902
Alex Main (P)	1918
Cy Malis (P)	1934
Bobby Malkmus (2B)	1960–62
Les Mallon (2B)	1931–32
Chuck Malone (P)	1990
Gus Mancuso (C)	1945
George Mangus (OF)	1912
Jack Manning (OF)	1883–85
Jeff Manto (3B)	1993
Harry Marnie (2B)	1940–42
Tom Marsh (OF)	1992, 1994–95
Doc Marshall (C)	1904
Rube Marshall (P)	1912–14
Doc Martel (C)	1909
Hersh Martin (OF)	1937–40
Jack Martin (SS)	1914
Jerry Martin (OF)	1974–78
Renie Martin (P)	1984
Carmelo Martinez (OF)	1990
Manny Martinez (OF)	1996
Ramon Martinez* (SS)	2005
Joe Marty (OF)	1939–41
Hank Mason (P)	1958, 1960
Roger Mason (P)	1993–94
Walt Masters (P)	1937
Paul Masterson (P)	1940–42
Greg Mathews (P)	1992
Eddie Matteson (P)	1914
Gary Matthews (OF)	1981–83
Dale Matthewson (P)	1943–44
Len Matuszek (1B)	1981–84
Al Maul (P)	1887, 1900
Ernie Maun (P)	1926
Dick Mauney (P)	1945–47
Tim Mauser (P)	1991, 1991, 1993
Derrick May (OF)	1997

Pinky May (3B)	1939–43
Erskine Mayer (P)	1912–18
Ed Mayer (3B)	1890–91
Paddy Mayes (OF)	1911
Jackie Mayo (OF)	1948–53
Mel Mazzera (OF)	1940
George McAvoy (—)	1914
Bake McBride (OF)	1977–81
Tommy McCarthy (OF)	1886–87
Tim McCarver (C)	1970–72, 1975–80
Al McCauley (1B)	1890
Bill McClellan (2B)	1883–84
John McCloskey (P)	1906–07
Don McCormack (C)	1980–81
Frank McCormick (1B)	1946–47
Moose McCormick (OF)	1908
Harry McCurdy (C)	1930–33
Ed McDonough (C)	1909–10
Roger McDowell (P)	1989–91
Chuck McElroy (P)	1989–90
Jim McElroy (P)	1884
Barney McFadden (P)	1902
Ed McFarland (C)	1897–1901
Jack McFetridge (P)	1890, 1903
Patsy McGaffigan (2B)	1917–18
Willie McGill (P)	1895–96
Gus McGinnis (P)	1893
Bob McGraw (P)	1928–29
Tug McGraw (P)	1975–84
Deacon McGuire (C)	1886–88
Stuffy McInnis (1B)	1927
Rogers McKee (P)	1943–44
Warren McLaughlin (P)	1900, 1903
Barney McLaughlin (SS)	1887
Jim McLeod (3B)	1933
Cal McLish (P)	1962–64
Billy McMillon* (OF)	1997
John McPherson (P)	1904
George McQuillan (P)	1907–10, 1915–16
Larry McWilliams (P)	1989
Lee Meadows (P)	1919–23
Louie Meadows (OF)	1990
Francisco Melendez (1B)	1984, 1986
Rube Melton (P)	1941–42
Rudy Meoli (SS)	1979
Hector Mercado* (P)	2002–03
Sam Mertes (OF)	1896
Jose Mesa* (P)	2001–03
Lenny Metz (SS)	1923–25
Irish Meusel (OF)	1918–21
Jack Meyer (P)	1955–61
Russ Meyer (P)	1949–52
Benny Meyer (OF)	1925
Mickey Micelotta (SS)	1954–55
Jason Michaels* (OF)	2001–05
Larry Milbourne (2B)	1983
Bob Miller (P)	1949–58
Cyclone Miller (P)	1884
Doc Miller (OF)	1912–13
Dots Miller (1B)	1920–21
Eddie Miller (SS)	1948–49
Elmer Miller (P)	1929
Hughie Miller (1B)	1911
Keith Miller (OF)	1988–89
Kohly Miller (2B)	1897
Ralph Miller (3B)	1920–21
Red Miller (P)	1923
Russ Miller (P)	1927–28
Stu Miller (P)	1956
Trever Miller* (P)	2000
Joe Millette (SS)	1992–93
Wally Millies (C)	1939–41
John Milligan (P)	1928–31
Kevin Millwood* (P)	2003–04
Al Milnar (P)	1946
Eric Milton* (P)	2004
Mike Mimbs (P)	1995–97
Clarence Mitchell (P)	1923–28
Fred Mitchell (P)	1903–04
Larry Mitchell (P)	1996
Johnny Mokan (OF)	1922–27
Bob Molinaro (OF)	1982–83

Fred Mollenkamp (1B)	1914
Alex Monchak (SS)	1940
Don Money (3B)	1968–72
Sid Monge (P)	1982–83
John Monroe (2B)	1921
John Montague (P)	1975
Willie Montanez (1B)	1970–75, 1982
Rene Monteagudo (P)	1945
Steve Montgomery* (P)	1999
Earl Moore (P)	1908–13
Cy Moore (P)	1933–34
Brad Moore (P)	1988, 1990
Dee Moore (C)	1943, 1946
Euel Moore (P)	1934–36
Johnny Moore (OF)	1934–37
Pat Moran (C)	1910–14
Mickey Morandini (2B)	1990–97, 2000
Seth Morehead (P)	1957–59
Keith Moreland (OF)	1978–81
Harry Morelock (SS)	1891–92
Lew Moren (P)	1907–10
Bobby Morgan (2B)	1954–57
Joe Morgan (3B)	1960
Joe Morgan (2B)	1983
Jim Moroney (P)	1910
John Morris (P)	1966
John Morris (OF)	1991
Jim Morrison (3B)	1977–78
Sparrow Morton (P)	1884
Walter Moser (P)	1906
Bitsy Mott (SS)	1945
Frank Motz (1B)	1890
Ron Mrozinski (P)	1954–55
Heinie Mueller (2B)	1938–41
Hugh Mulcahy (P)	1935–40, 1945–46
Terry Mulholland* (P)	1989–93, 1996
Moon Mullen (2B)	1944
Dick Mulligan (P)	1946
Joe Mulvey (3B)	1883–89, 1892
Manny Muniz (P)	1971
Scott Munninghoff (P)	1980
Bobby Munoz (P)	1994–97
Red Munson (C)	1905
Con Murphy (P)	1884
Dale Murphy (OF)	1990–92
Dummy Murphy (SS)	1914
Dwayne Murphy (OF)	1989
Ed Murphy (P)	1898
Ed Murphy (1B)	1942
Morgan Murphy (C)	1898, 1900
Pat Murray (P)	1919
Glenn Murray (OF)	1996
Tom Murray (SS)	1894
Danny Murtaugh (2B)	1941–43, 1946
Barney Mussill (P)	1944
Brett Myers* (P)	2002–05
Al Myers (2B)	1885, 1889–91
Bert Myers (3B)	1900

N

Bill Nagel (2B)	1941
Sam Nahem (P)	1942, 1948
Bill Nahorodny (C)	1976
Billy Nash (3B)	1896–98
Jim Nash (P)	1972
Earl Naylor (OF)	1942–43
Jack Neagle (P)	1883
Greasy Neale (OF)	1921
Cal Neeman (C)	1960–61
Ron Negray (P)	1955–56
Gary Neibauer (P)	1972
Al Neiger (P)	1960
Red Nelson (P)	1912–13
Tom Newell (P)	1987
David Newhan* (OF)	2000–01
Skeeter Newsome (SS)	1946–47
Gus Niarhos (C)	1954–55
Chet Nichols (P)	1930–32
Kid Nichols (P)	1905–06
Bill Nicholson (OF)	1949–53
Frank Nicholson (P)	1912
Doug Nickle (P)	2000–02

Bert Niehoff (2B)	1915–17
Tom Nieto (C)	1989–90
Al Nixon (OF)	1926–28
The Only Nolan (P)	1885
Dickie Noles (P)	1979–81, 1990
Jerry Nops (P)	1896
Leo Norris (SS)	1936–37
Ron Northey (OF)	1942–44, 1946, 1947, 1957
Lou Novikoff (OF)	1946
Ryan Nye (P)	1997–98

O

Dink O'Brien (C)	1923
Frank O'Connor (P)	1893
Harry O'Donnell (C)	1927
Lefty O'Doul (OF)	1929–30
Randy O'Neal (P)	1989
Skinny O'Neal (P)	1925, 1927
John O'Neil (SS)	1946
Joe O'Rourke (—)	1929
Prince Oana (P)	1934
Johnny Oates (C)	1975–76
Joe Oeschger (P)	1914–19, 1924
Jose Offerman* (1B)	2005
Chad Ogea (P)	1999
Bob Oldis (C)	1962–63
Omar Olivares (P)	1995
Gene Oliver (C)	1967
Al Oliver (OF)	1984
Steve Ontiveros (P)	1989–90
Eddie Oropesa* (P)	2001
Al Orth (P)	1895–1901
Fred Osborn (OF)	1907–09
Ricky Otero (OF)	1996–97
Jim Owens (P)	1955–56, 1958–62
Red Owens (2B)	1899

P

Gene Packard (P)	1919
Tom Padden (C)	1943
Don Padgett (C)	1947–48
Vicente Padilla* (P)	2000–05
Jose Pagan (SS)	1973
Donn Pall (P)	1993
David Palmer (P)	1988
Lowell Palmer (P)	1969–71
Stan Palys (OF)	1953–55
Al Pardo (C)	1988–89
Mark Parent (C)	1997–98
Dixie Parker (C)	1923
Frank Parkinson (2B)	1921–24
Jeff Parrett (P)	1989–90, 1996
Sam Parrilla (OF)	1970
Lance Parrish (C)	1987–88
Dode Paskert (OF)	1911–17
Mike Pasquella (1B)	1919
Claude Passeau (P)	1936–39
Gene Paulette (1B)	1919–20
Johnny Peacock (C)	1944–45
Frank Pearce (P)	1933–35
Harry Pearce (2B)	1917–19
Ike Pearson (P)	1939–42, 1946
Homer Peel (OF)	1929
Julio Peguero (OF)	1992
Eddie Pellagrini (SS)	1951
Roberto Pena (SS)	1968
Paul Penson (P)	1954
Luis Peraza (P)	1969
Tomas Perez* (2B)	2000–05
Tony Perez (1B)	1983
Yorkis Perez (P)	1998–99
Robert Person (P)	1999–02
Bill Peterman (C)	1942
John Peters (C)	1921–22
Kent Peterson (P)	1952–53
Leon Pettit (P)	1937
Pretzel Pezzullo (P)	1935–36
Bobby Pfeil (3B)	1971
Dave Philley (OF)	1958–60
Adolfo Phillips (OF)	1964–66
Buz Phillips (P)	1930
J. R. Phillips (1B)	1996
Taylor Phillips (P)	1959–60

Wiley Piatt (P)	1898–1900
Nick Picciuto (3B)	1945
Clarence Pickrel (P)	1933
Ty Pickup (OF)	1918
Ray Pierce (P)	1925–26
Duane Pillette (P)	1956
Horacio Pina (P)	1978
Lerton Pinto (P)	1922, 1924
Alex Pitko (OF)	1938
Togie Pittinger (P)	1905–07
Erik Plantenberg (P)	1997
Dan Plesac (P)	2002–03
Walter Plock (OF)	1891
Johnny Podgajny (P)	1940–43
John Poff (OF)	1979
Jennings Poindexter (P)	1939
Placido Polanco* (2B)	2002–05
Hugh Poland (C)	1947
Cliff Politte* (P)	1999–2002
Jim Poole (P)	1999
Al Porto (P)	1948
Mark Portugal (P)	1997–98
Lou Possehl (P)	1946–48, 1951–52
Wally Post (OF)	1958–60
Brian Powell* (P)	2004
Jake Powell (OF)	1945
Vic Power (1B)	1964
Les Powers (1B)	1939
Todd Pratt* (C)	1992–94, 2001–05
Mike Prendergast (P)	1918–19
Ray Prim (P)	1935
Tom Prince (C)	1999–2000
Chris Pritchett (1B)	2000
Mike Proly (P)	1981
Hub Pruett (P)	1927–28
Troy Puckett (P)	1911
Nick Punto* (2B)	2001–03
Blondie Purcell (OF)	1883–84
Jesse Purnell (3B)	1904
Shadow Pyle (P)	1884

Q

Tom Qualters (P)	1953, 1957–58
Paul Quantrill* (P)	1994–95
Tom Quinlan (3B)	1994
John Quinn (C)	1911
Rafael Quirico (P)	1996

R

Dave Rader (C)	1979
Don Rader (SS)	1921
Ken Raffensberger (P)	1943–47
Al Raffo (P)	1969
Pat Ragan (P)	1923
Frank Ragland (P)	1933
Pete Rambo (P)	1926
Elizardo Ramirez* (P)	2004
Edgar Ramos (P)	1997
Pedro Ramos (P)	1967
Goldie Rapp (3B)	1921–23
Shane Rawley (P)	1984–88
Johnny Rawlings (2B)	1920–21
Lou Raymond (2B)	1919
Randy Ready (2B)	1989–91, 1994–95
Leroy Reams (—)	1969
Art Rebel (OF)	1938
Gary Redus (OF)	1986
Jeff Reed (C)	2001
Jerry Reed (P)	1981–82
Milt Reed (SS)	1913–14
Ron Reed (P)	1976–83
Scott Reid (OF)	1969–70
Charlie Reilly (3B)	1892–95
Tommy Reis (P)	1938
Desi Relaford* (2B)	1996–2000
Butch Rementer (C)	1904
Jack Remsen (OF)	1884
Tony Rensa (C)	1930–31
Rip Repulski (OF)	1957–58
Carlos Reyes (P)	2000
Ken Reynolds (P)	1970–72
Ronn Reynolds (C)	1986
Flint Rhem (P)	1932–33

Chuck Ricci (P)	1995
Bob Rice (3B)	1926
Ken Richardson (2B)	1946
Lance Richbourg (OF)	1921
Pete Richert (P)	1974
Lew Richie (P)	1906–09
Steve Ridzik (P)	1950, 1952–55, 1966
Lee Riley (OF)	1944
Jimmy Ring (P)	1921–25, 1928
Frank Ringo (C)	1883–84
Charlie Ripple (P)	1944–46
Wally Ritchie (P)	1987–88, 1991–92
Hank Ritter (P)	1912
Ben Rivera (P)	1992–94
Eppa Rixey (P)	1912–17, 1919–20
Johnny Rizzo (OF)	1940–41
Joe Roa* (P)	2002–03
Mel Roach (2B)	1962
Dave Roberts (3B)	1982
Robin Roberts (P)	1948–61
Mike Robertson (1B)	1997
Bill Robinson (OF)	1972–74, 1982–83
Craig Robinson (SS)	1972–73
Don Robinson (P)	1992
Humberto Robinson (P)	1959–60
Felix Rodriguez* (P)	2004
Pedro Rodriguez (P)	1959
Ed Roebuck (P)	1964–66
Ron Roenicke (OF)	1986–87
Mike Rogodzinski (OF)	1973–75
Saul Rogovin (P)	1955–57
Cookie Rojas (2B)	1963–69
Scott Rolen* (3B)	1996–02
Jimmy Rollins* (SS)	2000–05
Pete Rose (OF)	1979–83
Bob Ross (P)	1956
Frank Roth (C)	1903–04
Jack Rowan (P)	1911
Schoolboy Rowe (P)	1943, 1946–49
Bama Rowell (2B)	1948
Charlie Roy (P)	1906
Luther Roy (P)	1929
Vic Roznovsky (C)	1969
Art Ruble (OF)	1934
Dave Rucker (P)	1985–86
Dutch Rudolph (OF)	1903
Scott Ruffcorn (P)	1997
Bruce Ruffin (P)	1986–91
John Russell (C)	1984–88
Dick Ruthven (P)	1973–75, 1978–83
Mark Ryal (OF)	1989
Blondy Ryan (SS)	1935
Connie Ryan (2B)	1952–53
Ken Ryan (P)	1996–99
Mike Ryan (C)	1968–73

S

Bob Sadowski (3B)	1961
Bill Salisbury (P)	1902
Manny Salvo (P)	1943
Juan Samuel (2B)	1983–89
Alejandro Sanchez (OF)	1982–83
Heinie Sand (SS)	1923–28
Ryne Sandberg (2B)	1981
Ben Sanders (P)	1888–89
Danny Sandoval* (SS)	2005
Jack Sanford (P)	1956–58
Ed Sanicki (OF)	1949, 1951
Benito Santiago* (C)	1996
Jose Santiago (P)	2001–02
Kevin Saucier (P)	1978–80
Jimmie Savage (OF)	1912
Ted Savage (OF)	1962
Carl Sawatski (C)	1958–59
Phil Saylor (P)	1891
Frank Scanlan (P)	1909
Mac Scarce (P)	1972–74
Russ Scarritt (OF)	1932
Steve Scarsone (2B)	1992
Jimmie Schaffer (C)	1966–67
Gene Schall (1B)	1995–96
Charley Schanz (P)	1944–47
George Scharein (SS)	1937–40
Dan Schatzeder (P)	1986–87

Jack Scheible (P)	1894
Danny Schell (OF)	1954–55
Bill Scherrer (P)	1988
Dutch Schesler (P)	1931
Lou Schettler (P)	1910
Curt Schilling* (P)	1992–2000
Freddy Schmidt (P)	1947
Mike Schmidt (3B)	1972–89
Gene Schott (P)	1939
Pete Schourek (P)	2002
Steve Schrenk (P)	1999–2000
Pop Schriver (C)	1888–90
Al Schroll (P)	1959
Rick Schu (3B)	1984–87, 1991
Ron Schueler (P)	1974–76
Wes Schulmerich (OF)	1933–34
Frank Schulte (OF)	1917
Ham Schulte (2B)	1940
Johnny Schulte (C)	1928
Howie Schultz (1B)	1947–48
Joe Schultz (OF)	1924–25
John Schultze (P)	1891
LeGrant Scott (OF)	1939
Lefty Scott (P)	1945
Jack Scott (P)	1927
Steve Searcy (P)	1991–92
Tom Seaton (P)	1912–13
Bob Sebra (P)	1988–89
Duke Sedgwick (P)	1921
Kevin Sefcik (OF)	1995–2000
Dick Selma (P)	1970–73
Andy Seminick (C)	1943–51, 1955–57
Ray Semproch (P)	1958–59
Paul Sentell (3B)	1906–07
Manny Seoane (P)	1977
Scott Service (P)	1988
Bobby Shantz (P)	1964
Jack Sharrott (P)	1893
Merv Shea (C)	1944
Nap Shea (C)	1902
Dave Shean (2B)	1908–09
Chuck Sheerin (2B)	1936
Keith Shepherd (P)	1992
Monk Sherlock (1B)	1930
Ben Shields (P)	1931
Jim Shilling (2B)	1939
Billy Shindle (3B)	1891
Dave Shipanoff (P)	1985
Costen Shockley (1B)	1964
Chris Short (P)	1959–72
Frank Shugart (SS)	1897
Toots Shultz (P)	1911–12
Anthony Shumaker (P)	1999
Harry Shuman (P)	1944
Ed Sicking (2B)	1919
Roy Sievers (1B)	1962–64
Tripp Sigman (OF)	1929–30
Carlos Silva* (P)	2002–03
Ken Silvestri (C)	1949–51
Curt Simmons (P)	1947–50, 1952–60
Wayne Simpson (P)	1975
John Singleton (P)	1922
Dick Sisler (OF, 1B)	1948–51
Pete Sivess (P)	1936–38
Ed Sixsmith (C)	1884
Ted Sizemore (2B)	1977–78
Jimmy Slagle (OF)	1900–01
Barney Slaughter (P)	1910
Heathcliff Slocumb (P)	1994–95
Roy Smalley (SS)	1955–58
Al Smith (P)	1938–39
Bill Smith (P)	1962
Bobby Gene Smith (OF)	1960–61
Charley Smith (3B)	1961
Edgar Smith (OF)	1883
George Smith (P)	1919–22
Jake Smith (P)	1911
Jimmy Smith (SS)	1921–22
Lonnie Smith (OF)	1978–81
Phenomenal Smith (P)	1890–91
Tom Smith (P)	1895
Lefty Smoll (P)	1940
Harry Smythe (P)	1929–30
Bill Sorrell (3B)	1965

Denny Sothern (OF) 1926, 1928–30
Dick Spalding (OF) 1927
Tully Sparks (P) 1897, 1903–10
By Speece (P) 1930
Tubby Spencer (C) 1911
Stan Sperry (2B) 1936
Hal Spindel (C) 1945–46
Paul Spoljaric (P) 1999
Jim Spotts (C) 1930
Jerry Spradlin (P) 1997–98
Homer Spragins (P) 1947
Jack Spring (P) 1955
Dennis Springer (P) 1995
Russ Springer* (P) 1995–96
Charlie Sproull (P) 1945
Eddie Stack (P) 1910–11
Tuck Stainback (OF) 1938
George Stallings (C) 1897–98
Charley Stanceu (P) 1946
Steve Stanicek (DH) 1989
Buck Stanley (P) 1911
Charlie Starr (2B) 1909
John Stearns (C) 1974
Morrie Steevens (P) 1964–65
Justin Stein (3B) 1938
Gene Steinbrenner (2B) 1912
Ray Steineder (P) 1924
Casey Stengel (OF) 1920–21
Dummy Stephenson (OF) 1892
Garrett Stephenson (P) 1997–98
Walter Stephenson (C) 1937
Bobby Stevens (SS) 1931
Dave Stewart (P) 1985–86
Glen Stewart (SS) 1943–44
Neb Stewart (OF) 1940
Kelly Stinnett* (C) 2003
Milt Stock (3B) 1915–18
Kevin Stocker (SS) 1993–97
Gene Stone (1B) 1969
Jeff Stone (OF) 1983–87
Ron Stone (OF) 1969–72
Lil Stoner (P) 1931
Ray Stoviak (OF) 1938
John Strike (P) 1886
Nick Strincevich (P) 1948
Dick Stuart (1B) 1965
Paul Stuffel (P) 1950, 1952–53
George Stutz (SS) 1926
Gus Suhr (1B) 1939–40
Ernie Sulik (OF) 1936
Frank Sullivan (P) 1961–62
Joe Sullivan (SS) 1894–96
John Sullivan (C) 1968
Tom Sullivan (P) 1922
Billy Sunday (OF) 1890
Rick Surhoff (P) 1985
George Susce (C) 1929
Gary Sutherland (2B) 1966–68
Jack Sutthoff (P) 1904–05
Dale Sveum (SS) 1992
Les Sweetland (P) 1927–30

T

Lefty Taber (P) 1926–27
Jim Tabor (3B) 1946–47
Doug Taitt (OF) 1931–32
Vito Tamulis (P) 1941
Danny Tartabull (OF) 1997
Fred Tauby (OF) 1937
Jack Taylor (P) 1892–97
Reggie Taylor* (OF) 2000–01
Tony Taylor (2B) 1960–71, 1974–76
Robinson Tejeda* (P) 2005
Kent Tekulve (P) 1985–88
Amaury Telemaco* (P) 1999–2001, 2003–04
Bob Terlecki (P) 1972
Tommy Thevenow (SS) 1929–30
Bobby Thigpen (P) 1993
Dick Thoenen (P) 1967
Bill Thomas (OF) 1902
Derrel Thomas (2B) 1985
Frank Thomas (OF) 1964–65
Roy Thomas (OF) 1899–1908, 1910–11
Tommy Thomas (P) 1935

Valmy Thomas (C)	1959
Erskine Thomason (P)	1974
Jim Thome* (1B)	2003–05
Jocko Thompson (P)	1948–51
Fresco Thompson (2B)	1927–30
Milt Thompson (OF)	1986–88, 1993–94
Sam Thompson (OF)	1889–98
Dickie Thon (SS)	1989–91
John Thornton (P)	1891–92
Cotton Tierney (2B)	1923
Mike Timlin* (P)	2002
Ben Tincup (P)	1914–16, 1918
Lee Tinsley (OF)	1996
Cannonball Titcomb (P)	1886
John Titus (OF)	1903–12
Al Todd (C)	1932–35
Bobby Tolan (OF)	1976–77
Freddie Toliver (P)	1985–87
Earl Torgeson (1B)	1953–55
Frank Torre (1B)	1962–63
Cesar Tovar (OF)	1973
Happy Townsend (P)	1901
Walt Tragesser (C)	1919–20
Gus Triandos (C)	1964–65
Manny Trillo (2B)	1979–82
Ken Trinkle (P)	1949
Coaker Triplett (OF)	1943–45
Michael Tucker* (OF)	2005
Chris Turner (C)	2001
Shane Turner (3B)	1988
Tuck Turner (OF)	1893–96
Wayne Twitchell (P)	1971–77
Jim Tyng (P)	1888
Turkey Tyson (—)	1944

U

Bob Uecker (C)	1966–67
Dutch Ulrich (P)	1925–27
Tom Underwood (P)	1974–77
Del Unser (OF)	1973–74, 1979–82
Ugueth Urbina* (P)	2005
Chase Utley* (2B)	2003–05

V

Gene Vadeboncoeur (C)	1884
Eric Valent* (OF)	2001–02
Fernando Valenzuela (P)	1994
Elmer Valo (OF)	1956, 1961
Ben Van Dyke (P)	1909
Andy Van Slyke (OF)	1995
Deacon VanBuren (OF)	1904
Fred VanDusen (—)	1955
Gary Varsho (OF)	1995
Jim Vatcher (OF)	1990
Emil Verban (2B)	1946–48
Joe Verbanic (P)	1966
Al Verdel (P)	1944
Johnny Vergez (3B)	1935–36
Tom Vickery (P)	1890, 1893
Shane Victorino* (OF)	2005
Bob Vines (P)	1925
Bill Vinton (P)	1884–85
Ozzie Virgil (C)	1980–85
Cy Vorhees (P)	1902
Ed Vosberg (P)	2000–01
George Vukovich (OF)	1980–82
John Vukovich (3B)	1970–71, 1976, 1979–81

W

Woody Wagenhorst (3B)	1888
Billy Wagner* (P)	2004–05
Gary Wagner (P)	1965–69
Hal Wagner (C)	1948–49
Eddie Waitkus (1B)	1949–53, 1955
Charlie Waitt (OF)	1883
Matt Walbeck (C)	2001
Ed Walczak (2B)	1945
Bob Walk (P)	1980
Curt Walker (OF)	1921–24
Harry Walker (OF)	1947–48
Marty Walker (P)	1928
Dave Wallace (P)	1973–74
Doc Wallace (SS)	1919
Huck Wallace (P)	1912
Mike Wallace (P)	1973–74

Lee Walls (OF)	1960–61
Augie Walsh (P)	1927–28
Jimmy Walsh (3B)	1910–13
John Walsh (3B)	1903
Walt Walsh (—)	1920
Bucky Walters (P)	1934–38
Ken Walters (OF)	1960–61
Lloyd Waner (OF)	1942
Bryan Ward (P)	2000
Joe Ward (2B)	1906, 1909–10
Piggy Ward (OF)	1883, 1889
Turner Ward (OF)	2001
Fred Warner (3B)	1883
Jack Warner (3B)	1933
Bennie Warren (C)	1939–42
Dan Warthen (P)	1977
Jimmy Wasdell (OF)	1943–46
Libe Washburn (OF)	1903
Buck Washer (P)	1905
Dave Watkins (C)	1969
Ed Watkins (OF)	1902
George Watkins (OF)	1935–36
Milt Watson (P)	1918–19
Eddie Watt (P)	1974
Frank Watt (P)	1931
Johnny Watwood (OF)	1939
Bill Webb (P)	1943
Lenny Webster (C)	1995
Herm Wehmeier (P)	1954–56
Dave Wehrmeister (P)	1984
Lefty Weinert (P)	1919–24
Phil Weintraub (1B)	1938
Bud Weiser (OF)	1915–16
Mike Welch (P)	1998
Harry Welchonce (OF)	1911
Bob Wells (P)	1994
Lew Wendell (C)	1924–26
Turk Wendell (P)	2001, 2003
Fred Wenz (P)	1970
David West (P)	1993–96
Jim Westlake (—)	1955
Wally Westlake (OF)	1956
Mickey Weston (P)	1992
Gus Weyhing (P)	1892–95
Mack Wheat (C)	1920–21
George Wheeler (P)	1896–99
Bill White (1B)	1966–68
C. B. White (3B)	1883
Deke White (P)	1895
Doc White (P)	1901–02
Sammy White (C)	1962
Mark Whiten (OF)	1995–96
Matt Whiteside (P)	1998
Jesse Whiting (P)	1902
Dick Whitman (OF)	1950–51
Pinky Whitney (3B)	1928–33, 1936–39
Bill Whitrock (P)	1896
Possum Whitted (OF)	1915–19
Del Wilber (C)	1951–52
Kaiser Wilhelm (P)	1921
Cy Williams (OF)	1918–30
George Williams (2B)	1961
Mike Williams (P)	1992–96, 2003
Mitch Williams (P)	1991–93
Pop Williams (P)	1903
Hugh Willingham (SS)	1931–33
Claude Willoughby (P)	1925–30
Bill Wilson (P)	1969–73
Glenn Wilson (OF)	1984–87
Hack Wilson (OF)	1934
Jimmie Wilson (C)	1923–28, 1934–38
Max Wilson (P)	1940
Hal Wiltse (P)	1931
Bobby Wine (SS)	1960, 1962–68
Darrin Winston (P)	1997–98
Jesse Winters (P)	1921–23
Rick Wise (P)	1964, 1966–71
Frank Withrow (C)	1920, 1922
John Wockenfuss (C)	1984–85
Andy Woehr (3B)	1923–24
Randy Wolf* (P)	1999–05
Bill Wolfe (P)	1902
Abe Wolstenholme (C)	1883
Harry Wolverton (3B)	1900–04

George Wood (OF)	1886–89
Pete Wood (P)	1889
Jim Woods (3B)	1960–61
Frank Woodward (P)	1918–19
Shawn Wooten* (C)	2004
Tim Worrell* (P)	2004–05
Russ Wrightstone (3B)	1920–28
Whit Wyatt (P)	1945
Johnny Wyrostek (OF)	1946–47, 1952–54

Y

Rusty Yarnall (P)	1926
Bert Yeabsley (—)	1919
Joe Yingling (P)	1894
Floyd Youmans (P)	1989
Bobby Young (2B)	1958
Del Young (SS)	1937–40
Dick Young (2B)	1951–52
Mike Young (OF)	1988

Z

Pat Zachry (P)	1985
Tom Zachary (P)	1936
Todd Zeile (3B)	1996
Charlie Ziegler (3B)	1900
Chief Zimmer (C)	1903
Jon Zuber (1B)	1996, 1998